CZECHOSLOVAKIA
IN COLOUR

anno incarnacônis dnice Millesimo CCxxxviij psctíssimu
patrin gregoriû papam nonu confirmatus est ordo fratrum
Cruciferor cum stella de regula sñ augustini que funda
uit adhuc iseculo existens xpia nissima uirgo Agnes
rogali genita ex progenie patre videlicet przemissio il
lustri rege bohemor Mater uero constancia sorore

CZECHOSLOVAKIA IN COLOUR

Photographs by Karel and Jana Neubert

Frontispiece.
1. A scene symbolizing the donation of the church of the Order of the Knights Hospitallers to the Grand Master Leo.
From the Breviary of Grand Master Leo, University Library, Prague

First published 1975 by
Octopus Books Limited
59 Grosvenor Street, London W 1

Text by Václav Kaplický, Libor Knězek,
František Kožík, Karel Michl, Jan Pilař,
Ladislav Stehlík, Josef Strnadel,
Jaromír Tomeček
Photographs by Karel and Jana Neubert
Illustrations selected by Dr Blahoslav Černý
Graphic design by Karel Pánek
© 1975 Artia, Prague

ISBN 0 7064   0403 3

Printed in Czechoslovakia
2/99/30/51

CONTENTS

Czechoslovakia, the homeland of both the Czechs and Slovaks — two nations with a very similar origin, language and history and with similar aspirations — lies in the centre of Europe, forming its very heart.

The peoples of Czechoslovakia are among the oldest inhabitants of Europe and for more than a thousand years have played an important part in its cultural development. The Czechs and Slovaks form a compact, economically and culturally advanced, socialist state. Nature seems to have endowed this small landlocked country with a variety of scenery as would normally be found in countries far distant from each other. Here, as if in the palm of one's hand, one can find practically every kind of natural beauty. Its rich variety creates a fascinating mosaic whose unique charm is one of the characteristic features of Czechoslovakia.

The towering peaks of the High Tatra Mountains can be contrasted with the wooded crests of the Šumava and Krkonoše (Giant) Mountains, the fairy-tale cone-like humps of the Czech Central Highlands, the romantic beauty of the Low Tatras and the Slovak Ore Mountains, the rising of the smaller hills and the poetic Czech-Moravian Highlands — all this contrasts strongly with the great stretches of fields and meadows in the lowlands, the uniformity of which is frequently broken by rolling hills and deepening slopes.

Czechoslovakia is a land of woods, groves and blossoming orchards, but it is at the same time a highly developed agricultural land, with vast stretches of golden wheat and barley, sugar-beet and potatoes, and with extensive hop-fields and vineyards from which originates the country's centuries' old reputation for beer and wine. It is rich, too, in lovely streams and rivers which come bubbling down from the mountains as lively trout streams, and flow on through towns and villages, carrying on their broad surface steamers and cargo vessels, joining this landlocked country to the seas. To compensate for the lack of a coast — the only natural beauty Czechoslovakia does not possess — thousands of fishponds were constructed long ago — some of them just tiny pools on village greens, others vast stretches of water, such as the South Bohemian ponds, the Rožmberk or the Svět pond at Třeboň. Then there are the giant artificial lakes of recent years behind the dams of power stations which have blended into the landscape, detracting nothing from its original charm.

The diversity of the different regions is borne out, too, by the diversity of the national costumes of the country people, the peculiarities of local dialects, the differences in the folk melodies, the fairy-tales, sayings and proverbs. Many of the regional characteristics connected with the life of the people have penetrated like underground rivers into their very soul and can only really be distinguished by sensitive observers.

None of these enchanting wonders would have existed had they not been fostered for centuries by the Czech and Slovak peoples. The birth of such a landscape, reflecting the culture of a people, which is a unique combination of what nature has given and man has shaped, is the gauge by which the maturity of the Czech and Slovak nations can be measured. If from time immemorial the Czech Lands were always far ahead of Slovakia in industrial and other spheres of development, a quarter of a century of socialist construction has levelled out these historically-rooted differences and brought a new life to the Slovak regions which has, almost overnight, transformed an area legendary for its backwardness and poverty into a flowering garden.

Czechoslovakia has its origin in such legends and tales as that of the first Czech prince who was a ploughman, in the unconquerable strength of the spirit reflected in the St. Wenceslas and Hussite chorals, the legendary outlaws Ondráš and Jánošík and the later Nikola Šuhaj who robbed the rich and gave to the poor. The continuity of these legends is strangely embodied in the ruined fortifications and castles which bear witness to the struggle for freedom right up to the ruins of Lidice, the village razed to the ground by the Nazis during the Second World War.

It is a country which is remarkable not only for what is on the surface, but for what is beneath it. It is here one can find great stalactite and stalagmite caverns, ice caves and underground labyrinths. The secret of Czechoslovakia lies, above all, in the soul of her people who have always been characterized by their love of peace, their deep humanity and their exceptional ability to absorb European influences and transform them into the spirit of their own two nations. Czechoslovakia is often described as a treasure-house of history and art. And it is from this background that artists, scientists and scholars have always drawn their inspiration, returning what they have drawn to the people in a new likeness.

THE LAND

Czechoslovakia is a landlocked country, its elongated shape giving it a frontier measuring 3,650 kilometres. It extends over an area of 127,860 square kilometres. As the crow flies it is 767 kilometres from its westernmost to its easternmost point and 468 kilometres from north to south.

The surface of the country is diverse and is comprised of two separate parts, differing in both character and development. The boundary between them runs down through the centre of Moravia from Ostrava in the north to Znojmo in the south. To the west of this dividing line extends the Czech massif, geologically much older than the eastern part of the Carpathian system. The Czech massif creates in Bohemia itself some lower ranges of highlands. Several times in the Pre-Cambrian and Paleozoic periods it was covered by the sea and laid bare again and as the sea receded it resisted folding. Breaks and rifts caused a connected range of mountains to rise around the fringe of the territory — the Šumava Mountains (highest peak 1378 m.), the Krkonoše or Giant Mountains (highest peak 1601 m.), the Bohemian Forest (1042 m.), the Ore Mountains (1244 m.) and the Jeseníky (1491 m.). The influences of water and the atmosphere lowered the height of the Czech massif and gave it the form it has today.

The eastern part of the country is geologically much younger and therefore has a quite different character. It is created by the Carpathian range which rose up at about the same time as the Alps. For this reason the whole of Slovakia is crossed by almost parallel ridges of mountains. The highest of these ranges are the High Tatras (their highest peak and the highest in the whole of Czechoslovakia is Mount Gerlach, 2654 m.), the Low Tatras (highest peak 2043 m.), the Slovak Ore Mountains (1476 m.) and the Western Beskydy (1323 m.). Czechoslovakia's territories are crossed by Europe's principal watershed from which rivers flow into three seas. The Elbe and the longest Czech river, the Vltava (435 kilometres), drain Bohemia and carry away its waters to the North Sea, the Oder takes the waters of Silesia and part of Moravia to the Baltic Sea and the Danube which forms a natural frontier in southern Slovakia carries the waters of Slovakia and part of Moravia to the Black Sea.

In the basins of the great rivers the Elbe, the Morava and the Danube lie the country's most fertile lowlands. In the Šumava Mountains there are eight glacial lakes, the biggest of which, Black Lake, covers an area of 18 hectares (nearly 47 acres) and in the Tatras there are as many as 125 lakes. The biggest of the man-made lakes is Rožmberk (721 hectares). The most noteworthy of the great reservoirs are the Slapy, Orlík and Lipno on the River Vltava; the Orava Lake in northern Slovakia and the lake at Vranov in Moravia on the River Dyje.

The very diversity of nature resulting from long-lasting geological development means that Czechoslovakia has a tremendous variety of fauna and flora. Almost all types of Central European flora and fauna, apart from coastal vegetation, can be found here. For instance, there are some forty thousand kinds of animals and birds and around three thousand varieties of plants.

An entire third of the country's territory is covered with forest. With the exception of the dwarf pine vegetation in the high mountain areas and protected virgin forests and meadowland groves, the woods are carefully cultivated.

Czechoslovakia's natural surroundings have been described as the key to the study of the post-glacial development of all Central Europe's flora and fauna.

Czechoslovakia's landscape is one of the country's most prized possessions and so its protection is ensured by the state and embodied in the constitution. Not only are the wealth of forests and waterways, bird life and rare plants protected, but care is taken to see that industrialization does not harm the beauties of the landscape nor pollute the environment so that man can have truly ideal surroundings.

And so today one can find in Czechoslovakia extensive territories which have been declared national parks. They include areas such as the Šumava Mountains and the High Tatras which are of value to the natural sciences and which have so far been little changed by civilization. At present, there are 522 protected areas, including a number of nature reservations. The state gives its protection to forests, to rare flora and fauna or any that are in danger of extinction. It also protects unusual rock formations, systems of underground stalactite and stalagmite caverns and ice caves, peat bogs with vegetation of a special kind, bird sanctuaries on the fishponds at Třeboň in south Bohemia and Lednice in south Moravia, especially interesting land formations, erosive areas and some individual ancient trees and rocks.

Czechoslovakia's beautiful natural setting, which many years have transformed into what might be called one vast park, is protected for man so that he can find in it health and recreation. The intention of conservationists is to see to it that man can live in an environment which has come into being as the result of the harmonious development of natural and social conditions and to ensure that this environment is neither devastated nor plundered by man.

◀ *2. Mrázov Pond near Teplá, West Bohemia*   *3. The Devil's Wall, above the upper reaches of the River Vltava*

THE CULTURAL
LANDSCAPE

Old chronicles as well as fragmentary reports of travelling merchants from abroad bear witness to the fact that the territories in the centre of Europe, for centuries termed the Lands of the Czech Crown and the Lands of Upper Hungary, were known long ago throughout the world.

Although the area in which diverse ethnic groups and cultures came together has yet to be fully documented, it is clear that this part of Central Europe has a cultural history going back for more than a thousand years. Gradually the Czech and Slovak elements came to the fore and there was, at the same time, a natural coming together of the neighbouring German, Polish, Hungarian and Ukrainian groups.

It is a question not only of historical but also of ethnical import why this unit always succeeded in maintaining a certain measure of integrity. Seen against the background of history as a contradictory but continuous process, it has been confirmed that there were certain geographical and ethnical factors which enabled the indigenous population of this area to survive the storms and whirlwinds of history. These factors were especially strong among the people who regarded the soil not only as the giver of life but as representing the land and its culture. It is no accident that in this small part of Europe progressive ideas assimilated from elsewhere have for centuries been converted into reality with a remarkable vigour, affecting not only the immediate surroundings, but the rest of the world as well, thus richly repaying the debt they owe to their sources. This is the case in the sphere of culture and the arts, in economic progress, scientific and technical discoveries and also in great social and ideological movements, such as, for example, the Hussite movement.

The Czech Lands and Slovakia, however, should naturally not be considered outside the context of European development. The dilemma facing these lands at the beginning of their history, exemplified by the conflict between Byzantine culture and the culture of Roman Catholicism, in various modifications during the course of history found its reflection in the spiritual and material climate of the country. The fact is that the western Slavs who inhabited this area remained bound, by their very Slavonic character, to the north-east and east, although for centuries they were dependent on the Latin and Germanic western world.

This country is a splendid example of the concentration not only of diverse natural forms, but also of social groupings. Czechoslovakia contains within itself the whole complexity of cultures which gradually harmonized with things created by nature and by man. There are footpaths and roads as old as time itself, repaired, restored and changed in various ways, towns and villages, isolated churches with little graveyards on the hilltops, which compete with prehistoric mounds and barrows; Renaissance and Baroque parks, little woods planted for the feudal lords, the remains of virgin forests; there are waterways along whose banks life has flowed on for centuries, leaving characteristic traces of the various epochs, lakes — old and new, mountain and lowland, the great cascades of dams and power stations created on rivers in modern times; there are also the dense

forests on the frontier ridges, deserted till the Middle Ages, and the wooded mountains of Central Slovakia which have only recently been exploited for economic purposes. To this very day the vast parklands as well as a great deal of former church property are open to the public. Monuments to the co-existence of man with nature are also provided by the melancholy moors of South Bohemia with their lovely villages of Baroque farmsteads and beautiful tiny shrines at countless crossroads, or the splendid ruins of the seats of powerful lords in the highland plains of the Spiš area of Slovakia. These older traces of man's involvement with nature are mingled with traces of a much later date, from the time of the industrial revolution. We find the vast production plants which overshadow the once famous centres of medieval mining and foundry-working in Bohemia and Slovakia and the modest but once important manufacturing enterprises dating back to the beginnings of industrial production in various parts of the same territories. Alongside these resources with which man adapted and subordinated nature to his own needs, we find tiny, less easily recognized, traces of the union of man and nature typical of this land. From them we recognize how for centuries respect for a tree deliberately planted in a certain place was passed from father to son as was respect, say, for a pathway along which many generations have walked through dense mountain forests; or how a little trough of a stream by which generation after generation of children have grown up is loved and preserved. In this continuity of tradition in which an object can assume a special spiritual meaning there is a growing recognition of the relationship between man and the landscape from which he springs, which is typical of and indeed essential for the people of a small country such as this. It provides tangible proof — even though sometimes merely symbolic — of the lasting nature of human labour and the relationship between man and the community.

4. West Moravian landscape near Tišnov

5. Head of a Celtic hero. National Museum, Prague ▶

EARLY MAN IN CZECHOSLOVAKIA

The geographical position of the country at the crossroads of main routes of communications led to the uneven distribution of human settlement and uneven development of cultural trends throughout early history. The eastern part of the state received civilizing influences from the central Danubian regions and the Balkans, whereas Bohemia and the western and northern parts of Moravia were more inclined to be orientated towards the region of the Upper Danube and areas to the north, such as Silesia, Lusatia and Saxony. As a result, especially in more recent times, we quite often find two peoples of different origin and with different cultures — one inhabiting the north, the other the southern half of Bohemia and the adjacent parts of Moravia.

Few reliable relics of the Early Stone Age — the Lower Paleolithic Age (some 600,000 to 150,000 years ago), testifying to the presence of the earliest man — Pithecanthropus — remain in Czechoslovakia. There are stone tools made of materials which were not typical (flint and quartz), or showing unusual techniques of craftsmanship, as well as some more typical tools of undetermined stratigraphic origin, but there are no actual traces of Early Stone Age man himself.

The situation becomes clearer as regards the Middle Paleolithic Era and the beginnings of the Upper Paleolithic (150,000 to 40,000 B. C.). There have been occasional skeletal finds relating to the inhabitants of that period — Neanderthal Man — both in Moravia and Slovakia and more frequent finds of chipped stone tools in cave dwellings. Tools such as these are associated with the Mousterian culture typical of Neanderthal Man.

The development of the society of game hunters culminated in the final stages of the Upper Paleolithic Era, towards the end of the fourth and last Ice Age. During the periods of the Gravettian, Magdelanian and, in Slovakia, the Szeletian cultures, people of the same type as the modern man, *homo sapiens*, lived on the territory of present-day Czechoslovakia. They were probably already organized in matriarchal clans. The hunting of big herds of animals made it necessary for people to organize themselves into bigger co-ordinated groups. The game lived mainly on the loess soil of the Moravian dales. It is here that a number of camping sites of these Upper Paleolithic hunters have been found — at Dolní Věstonice, Pavlov and Přerov-Předmostí. Finds of specialized stone tools and especially early examples of work approaching art (early man did not know art as such) testify to the highly developed talents of the people of that epoch, their ability to think abstractly, their imagination, manual skill, keen powers of observation, memory and the beginnings of religious ideas. No wall paintings, drawings or engravings from this period have been found on Czechoslovak territory. What have been found here are extremely interesting small examples of sculpture, such as the tiny statuettes, the famous Venus from Dolní Věstonice in South Moravia, and the representations of whole groups of animals, frequently quite complex in composition, engraved on animal bones.

The Gravettian culture of Central Europe had more links with the East of Europe than with the West European Frankish-Cantaberian circuit. Upper Paleolithic hunters appear to have moved from east to west. As the glaciers receded to the north, the climate of Central Europe underwent considerable changes. Herds of game moved northwards and the hunters followed them.

In the fifth millennium B.C., the earliest agricultural civilization appeared in what is now Czechoslovakia. Professor V. Gordon Childe described the transition from the Paleolithic to the Neolithic Age as the Neolithic revolution. Man ceased to hunt and just live off the land passively as a parasite and started to cultivate it and produce his livelihood. This significant turning point in man's history occurred in the Near East as early as the eighth and seventh millennia B.C. and it was from that area that the first actual farmers came via the Balkans into Central Europe. They came with their skill in constructing their long rectangular dwellings divided into several sections housing individual families. They were made of wooden piles, plaited walls and had saddle-shaped roofs. The earliest pottery used by these peoples was decorated with geometrical designs, engraved or painted spirals, zig-zags and meanders. They also brought with them their knowledge of basket-making and weaving. In their religious ideas these earliest farmers already recognized a god or rather a goddess — the giver of life and fertility. Their form of social organization was the matrilineal clan. Dating from the Upper Neolithic Era (the period of the culture of painted pottery) at the turn of the 4th and 3rd millennia B.C. many finds have been made in south-western Moravia of stylized clay figures mostly representing women in adoration.

The Eneolithic or Copper Age (2500—1800 B.C.) was a period of great ethnic migrations and social and economic upheavals in Central Europe. The cultures of the farming population in the Danube basin died out and many groups of herdsmen, probably already organized in patriarchal clans, penetrated into Czechoslovak territory from both east and west. There were people whose pottery was decorated with cord (the high necks of their vessels were decorated with the imprint of cord) and who came from the north-east, and the Beaker folk, who spread throughout western Europe, probably from North Africa. Those with the corded pottery were a fighting people, equipped with flat war-axes made of stone and less frequently of copper. The Beaker folk with the pottery in the form of upturned bells of reddish-brown clay, imprinted with ornamentation in the form of horizontal stripes filled in with white, were armed with bows. In the Eneolithic Era ritual burials became common. Bodies were not cremated and were buried unburned, on their sides, in a crouching position. The patriarchal organization of society was also reflected in their religion, with male gods and personifications of the sky, its manifestations (thunder and lightning) and celestial bodies taking on increasing significance.

Although Eneolithic means the Copper Age, metal finds (gold was, next to copper, the most frequently used metal) are rare. Not until the Únětice culture of the Early Bronze Age (1800 to 800 B.C.) when the civilizations, cultures, and most likely ethnic standards, too, began to intermingle, did metals and their production become more common. Copper was soon replaced by bronze. The cultural orientation on the Danube region and the Balkans remained unchanged. The country began to play a part in long distance trading. Moravia was crossed by the important Amber Route along which amber was transported from the Baltic coast to the shores of the Mediterranean and beyond to Egypt and Syria. In Central Europe, Egyptian faience heads began to appear, bronze pins in Syrian shapes and spiral motifs of Mycaenean origin appeared in the geometrical ornaments of bronze tools and implements.

The cultures of the urn fields of the Middle and Late Bronze Age were brought into Czechoslovakia by people from the north, from Silesia and Lusatia. Large numbers of these agricultural people concentrated mainly in the northern half of Bohemia and Moravia to such an extent that the density of settlement in some areas was even greater than today. At the turn of the second and first millennia B.C., the development of a society based on clans reached its climax. The people of the urn fields culture were well organized and were already building strongholds on hilltops for purposes of defence, but they were not a fighting people. They cremated their dead, laying them to rest on extensive burial grounds. At that time there were still no traces of any marked social differentiation. Contacts with the East continued, though they were less intensive. Elements of the Mediterranean and Balkan cult of the Sun emerged, culminating at the beginning of the first millennium B.C. (bronze ritual chariots with depictions of the Sun and bird motifs).

Marked differentiations in primeval society, taking it to the threshold of a class society, came about in the Early Iron Age, also known as the Hallstatt Period. Although the use of iron spread from the Mediterranean before the end of the second millennium, it did not reach Central Europe until the eighth century B.C. and was not in general use till a century later. A wave of professional warriors came into existence who subjugated the agricultural population and built strongholds on the heights in the manner of Greek castles. Bohemia and Moravia lay on the western fringe of this upsurge of civilization. Italy supplied the aristocracy of warriors with wine, luxury bronze utensils, and Greek pottery and jewels. In Bohemia and Moravia we find the magnificent graves of princes with chariots, countless utensils, and wonderful harnesses and weapons. In the territory between western France and Bohemia, the first historical nation was beginning to take shape — the Celts who continued to occupy the territory until the beginning of the Christian era.

Although the warriors of the Late Hallstatt period were in all probability Celts, specifically Celtic culture with its own forms of artistic expression came into being only in the course of the fifth century B.C. We term it the La Tène culture, after the trade centre, La Tène, on the shores of Lake Geneva. Its beginnings in Bohemia at the turn of the fifth and fourth centuries B.C. are princely tombs beneath barrows, with cast bronze ornaments, decorated with masks, animal motifs or strongly stylized elements of plant origin — known as fish-bladder motifs. All these elements, forming entities of a high artistic level executed in small ornaments by the technique of wax casting, are examples of what is referred to as the old La Tène style. Celtic production — and not only artistic production — culminated in the period of the oppida, the oldest settlements of an urban type in Czechoslovakia, usually built on hilltops in the first century B.C. The Celts stabilized the shape of most iron implements which has remained unchanged to this day (the spade, the axe, the hammer, etc.), they mined iron ore and knew how to smelt and forge it and they minted the first currency in this country in the form of Macedonian coins. They developed large-scale production of tools and metal ornaments (bracelets, clasps) in the central workshops of the oppida. A rare find in Bohemia was a Celtic stone carving of the head of a god or hero of sandy marl. The flat, ornamental and entirely decorative approach to the depiction of the man's head only remotely suggests the lesson learned from Mediterranean models. West of the Rhine, Celtic sculpture is extremely rare.

At the beginning of the Christian era, Teutonic tribes — a union of tribes known under the term Marcomanni, established in about 15 A.D. — occupied Bohemia and, shortly afterwards, Moravia. The Celts receded towards the Danube, but in the meantime Roman legions had already reached this area and the Danube became the frontier of the Roman Empire. Celtic power crumbled without offering serious resistance. The oppida were captured and occupied for some time by the Teutonic conquerors, but the workshops stopped producing for good. In the first half of the first century A.D. this lack was compensated for a short time by bronze utensils imported from the workshops of southern Italy. At about the same time, the potter's wheel, which had first appeared in the Late La Tène period, completely disappeared (it was not used again until the ninth century). Since the lands never formed part of the Roman Empire, it is unusual to find Roman luxury goods on the territory of Czechoslovakia. Occasionally we come across moulded pottery with a shiny surface and of a reddish colour, most often shaped as dishes, with figural designs or just plant ornaments in the lower half of the vessels.

During the great ethnic migrations caused by the invasion of Europe by the Huns in 375 A.D., the picture of the settlement of these territories changed rapidly. Of Teutonic tribes, the Langobards appeared in Bohemia and Moravia in the second half of the fifth century, while the Marcomanni tribes moved south-west to what was later to become Bavaria.

The first Slav tribes penetrated into the land from areas north of the Carpathian arc in about the year 500. They still came across Germanic inhabitants but these completely abandoned the country in the sixth century and moved to the former Roman provinces. The oldest Slav culture was simple, characterized above all by crude hand-shaped pottery of what is known as the Prague type. There were no differentiations in Slav society at the time of its expansion, the people being engaged solely in cultivating the land. At the close of the sixth century, Slav farmers who had settled in the eastern half of Czechoslovakia became dependent for a long time on the Nomadic Avars of Asiatic descent, who appeared in the Danube basin in the year 568. The Slav tribes in Czechoslovakia did not undergo any economic, cultural or political development until the second half of the eighth century, when Avar power began to disintegrate. Two expeditions of Charlemagne against the Avars in the last decade of the eighth century put a definite end to their rule. Christianity spread to Moravia, Slovakia and later to Bohemia, with local princedoms merging and strongholds being established as defensive and administrative centres. The first Slavonic state — the Great Moravian Empire — came into being — ruled by the indigenous Mojmír dynasty (830—906 A.D.). Gradually a specific culture, with its roots in the national heritage, developed. The first stone churches, adorned with frescoes, were built, while gold and silver jewelry as well as bronze and silver adornments to armour were produced in the forging shops of the strongholds. During the ninth century the state began to play a part in European development, entering into contact and conflict with its neighbours. It was in this century, too, that Byzantine missionaries brought the Glagolithic script, based on the Greek alphabet, to the Great Moravian Empire, so laying the foundations for Slavic literature. The ninth century thus marks the turning point in Czechoslovakia between primeval times and the truly historical era.

6. *Kašperk Castle, South-West Bohemia*

7. *The flying buttress system of St. Vitus's Cathedral, Prague* ▶

MAN'S ENVIRONMENT (Architecture)

In all periods of history, architecture has created man's environment. By its very nature, a structure encloses a certain space, at the same time influencing and shaping the space around it. The intermingling of units of the landscape that have been created with a deliberate purpose with components of a natural origin is a characteristic of a civilized country such as Czechoslovakia. Centuries of work and of life itself have left few spots untouched by the hand of man. Historic buildings with varying functions and of varying importance are thus bound together, not only by the typical intertwining of one historical style with another, but also by an organic interaction with the features of the surrounding landscape in its infinite variety.

Romanesque architecture on Czechoslovak territory covered roughly the period from the end of the ninth to the middle of the thirteenth century. Settlements were based on older foundations as was the layout of the basic network of roads which in the Czech Lands gradually focussed around Prague, which acted as the junction of the entire network. This corresponded to the economic, commercial and political significance of this newly forming centre following the disintegration of the Great Moravian Empire. The majority of ecclesiastical buildings of that period that have been preserved are rotundas and small churches with tribunes. It was no chance occurrence that they came into being in the areas covered by the Great Moravian Empire (the Znojmo rotunda with its wonderful frescoes depicting the Přemysl legend, dating from the year 1134, the Rotunda of St. George at Skalice at the foot of the Small Carpathians, the brick abbey church at Diakovce in south-west Slovakia), or in the regions of the next stage of social development in the Czech feudal state (rotundas in West and Central Bohemia). Unlike the situation in western countries, Romanesque basilicas have not been preserved here on any scale, although evidence of their existence is provided by structural fragments in Gothic ecclesiastical centres, some of them rebuilt in Baroque style (the monasteries at Doksany, Kladruby, Sázava, Rajhrad, Želiv, etc.). Of basilicas preserved outside Prague itself, a typical example of great purity is provided by the village church at Tismice, as well as the basilicas at Milevsko and Teplá and the monumental basilica at Třebíč. Small churches with tribunes contain a surprising wealth of detail (the capitals of pillars and the columns themselves, windows and portals). This is also the case with secular buildings (the Castle of Olomouc, the Palatine Chapel and Palace in Cheb, etc.). An extremely high standard of Romanesque architecture is to be found in Prague, where besides a good deal of fragmentary evidence there are well preserved ecclesiastical buildings (the Benedictine Convent Church of St. George) and remnants of princely edifices at Prague Castle and at Vyšehrad. Most noteworthy, however, is the wealth and architectural beauty of a number of Romanesque houses (the Old Town, the Havel district), as well as the Queen Judith stone bridge dating from the second half of the twelfth century.

Little Romanesque churches, for purposes of convenience, were usually situated on hilltops, thus becoming a typical feature of the landscape.

The Gothic period, from the middle of the thirteenth to the late sixteenth century, was closely associated with the growth of towns both in the Czech Lands and Slovakia. These new centres waged a successful struggle for administrative and economic independence. Royal towns, in particular, grew apace (Mělník, Hradec Králové, Pilsen, Žatec, Písek, Olomouc and Brno). In Slovakia, towns were built with special regard to the danger of Turkish invasion (Bratislava, Nitra, Zvolen, Trenčín). Towns with special mining privileges (Kutná Hora, Jihlava, Banská Štiavnica, etc.) as well as subject towns underwent great developments. The foundation of the New Town of Prague by Charles IV (1348) must be regarded as a unique feat of urban planning.

The Gothic style with its new conception of space was dominant in architecture. In the fourteenth century, a number of outstanding architects came to Bohemia at the invitation of Charles IV, who was then ruler of the Holy Roman Empire. One of the most outstanding was Peter Parler, who followed up the work of Matthias of Arras in the building of Prague Cathedral, and, with the other buildings he designed in Bohemia, determined further developments. A number of churches were reconstructed in the towns and new churches were built, along with monasteries, burghers' houses and castles, with all their connected buildings belonging to the crown or to powerful feudal families. At the end of the fifteenth century other outstanding architects who had a great influence on Late Gothic in the Czech Lands appeared on the scene. In addition to Matěj Rejsek, responsible for the Powder Tower in Prague, there was Benedict Ried of Piesting, who built Kutná Hora, and in particular St. Barbara's Cathedral. A number of new parish churches and abbeys in Bohemia were splendid examples of Late Gothic such as the Zlatá Koruna (Gold Crown) Monastery, the monastery at Vyšší Brod and the parish churches of Kadaň, Hradec Králové and Soběslav. Late Gothic castle chapels can be seen at Zvíkov, Křivoklát, Orlík and burghers' houses at Tábor, Žatec, Znojmo, Prague, Olomouc, etc. In Slovakia, too, a wide range of examples of architecture came into being that to this day greatly influence the appearance of Slovak towns and the countryside as well, from churches to feudal castles (Spišské Podhradie, Žehra — the Church of the Holy Spirit with its unusual frescoes at Čejčovice, St. James's Church in Levoča, Bardejov, Bratislava) as well as burghers' houses (Levoča, Poprad, Banská Štiavnica and Kremnica).

The Gothic style survived for a long time outside the main centres and it continued to have an influence on details even during the period of Renaissance architecture which never took a great hold in the Czech Lands. The Renaissance struck far deeper roots in Slovakia, especially in the eastern part. It left its mark on feudal seats and above all burghers' houses and civic buildings which in Eastern and Central Slovakia are reminders of the culmination of Renaissance in the sixteenth and seventeenth centuries. Proof of this is provided by churches and belfries with their typical attic storeys, town halls, burghers' houses and the seats of the aristocracy in many Slovak towns. Many small feudal seats in the Renaissance style can be found in the Slovak regions. But only a few buildings in pure Renaissance style have been preserved in the Czech Lands. It is true that we can find some castles with traces of this style. But there are more burghers' houses and even complete urban groupings which, in combining a mixture of styles, produce an indigenous form of expression known as "Czech Renaissance". In Litoměřice, Prachatice, Třeboň, Nové Město nad Metují and Telč many picturesque town halls and burghers' houses have gables, tessellated façades, graffiti decorations, attics, towers and arcades.

What did become firmly rooted in the Czech Lands, however, was Baroque that developed from the seventeenth to the end of the eighteenth century when features of the Rococo period began to prevail. Italian and other foreign architects and craftsmen who were invited to the Czech Lands in the period when Renaissance architecture was in great demand became assimilated in their adopted country and its environment during the Baroque period. The new social and economic structure provided wonderful opportunities for the building of monasteries and churches in towns and villages, as well as mansions, including the laying out of their parks. The new feudal rulers who, during and after the Thirty Years' War, had seized possession of estates in Bohemia, Moravia and Silesia, provided the funds. Original ideas, based on the illusionism of Italian Baroque, found here not only fertile soil but also opportunities for further development, unique in Europe. Architects like K. I. Dientzenhofer had a great influence on the appearance of the entire landscape as well as on individual towns. At other times they would counter dynamic trends with a concept of tranquil mass as did for example J. B. Mathey. The painters and sculptors who helped to complete these monumental structures were ideal cooperators. Architects of Czech origin, like F. M. Kaňka, appeared from time to time among the foreign architects. Where this systematic and detailed cooperation of different arts in architecture and landscape gardening did not result in completely new structures, the new style influenced the renovation of façades and left its imprint on the general appearance of towns whose architectural core was based on an older layout. Baroque, more than any previous style, changed the countenance of the landscape through its discovery of a consistent way to relate interior and exterior architecture. It also influenced the appearance of Slovak towns, though in a less radical manner. There we can find isolated examples outstanding for their individuality. During this period, many great foreign personalities in world architecture were working in the country, men such as J. B. Fischer of Erlach. Proof of how deeply Baroque penetrated into the country is provided by the fact that the peoples of the Czech and Slovak countryside, who were still subject peoples, began to develop their own means of expression through folk architecture. Sporadic examples of this can be found in older farm buildings and more especially in wooden churches in which the Gothic style often survived. Examples of ecclesiastical and secular architecture, dating from the seventeenth and eighteenth centuries in East and Central Slovakia, as well as functional timber buildings, farm buildings and small consecrated stone structures of Moravian and Czech folk architecture in Baroque style, bear witness to the growing inventiveness of folk craftsmen and how they could adapt a given style to their own needs. In this way, in the eighteenth and later in the nineteenth century, an important background to folk art came into being in the different localities and regions.

Classicism reacted to the decorative sophistication of Rococo by a sobriety in the outer lines of buildings and stress on usefulness within. Only in the layout of parks did the romantic beauty of natural surroundings come into its own, the scenery of the Czech Lands and Slovakia offering ample scope for this. It was not accidental that, at a time when the architecture of the two parts of the country was becoming more similar in the spirit of the stylistic changes that were coming about (Classicism, Empire, Biedermeier) and, later on, in an indiscriminate mixture of styles, an ugly element began to invade urban areas in the housing built for the newly emerging working class. In the countryside some beautiful residences were still being designed for the aristocracy and there were still a few important buildings in the towns being constructed. It must be taken into account, of course, that at a time when the new element of national revival and social liberation with its accompanying upsurge of culture and the arts was beginning to foment, both the Czech Lands and Slovakia were forced into the position of being periphery regions of the Austro-Hungarian monarchy. As far as complete urban units are concerned, we should take note of the development of spas and watering places in the second half of the nineteenth century. At that time some new personalities were coming to the fore in architecture. In the Czech Lands they included Josef Zítek (the National Theatre in Prague, Karlovy Vary Colonnade), together with other representatives of a new generation, who succeeded in mastering stylistic inter-mixtures of the past while at the same time seeking their own indigenous form of expression. The rapid growth of industry and commerce increasingly meant not only the creation of urban agglomerations which completely disregarded the social needs of the ever more sharply differentiated classes of society, but also the erection of new technical and industrial structures which mercilessly invaded the landscape.

This was strongly opposed by the younger generation with their social programme and their desire to give urbanism a new appearance and to utilize newly discovered building techniques. The first indications of these new trends can be found in the work of "Art Nouveau" architects who aimed at new decorative forms and new concepts of style. An outstanding personality who laid the foundations of modern Czechoslovak architecture was J. Kotěra. He designed individual functional buildings as well as entire housing estates and urban units with a truly social concept. His pupils (O. Novotný, J. Gočár, P. Janák) followed in his footsteps, sometimes seeking a solution in close ties with Cubism, the application of which in architecture became a Czech speciality.

In the twentieth century, it was a generation of modern architects, who despite having little scope to implement their plans, included their dreams of a new type of functional architecture in their plans in the 1920's. In some of the buildings, completed in this period, and above all in the housing estates, these architects (O. Starý, J. Kroha, B. Feuerstein, O. Tyl, K. Honzík, J. Havlíček, J. Fuchs and others) put into practice new urbanistic conceptions of modern housing, combining efficiency with aesthetic values. Among these achievements, which include outstanding works by such internationally recognized architects as Mies van der Rohe in Brno and Adolf Loos in Prague, we should not forget to mention the fine garden city of Baba in Prague. It was not possible for the generations between the two world wars to put their progressive creative and social projects into practice on an adequate scale. Czech and Slovak architects were only able to do this during the post-Second World War period of socialist construction. The demands for new housing estates and entire new towns gradually overcame divergences in ideas of how to find new popular decorative expression, and enabled both the older and the rising generation of architects to construct new housing, new cultural and industrial buildings and revolutionary technical and agricultural projects. Architects once more applied themselves to the task of creating a living environment for the people, linking town and countryside and villages with their immediate natural surroundings. In many spheres, architecture, as art of great social and cultural importance, was faced with many new tasks which in several cases were carried out on a level equalling world standards.

THE SCULPTORS' HANDS

Far too little of the art of the sculptor during the Romanesque period in Czechoslovakia exists, though there is written evidence of it. During that epoch, sculpture was an organic part of architecture and was also closely connected with arts and crafts. Yet those examples which have been preserved testify to the skill of their creators; for example, the stone carving above the altar of the Adoration of the Virgin Mary by Přemysl Otakar I and the Abbess Agnes, dating from the early thirteenth century, the bas-relief on the Lesser Town bridge tower in Prague, dating from before 1250, and the figure of a lion in Spišská Kapitula, dating from the same time. From the very beginning of the fourteenth century the development of Gothic sculpture grew out of a background of certain traditions and thanks to social progress at the time and to commissions from the Church and secular rulers, in particular the court, there was a rapid growth in artists who created Madonnas and figures of Christ and of the saints. Splendid works by Peter Parler's lodge began to make their appearance, including unusual sculptured portraits. From around the year 1400 on, we find Madonnas with lovely human features which are examples of what is known as the "Beautiful Style". In addition to the pleasing character of Gothic sculpture, it also contains an element of the dramatic and a lively manner of dealing with the themes in hand, closely connected with real life experiences. In Western Slovakia and in the neighbourhood of Košice, stone statuary designed to form part of the entire architecture of a building played an important part. Some of the artists, such as Master Štefan, were no longer anonymous. The fourteenth and fifteenth centuries brought with them the development of wood-carving which can be seen, in particular, on the altars of churches in Central and Eastern Slovakia. Among the work carried out by artists in these regions during the fifteenth and sixteenth centuries, the work of Master Pavol of Levoča, at the turn of the two centuries, stands out and testifies to the continuity between late Slovak Gothic style and Renaissance art. The Renaissance left some examples of sculpture in Bohemia and even more in Moravia, especially work closely linked with architecture (tomb-stones and memorial tablets). Both native and foreign masters played their part. As well as stone-work, we find the use of stucco and of metal which again became an attractive material for works of sculpture. The situation was similar in Slovakia where the Renaissance lived on in sculpture even longer than in the Czech Lands. The surprisingly vigorous arrival of Baroque on the scene was made possible by the many opportunities for building new complexes of structures, churches and monasteries and by the penetration of works of sculpture into towns and the open countryside. Among the many materials used we find that malleable sandstone prevails. We come across works by great artists who were active in Bohemia, Moravia and Silesia, such as F. M. Brokoff, the author of monumental works of statuary of static richness, and Matthias Braun, who created the unique and dramatic groups of statuary at Kuks. In Slovakia, where Baroque sculpture developed during the second half of the seventeenth century, it underwent similar developments. Two outstanding artists who not only influenced sculpture in Slovakia but also in neighbouring countries were G. R. Donner, who worked in Bratislava at the beginning of the eighteenth century, and F. X. Messerschmidt, who worked in the same city at the close of the century and who was responsible for a number of strange gargoyle-like heads.

The decline of Baroque sculpture, which was especially marked in the Czech Lands, in the nineteenth century was caused mainly by a lack of demand. So sculptors had to devote themselves principally to minor tasks, such as tombstones or decorative ornamental carvings. This decline in sculpture, during which most of the big workshops were closed, was particularly noticeable in the regions of Moravia and Slovakia.

In the second half of the nineteenth century, the art of the period of national revival and its ideas produced one great Prague sculptor of European stature, J. V. Myslbek, whose portraits, bas-reliefs and monuments laid the foundations for modern Czech sculpture. Towards the end of the nineteenth and the beginning of the twentieth century, his pupils and successors gave sculpture a new breadth, fullness of content and variety of form, as part of Art Nouveau trends (F. Bílek, L. Šaloun), in the lyrical interpretation of classically simplified form (J. Štursa), or in the new forms of Cubism (O. Gutfreund). In this way, Czech sculpture in the 1920's made an original contribution to modern European art. Slovak sculpture, too, at the end of the nineteenth century and in the first half of the twentieth, began to explore new ways and, under the influence of Czech art, it found its own forms of expression and breadth of creation in the most recent period, through certain great artists (J. Kostka and R. Uher, for example) and because of the same new opportunities for broad social application which also gave encouragement to art in the Czech Lands.

◄ *8. M. B. Braun: "The Nativity of Christ". Bethlehem, near Kuks*

9. B. Kubišta: "Quarry at Braník". National Gallery, Prague

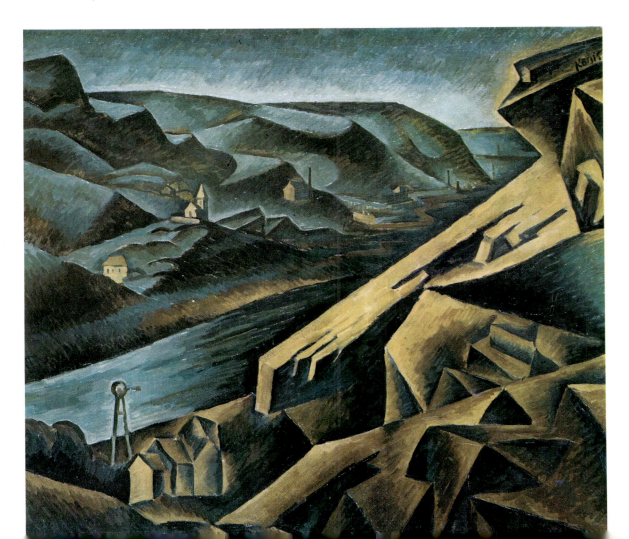

THE PAINTERS' EYES

The earliest beginnings of Romanesque painting in the Czech Lands and Slovakia can be found, above all, in beautiful illuminated manuscripts such as the Vyšehrad Codex, the Wolfenbüttel Manuscript and the Gumpold Legend of St. Wenceslas. Western and Byzantine influences are also to be found in rare but important murals like St. Catherine's Rotunda in Znojmo and St. George's Basilica in Prague. Some thirteenth-century illuminations indicate the originality with which different influences and currents were adopted and presented. Similar developments can be found in Slovakia, where there are mural paintings, such as those at Diakovce and Žehra, which are astonishing for their monumentality and breadth of conception. The Gothic era saw a great upsurge of painting in both parts of the country. The growing demand for the illumination of books led to the opening of more workshops; there was an ever greater variety of decorative expression using figural motifs and combinations of drawing with coloured patterns. Examples of this are the manuscripts of the scribes of Queen Rejčka, the Passional of the Abbess Cunegunda and the Velislav Bible, as well as illuminations dating from the culmination of Gothic in the fourteenth century. This trend continued in the fifteenth century and led to the creation of magnificent illuminated books in the sixteenth century, in the spirit of a style that was already on the decline. Mural paintings underwent a similar development. This art began to depart from the linear approach (Jindřichův Hradec) associated with the illumination of books, and moved towards the grandiose cycles of the period of high culture during the reign of Charles IV, in which the setting began to play an important role, as in the Karlštejn Castle, the Emmaus Church in Prague and St. Wenceslas's Chapel in the Prague Cathedral. Art at the end of the fourteenth and the beginning of the fifteenth centuries culminated in remarkable examples of late Gothic painting which already contained the seeds of the Renaissance period (Kutná Hora, St. Barbara's Cathedral). Czech panel painting was of exceptionally high quality, having been promoted in the early fourteenth century by commissions from the church hierarchy, from the court and later from the nobility. The magnificent cycle of paintings by the Master of Vyšší Brod is evidence of the growing maturity of highly personal views on art which found further expression in the lyricism of the spiritual paintings of the Master of Třeboň and the more vigorous approach of the court painter, Theodorik. The end of the fourteenth and the beginning of the fifteenth centuries brought many examples of the "Beautiful Style", especially in panel paintings of Madonnas. At the same time, themes concerning suffering were much more forceful, an evidence that art was beginning to respond to real life experience. The Gothic lingered on well into the sixteenth century in the illumination of books and in panel paintings in the Czech Lands. This brings us, after 1500, to other remarkable artists like the Master of Litoměřice, in whose works we may find indications of contact with the ideas of the Renaissance. From the early fourteenth century in Slovakia, as in the Czech Lands, Gothic art took over outside themes in mural painting (Spišská Kapitula, Dravce, etc.) and in the art of illuminating books. In both these branches and, above all, in panel paintings, highly individual expressions could be seen, based on the strength of particular artists. Although painting was hitherto dependent on commissions from the court and the Church, during the fifteenth and sixteenth centuries town councils, too, began to commission work, especially in rapidly developing mining centres. The Renaissance came to Slovakia earlier than to the Czech Lands, at the turn of the fifteenth and sixteenth centuries. This was thanks to the Italian masters invited to the country and to the spirit of the court of Matthias Corvinus which the feudal lords, secular and ecclesiastical, strove to imitate in the so-called "Upper Lands" of Hungary. The tradition of Late Gothic lingered on for a long time in Czech Renaissance painting: the new style was initiated not only by Italian artists but by local painters, firstly in great mural paintings in churches and in secular buildings (frescoes and graffiti). This style then faded out in the short-lived period of Mannerism at the Royal Court of Rudolph II where outstanding local and foreign artists intermingled. Baroque painting, like other forms of Baroque art, expressed the new aesthetics of style which dominated the Czech Lands throughout the seventeenth and eighteenth centuries. It spread throughout the whole country, affecting everything from the altars and walls of village churches to the magnificent ecclesiastical and secular edifices of towns, monasteries and castles. This multiplicity of creative art, though not always of the same standard, led to the cooperation of painting with other forms of art. At the same time this period made it possible to carry out exceptional tasks and thus to mature to levels second to none in Europe. Among such artists who emerged in the early seventeenth century we should mention the graphic artist Václav Hollar, a sensitive observer of events and of the landscape, and, later on, the painter Karel Škréta, who with sobriety and in his own individual way developed North Italian stimuli with a monumental approach. At the turn of the seventeenth and eighteenth centuries, the most outstanding figure was Petr Brandl, a dramatic interpreter of religious themes, who in his portraits carried on the tradition initiated by Škréta. In addition to many other Czech Baroque painters we should mention at least V. V. Reiner, a painter of frescoes, whose works are striking for their purity of colour and sense of composition. During the Baroque period, a great many foreign artists worked in Slovakia, including some truly outstanding figures such as A. F. Maulpertsch and J. L. Kracker. At the same time the Baroque portrait painter, Jan Kupecký, worked outside his native land for the greater part of his life. The wealth of Baroque paintings and murals in Eastern Slovakia was supplemented, even from medieval times, by vividly painted icons related to the Orthodox faith. The gradual advance of Romantic painting in the early nineteenth century, which had some remarkable exponents in the Czech Lands, came to a peak in the middle of the century as a result of the national revival movement. It is in this context that we meet the Romantic artist, Josef Mánes, whose paintings and drawings inspired the next generation as well as individual artists to give expression to ideas about the Czech past and present. The most remarkable was Mikuláš Aleš, an artist with roots in the folk traditions of his people, who was active towards the close of the nineteenth century. Others worth mentioning include Josef Navrátil, an artist of unusually intense sensitivity, employing a rich range of colours in his paintings and murals, and the figuralist Karel Purkyně who, in the concept of his pictures and the intensity of his expression of psychological tension, was a forerunner of the era of realism. The generation of the 1880's distinguished itself in monumental painting. In Slovakia, too, an important role was played by artists who contributed to the national revival movement, such as J. B. Klemens and P. Bohúň, or by those who gave monumentality to everyday themes (D. Skutecký). At the beginning of the new age, it was the artistic generation of the 1890's which took the lead in the Czech Lands. Such artists as the original interpreter of Impressionism, Antonín Slavíček, and the creator of gentle decorative works with an underlying symbolism, Jan Preisler, came to the fore. Even before the First World War, Cubism had penetrated into the country with the works of several striking artistic personalities (B. Kubišta, E. Filla, etc.). Developments in painting in the first half of the twentieth century made possible a confrontation of different trends and directions. Surrealism found specific expression, as did the work of artists who went beyond the framework of existing styles (F. Kupka, J. Lada, J. Zrzavý, J. Šíma and others). From the 1920's on Slovak painting began to seek and find its own path, closely linked with the character of the land, its landscape and its people. From the pioneering work of Martin Benka, it began to take on breadth and to respond in an original way to modern trends in the visual arts (L. Fulla, M. Galanda, M. A. Bazovský). During the nineteenth and especially during the twentieth century, drawing and graphic art, both in their own right and in connection with book illustration, have yielded a number of outstanding works. Art in Czechoslovakia in the present epoch is making full use of this broad basis to continue its development and give a new social content to painting, graphic art and the illustration of books.

10. J. Čapek: From the cycle "Yearnings". National Gallery, Prague

11. Central Bohemian landscape near Líteň ▶

BOHEMIA AND MORAVIA

The memory of the ancient country, where the historic lands of Bohemia and Moravia lie, is hidden deep beneath the deposits left by a thousand years of history. All the secrets uncovered from the depths indicate that the area of today's Bohemia and Moravia were endowed by nature with all the proper preconditions for human settlement.

In about the middle of the first millennium the first Slavonic tribes came here from the area lying between the Oder and Dnieper rivers. The Byzantine historian, Prokopios, who between the years 527 and 536 A.D. took part in military expeditions to these parts, mentions the Slav settlers in his history. "These peoples", he writes, "these Slavs and Ants, are not ruled by one man, but from time immemorial they have lived democratically and therefore all matters — both pleasant and difficult — are always discussed jointly . . . Both tribes share a single tongue which is harsh and barbaric. They are not in any way evil or malicious but rather sincere and frank as are the Huns . . ." Another report about the first half of the seventh century can be found in a Frankish chronicle. About the year 660, the chronicler writes: "In the fortieth year of the rule of Chlothar (623—624), a man by the name of Samo, a Frank from the Senon region, took with him a number of merchants and went among Slavs who were called Wends to trade with them . . . When the Wends waged war against the Huns, the merchant Samo went with their army. The Wends, seeing how useful Samo was, chose him as their king and he ruled over them happily for thirty-five years. Under his rule, the Wends fought many battles against the Huns and thanks to his advice and good services, they were always victorious. Samo had twelve wives of Slav origin who bore him twenty-two sons and fifteen daughters."

The most ancient Czech chronicler, Cosmas, in his history written in Latin at the beginning of the twelfth century, recounts the original tribal legends about the coming of the first Slavs to Bohemia, the story of the first princes and tales about the first Czech rulers of the Přemyslid line. Even though we are enchanted mainly by the beauty of these legends and myths, it is a fact that archaeologists later found traces of early Slav fortified settlements at the very places Cosmas mentioned in his chronicles.

It was only at the beginning of the ninth century that conditions became ripe for the formation of a great Slav state covering the territories of Moravia, Western Slovakia, parts of Hungary, Poland, Silesia and Bohemia. Mention of the first Moravian ruler known to history, Prince Mojmír (830—846), who joined the princedom of Nitra to the Moravian state, driving out Prince Pribina, is to be found in a letter from the Bishop of Bavaria to the Pope. The most outstanding rulers of the Great Moravian Empire, Rastislav and Svatopluk, are referred to in the Fulda chronicles and in a papal bull issued by Pope John VIII, adjusting relations between the Diocese of Moravia and the Holy See and permitting the use of the Slavonic liturgy.

Rastislav, who, in 863, invited two missionaries from Salonika in Macedonia, Constantine and Methodius, to the Great Moravian Empire, fought against the insistence of the use of the incomprehensible Latin tongue, as well as the powerful influences of his western neighbours. The missionaries created for the Czechs the glagolitic script and translated into Old Slavonic the majority of ecclesiastical texts. Various legends were taken down in this language, including the legend of the life of St. Wenceslas.

The Great Moravian Empire, one of the early medieval feudal states, collapsed in the years 903—906 under the onslaught of Magyar invaders. But the heritage it left had a great influence on future developments. Not only was it a powerful domain, but its culture achieved a remarkable level. The jewels, swords, vessels and whole temples discovered by Czech archaeologists have aroused the admiration of the whole of Europe. Constantine and Methodius were not only the originators of the Slavonic liturgy, but also of the Czech and Slovak literature, the first examples of which date from the ninth century. Their disciples, who were after Methodius' death (885) driven into exile, spread the new script to the Bulgarians, Serbs and Russians and thus laid the foundations for Slavonic literature.

After the collapse of the Great Moravian Empire, the history of the Czechs and Slovaks for a long time developed along separate paths. The centre of gravity of political and cultural development shifted from Moravia to Bohemia. At the end of the ninth and at the beginning of the tenth century, after a long and bitter struggle to unite the various Slavonic tribes living on the territories of Bohemia, the rulers of the Czech tribes established an independent state. It was headed by princes of the Přemyslid dynasty who established their seat in Prague. In the eleventh and twelfth centuries, the Czech medieval state, basing its defences on princely fortresses, gained a strong position among the feudal domains of Europe. In the year 1085, Vratislav II was the first to be given the title of king. In 1212 Přemysl Otakar I became hereditary king with the right to elect the Holy Roman Emperor. The Golden Bull of Sicily (1212) settled relations between the lands of the Czech Crown and the Holy Roman Empire.

The discovery of rich silver deposits on Czech territory led in the thirteenth century to an unprecedented increase in the power of the last Přemyslids. They closed their gap with Europe and with the help of foreign colonizers and Italian and French architects, constructed a network of fortified Gothic castles on the hilltops of Bohemia and Moravia. Many royal towns were established, along with monasteries, churches and fortified manors. The Kingdom of Bohemia became one of the most important powers in Europe. Přemysl Otakar II gained the territories of Austria, which remained part of the Czech crown lands for a long time, and the last-but-one of the Přemyslids, Wenceslas II, joined to the Czech crown the crowns of Poland and Hungary. When in 1306 the male line of the Přemyslids died out, rulers of the Luxembourg family came to the Czech throne. John of Luxembourg, husband of Eliška Přemyslovna, saw his main role in waging war and in the ideas of chivalry of the Europe of his day. His son, Charles IV (1346—1378) led the Czech state to the peak of its political power. When he also gained the crown of the

Holy Empire, Prague became the virtual centre of Europe, where the greatest figures in the cultural world of the time met. The first university in Central Europe was in Prague (1348). The majestic Cathedral of St. Vitus at Prague Castle was being constructed, fortified castles were built as well as towns and cities. Architecture flourished and literature and the arts were promoted.

Conflicts which came about at the end of the fourteenth century within Czech feudal society and the Church culminated in the first decades of the fifteenth century in the powerful Hussite revolutionary movement. The burning at the stake of John Huss, Master of Prague University and principal spokesman of the Czech Reformation, at Constance in 1415 on the orders of the ecclesiastical consilium, fanned the flames of revolution in the Kingdom of Bohemia. Under the military leader, Jan Žižka, a people's army was organized which not only by its military skill, but also by the strength of its ideas, defeated the much stronger armies of the German crusaders. In the Hussite town of Tábor, a new society came into being, based on the principles of equality for all people. From 1421 to 1434, Hussite troops resisted the superior strength of feudal and ecclesiastical Europe. Revolutionary Bohemia sent out manifestos to various countries on the continent.

When the feudal and ecclesiastical hierarchy of Europe realized that the Czech nation could not be defeated by force of arms, they prepared to compromise and embarked on the tactic of making false promises. The next hundred years were full of battles with defeats alternating with more hopeful periods, such as the reign of the Hussite king, George of Poděbrady (1458—1471). This monarch sent a message to the King of France, Louis XI, in which he proposed the establishment of an association of Christian rulers capable of restricting the intrigues of the Papal See and ensuring a negotiated peace in Europe.

However, when in the year 1526 Ferdinand of Habsburg ascended the Czech throne, a period of nearly four hundred years of the darkest reactionary rule began for the Czech Kingdom, which gradually pared away the country's independence and brought it under the direct rule of the multi-national Habsburg monarchy. During the first hundred years of Habsburg rule, Hussite ideas still guided the anti-Catholic opposition in all internal conflicts and sustained the spirit of revolt and resistance among the people. This was a period when the power of the nobility and the burghers was growing and the re-opened silver mines led to the flourishing of towns and cities and to an upsurge in the arts. The development of the Czech language could be seen in all beauty in the translation of what was known as the Kralice Bible. The Imperial court of Rudolph II in Prague was a gathering place for such world-renowned scholars as Jan Kepler and Tycho Brahe.

Catastrophe came in the year 1620, when the uprising of the Czech Estates who had wanted to depose the Habsburgs from the Czech throne was defeated at the Battle of the White Mountain.

Then followed a period known by the common people as the "Time of Darkness". What the Habsburgs had failed to do before, they now succeeded in achieving with considerable assistance from the Catholic Church by methods of terror hitherto unprecedented in Czech history. Twenty-seven Czech noblemen who had led the rising were executed in Prague's Old Town Square. The only religious faith that was permitted was Catholicism. A royal decree was issued, containing the following words: "If anyone within the stated period of six months has not come to terms with us and our Holy Catholic faith . . . we will neither permit nor allow such a person to continue to reside in our hereditary Kingdom of Bohemia or to retain possession of his property, for prior to leaving our Kingdom of Bohemia they must sell their property to their relatives or other Catholic members of the population . . ."

There was a wave of mass emigration, the country losing such outstanding figures as Jan Amos Komenský (Comenius), the great philosopher and educationalist. Granting equal status to the German language led to much stronger and more rigid Germanization of the Czechs. The Church dispatched Jesuit inquisitors to Bohemia to use force, craft and the splendours of Baroque to re-Catholicize the Czech heretics, for by that time hardly one in five of the population had proclaimed the Catholic faith.

The plebeian Czech nation did not yield even to this concentrated onslaught, even though as a state Bohemia had ceased to play an independent political role in Europe, and even though after the unending wars which ebbed and flowed across its territory, the population had been virtually decimated so that hardly a million and a half souls remained. The yearning for freedom and justice lived on in the literary production of the people, coming to life in peasant uprisings, and was preserved in the countryside among the common folk. These tiny embers, smouldering in the ashes of suffering and hardship, were again fanned into flame at the end of the eighteenth century during the period of enlightenment which in Bohemia developed into an era of national revival. Once again the Czech language was revived and culture and learning again began to restore the broken links with the glorious period of the nation's history. Despite the efforts of Vienna to centralize and Germanize its subject nations, the process of creating the Czech nation was reaching a peak. The movement for national liberation inevitably led to the establishment of the Czechoslovak Republic in 1918 when the Czechs and Slovaks once more came together in an independent state.

The first twenty years of independence, however, did not fulfil the hopes which had been kindled by the new-found freedom and by the Great October Revolution, whose ideals strengthened the age-old democratic traditions of the Czech nation. Only the Communist party which came into being in 1921 fought for the just demands both of the working class and the whole nation.

The period of bourgeois government collapsed in fiasco after the Munich dictate of 1938 which destroyed the united republic, soon to become a prey to Hitler's Germany. Six years of fascist occupation during which some of the finest sons of the nation were sacrificed ended thanks to the eventual victory of the Soviet Army and the other Allied forces. On 9 May, 1945, Prague, in the throes of an uprising against the Nazis, welcomed the first Soviet tanks. With them came freedom and the dawn of the new era of socialism.

12. Prague Castle and the rooftops of the Lesser Town

PRAGUE

Praga caput regni they used to say in days gone by. Indeed, all the greatest events of Czechoslovakia's history took place within its venerable walls. All styles of architecture have left their mark here. Prague never succumbed completely to any one of them, but blended them all into a single stirring harmony.

The oldest buildings in Prague date back to the period more than a thousand years ago when the first Christian princes founded modest sanctuaries on the spots they had chosen for their tombs. There are several Romanesque rotundas from the tenth century and the first little church was built on Hradčany Hill by Prince Bořivoj towards the end of the 9th century. On the rocky knoll overlooking the settlement, the Přemyslids began to build their fortified seat. Each period added something to it. Hollows were filled in, the ground level rose, so that by the time of Charles IV the ground-floor was on the same level as the highest floor of the fortified palace built by Spytihněv II three centuries earlier.

Most impressive of all are the ecclesiastical buildings at Hradčany. St. Vitus's Cathedral is a treasure of Gothic art and architecture. King Charles IV (1346—1378) who was at the same time Holy Roman Emperor, cherished Prague and chose it as his seat, transforming it into a large and splendid city. Where the Chapel of Prince Wenceslas once stood, he had a cathedral built worthy of the seat of an archbishop. The first to work on it was Matthias of Arras who built the ring of choir chapels. When he died ten years later (1352), he was buried in the unfinished building and Charles IV invited young Peter Parler from Gmünd to continue the work. Parler, who settled down in Prague, devoted his entire life to the edifice. His Gothic style expressed a free-flowing fantasy and all the decorations of the Cathedral came from his lodge where his four sons worked with him. Twenty-eight columns bear the weight of the vaulting of the nave with its windows and its arcades over which runs the portrait gallery or triforium containing twenty-one busts of famous ecclesiastical and secular notables. The Cathedral has a nave and two aisles, a transept, and a gallery and the ring of chapels behind the choir. The building turns its most impressive face towards the city. It was on this side that Parler placed the porch and the tall tower, and the Golden Gate with its magnificent Venetian mosaics.

For a long time work on St. Vitus's Cathedral remained at a standstill. This was at the height of the Hussite movement which was sparked off by the burning at the stake of John Huss in 1415, when the country had to be defended in the struggle for freedom and purity of conscience. Only after the flames of war had died down, in 1502, did the builder Benedict Ried complete the bold vaulting of the Vladislav Hall, the most splendid masterpiece of Late Gothic, the windows of which show the first Renaissance motifs north of the Alps. This hall is now the scene of the election of presidents of the Czechoslovak Republic.

Further hard times awaited Prague and its castle. After the rising of the Czech Estates against the Habsburgs in 1618 and the ill-fated Battle of the White Mountain in 1620, the Czech Lands were condemned to a period of darkness which was to last for almost three hundred years. The Cathedral lived through the country's history with its people. Calvinist preachers who came here with Frederick of the Palatinate, the "Winter King", stripped it of all its ornaments. A hundred years later, the victorious Catholics, in their turn, contributed the silver tomb of the Counter-Reformation saint, John of Nepomuk. Prague by that time had ceased to be the royal seat and the castle was deserted. Under Maria Theresa and Joseph II, the castle was rebuilt in Neo-Classical style. Not until the nineteenth century was the Cathedral crowned with two spires, stained glass windows and ornamental grills. The whole edifice was actually not completed until 1929 — that is to say six centuries after it was begun. Beneath Collin's marble mausoleum in St. Vitus's Cathedral on which lie figures depicting Ferdinand I and Anne Jagiello are metal coffins containing the remains of the rulers who made the greatest contribution to the Czech history: Charles IV, his son Wenceslas IV and George of Poděbrady.

Charles IV, in particular, was a great collector of holy relics and works of art, with which he then adorned St. Vitus's Cathedral. Unhappily the valuable collections were often moved in times of war and much of the gold and silver was used to pay armies of mercenaries. After the defeat of the Reformation, thousands of Saxon, Bavarian and Swedish carriages took away irreplaceable jewels which were never returned, and so Prague ceased to be the "Golden City". Part of the treasures that have been preserved are exhibited in the second courtyard of the castle in the Chapel of the Holy Rood. There are objects made of gold and crystal, reliquaries and various utensils. All of them testify to the high standard of medieval art in Bohemia.

The heart of the Cathedral is the tomb of St. Wenceslas, the Prince who was murdered by his brother Boleslav in 925 or 935, and whom the people chose as the patron saint of their country for his love of peace and his wisdom. Over this tomb which had once been lodged in the Romanesque rotunda, Peter Parler built a chapel which is a masterpiece of Czech Gothic art. The unusually high walls with tiny windows are decorated with amethysts and jaspers set in gilded plaster, while above them on the walls is a cycle of paintings by an unknown

13. The third courtyard of Prague Castle with St. Vitus's Cathedral

14. The east end of St. Vitus's Cathedral with a ring of choir chapels

15. Central nave and choir of St. Vitus's Cathedral ▶

16. The crown jewels of the Kingdom of Bohemia   *17. The St. Wenceslas's Chapel in St. Vitus's Cathedral* ▶

master of the Czech medieval school on the theme of Christ's Passion. Above the cornice another painter completed the decorations in Renaissance style. The ornamentation of the chapel includes the fourteenth-century sepulchre of St. Wenceslas and a statue of the saint carved possibly by Peter Parler himself and his nephew Henry.

From the corner of the chapel a staircase leads up to a room where the crown jewels of the Kingdom of Bohemia are kept behind seven locks. The crown which Charles IV commissioned in the middle of the fourteenth century is said to be of greater value than the whole Cathedral. In times of unrest the crown was taken elsewhere for safekeeping, but the Czech people carefully followed its fate. When, after the end of the Austro-Prussian War (1866) the government had it taken back to Prague from Vienna, it was done in the dead of night. Nevertheless, village patrols were vigilant and fires lit on the hilltops marked the progress of the precious treasure.

As we leave the Cathedral we come at every step upon places steeped in history. In the third courtyard whose paving stones cover a labyrinth of passage-ways, cellars, old fortifications and burial places, stands a lovely little Gothic statue of St. George and the Dragon dating from the year 1373. A granite monolith in the simple beauty of stone honours the victims of the First World War. Behind the Cathedral, where there is an unbelievable maze of buttresses, finials and stone decorations, we come upon the spot where the stone throne of the ancient princes used to stand. On the opposite side the square is flanked by the Romanesque Basilica of St. George. The silhouette of its twin towers is a characteristic feature of the panorama of Hradčany.

The tiny "dolls' houses" in Golden Lane, built on to the wall of the sentries' walk in the fortifications over Stag Moat back in the seventeenth century, used to house the castle guard and goldsmiths. Behind Golden Lane stands the notorious prison, known as the Dalibor Tower. It is possible to go right down into its lowest dungeons.

The Renaissance period also left its mark on the castle complex. The lovely Renaissance Summer Palace was built by Ferdinand I for his young wife Anne, daughter of Vladislav Jagiello, who brought him the Crown of Bohemia as part of her dowry (1526). The Italian architect Paolo della Stella designed it with open arcades as if for the climate of Italy. Fancy dress balls and firework displays used to be staged here. It is now an art gallery.

In the garden of the Summer Palace, which the people refer to as the Belvedere, there is a metal fountain, cast in 1573 according to a design by Francesco Terzio by Tomáš Jaroš of Brno, who also cast the biggest bell in the tower of St. Vitus's Cathedral (it is called Sigismund and it weighs 135 metric centners). As the water springs from the fountain and strikes the metal, it makes a pleasant sound which has earned it the name of the "Singing Fountain".

32

19. *The little houses in the Golden Lane*

20. *Golden Lane at Hradčany, Prague*

◄ 18. *The Vladislav Hall at Prague Castle*

Another curious building in Prague is the Renaissance Summer Palace Hvězda (Star) which Ferdinand's son had built for his mistress, Philippine Welser, in the shape of a six-pointed star with rhombus-shaped chambers.

After the Battle of the White Mountain, the Protestant nobles lost their property, which was then easily acquired by Spanish and Italian commanders of the armies of the Catholic League. In building their palaces they wanted, above all, to express the strength of their victorious ideology. Entire districts were razed to make way for these new palaces, the largest of which was built for Albrecht of Wallenstein. However, the pomposity of the new style soon yielded to the elevating influence of the environment. Artists refused to comply with the self-important aims of the powerful, preferring instead to give expression to their own experience. The façades of the houses took on wavy lines, the interiors of cathedrals and churches came to life and the faces of carved saints reflected passion. Their robes were executed with flowing lines, female saints acquired a look of gracious-ness and the lips of Madonnas seemed waiting to receive a kiss. Sculptors such as Braun and Brokoff endeavoured to give dramatic expression to the yearnings of the human spirit.

Many churches in Prague spoke this language. The architect K. I. Dientzenhofer strove to counterbalance the majesty of Hradčany Castle by creating the cupola and tower of St. Nicholas's Church in the Lesser Town. The Church of Our Lady of Victories contains the little statue of the Infant Jesus of Prague, which is an object of veneration, especially abroad. The rich interior of St. James's Church is a perfect setting for concerts of church music. Another unique building in Prague is the Loreto. First a copy of Bramante's Santa Casa was erected here, to which were then added the cloisters, monuments, chapel, the building proper and the tower with its famous carillon. In 1626, the Lady Benigna of Lobkowicz made the first donation for the building and from then on the Loreto treasure grew apace. Today it includes many gold and crystal objects, the most valuable of which is what is known as the "Prague Sun" (1698), a monstrance which is set with 6,222 diamonds.

The main approach to the Castle is from Hradčany Square. When in 1541 a great fire destroyed a consid-erable part of the Lesser Town and part of the Castle itself, as well as the houses in Hradčany Square, powerful

21. *The Renaissance Queen Anne's Summer Palace, Hradčany, Prague*

22. *Baroque diamond-studded monstrance from the Loreto treasury*

23. *The front of Loreto Church, Hradčany*

25. Master of the Lamentation of Žebrák: "The Lamentation of Christ of Žebrák", National Gallery, Prague

noblemen seized the opportunity to build great palaces on this convenient site, which had hitherto been used as a market place. The Renaissance Schwarzenberg Palace today houses the Museum of Military History. Baroque is represented by the Tuscan Palace and Rococo by the Archbishop's Palace.

In the Šternberk Palace, as early as at the beginning of the eighteenth century, there was a picture gallery established by art-loving noblemen. Today it is the headquarters of the National Gallery and its collections. It contains outstanding works of Czech Gothic art and of seventeenth- and eighteenth- century Baroque (paintings by Škréta, Kupecký, Rainer, etc.). Among pictures by artists from other lands exhibited here are the works by Italian, German, French, Dutch and Flemish masters. The sensitive arrangement of the paintings in the spacious, well-lit halls makes a walk through the National Gallery an unforgettable experience.

Just beneath the Castle is the little-known picturesque district called Nový Svět (the New World). Poor townsfolk used to live here and it has preserved many of its old features. Its simplicity is in stark contrast to the majesty of the Castle and the magnificence of the Černín Palace.

Another place which bears witness to the past is Strahov. The building was formerly a Premonstratensian Monastery and the visitor is still reminded of this today by its vast library. It now houses the Museum of Czech Literature which contains a splendid collection of literature produced by the nation throughout the ages.

In the Renaissance period parks and gardens were treated as works of art. Rudolph II wisely provided his Golden Prague with refreshing flower gardens and shady avenues. Following the example set by the royal gardens, the noble owners of the palaces in the Lesser Town uprooted the vineyards on the slopes and replaced them by the terraced gardens, which adorn Prague to this day. In the summer months concerts are frequently performed in the unique natural setting of these lovely gardens. One of the most beautiful is also the smallest. It is called the Vrtba Garden and is situated beside the house which used to belong to Kryštof Harant of Polžice, a fine Czech composer, who was beheaded when accounts were settled after the Battle of the White Mountain. From here one can move on to the Seminary Garden and to Petřín Hill, which rises over the city like a rolling green wave. Here can be found not only the historic Hunger Wall, which Charles IV ordered to be built to

26. *The terraces of the Kolovrat and Ledeburg Gardens in Prague's Lesser Town*

provide work for the poor, but also an ancient church, an observation tower, a maze of mirrors and extensive rose gardens.

The most beautiful walk in Prague is across Charles Bridge. The approach to the bridge from the Lesser Town is guarded by a gateway with two towers, the smaller of which is of Romanesque origin. It was built simultaneously with the construction of the original Judith Bridge in the third quarter of the 12th century. At the Old Town end of the bridge on the first pier stands another tower. This was the work of Peter Parler and the design and construction of the tower itself, as well as the sculptured saints and kings and their emblems which adorn it, have made it one of the loveliest medieval towers in Europe. The tower is open to the public and from it one can get a splendid view of the city. On the top floor can be found the marks of medieval stonemasons, the initials of prisoners held there and also some illegible inscriptions evidently intended to keep away evil spirits.

Charles Bridge provides an eloquent example of how the genius of locality can master and blend together contrasting styles. From 1668 to 1715, the monasteries, the Jesuit College and various faculties had thirty groups of Baroque statuary placed along the bridge to bear witness to the defeat of the Reformation. But the original purpose of the statues was soon forgotten and the people of Prague came to regard the works as their own. The statues became rooted in the walls of the bridge like an avenue of ancient trees that had always belonged here. The bridge became a popular spot for leisurely strolls. Its five hundred and twenty metres are full of delightful impressions. The view in every direction brings closer the intoxicating beauty of the Vltava and its banks. One can step down from the bridge on to Kampa Island, where the city goes right down to the level of the water as it did in days of old. On the other side is a branch of the Vltava known as the Čertovka, which washes the foundations of the old houses in what is called Prague's Venice.

Beyond the Bridge Tower lies Křižovnické náměstí (the Square of the Knights Hospitallers) whose small area is flanked by several remarkable structures. The Monastery of the Knights Hospitallers and the Church of St. Francis stand next to St. Saviour's Church, the façade of which is guarded by statues of the country's patron

27. The River Vltava in the centre of Prague

28. *Baroque statue of St. Lutgard by M. B. Braun on Charles Bridge, Prague*

saints. A little further on is the entrance to the Clementinum, once a Jesuit bastion, which today houses the immense State Library. Next to the Castle, this is the biggest complex of historic buildings in the city.

The Old Town has kept its ancient atmosphere in its narrow streets, courtyards and gateways, which often look like some picturesque stage sets for a thrilling drama.

This atmosphere can be felt most strongly in what used to be the Jewish quarter. In the Middle Ages, Jews made up quite a large proportion of the population, but they were never very secure. Sometimes they would be driven from the city and would lose their possessions, then they might be allowed to come back again and rich individuals often became the king's creditors. As time went on, the ghetto vanished as a result of building reconstruction and all that remained were a handful of synagogues, a town hall and the Jewish cemetery. Yet these are among the most remarkable ancient buildings in Prague.

The Old-New Synagogue from the thirteenth century is one of the oldest Jewish houses of prayer in Europe and it is one of the most unusual Gothic structures in Prague. Only a little light penetrates the narrow windows into the two-naved hall. The dark walls, which, it is said, have never been cleaned so that traces of blood from anti-Jewish pogroms should not be erased, envelop the interior of the Synagogue in a shroud of sorrow and mystery.

In the Jewish Cemetery some twelve thousand gravestones set here between the fifteenth and eighteenth centuries are crowded together. The grave most frequently visited is that of the legendary Rabbi Yehuda Löw

29. *The Old Town Bridge Tower, Prague* ▶

ben Bazelel, who is said to have created and brought to life the clay figure of the Golem. Into the crevices in Rabbi Löw's tombstone visitors often place slips of paper on which they have scribbled their secret wishes. Evidence of the era of Rudolph II is provided by the fact that another synagogue bears the name of Mordechai Maisel who was, in this time, the richest man in Prague.

The Powder Tower, the Bridge Tower's younger sister, provides entry to the Old Town from a modern crossroads. Celetná Street, through which coronation processions used to pass, leads to the Old Town Square which is the virtual heart of the city. The historic Old Town Hall used to be the scene of the election of kings, of courts of law, of murders and revengeful bloodshed. After the Battle of the White Mountain, the pavement in front of the Old Town Hall was the scene of the mass execution of twenty-seven Czech noblemen who had led the uprising against the Emperor. Their heads were displayed for several years in cages hung from Prague towers. One entire wing of the Old Town Hall was destroyed by fire in the final stage of the Second World War. Foreign visitors patiently wait in front of the Town Hall's tower for the hour to strike and the procession of apostles to make their appearance in the windows above the Astronomical Clock. But Czech people have the additional knowledge that the greatest treasure of the clock is the almanach painted round it by Josef Mánes, one of the foremost Czech painters of the nineteenth century.

In the centre of the square stands the monument to John Huss, which was unveiled in 1918. Since then it has been a silent yet eloquent inspiration to the people in their times of trouble.

The Old Town Square could be a text-book of architectural styles. To this day treasures of the Gothic and Romanesque periods are still being uncovered as façades are renovated. The destruction of part of the Town Hall in one corner of the square has opened the view on to the Church of St. Nicholas, built by Kilian Ignatz Dientzenhofer. However, it is the Church of Our Lady Before Týn, commonly known as the Týn Church, that dominates the square. Its entrance is concealed behind houses, over the gabled façades of which the silhouette of the Church's front with its twin towers rises. The Týn Church used to belong to the followers of the Chalice (the Utraquists), but when the Emperor Sigismund ascended the throne he had a gallows made of its roof

◄ *30. The Old-New Synagogue in Prague's Old Town*

31. The Old Jewish Cemetery, Prague

32. *Prague's Old Town Square, the astronomical clock and the Church of Our Lady Before Týn*

33. *Baroque statues of antique gods and goddesses at Troja, Prague*

beams from which to hang Hussite warriors. After the defeat of the Protestants, the statue of King George of Poděbrady was thrown down from the church tower. Inside can be found the tomb of the great Danish astronomer, Tycho Brahe, who discovered a new star during his stay in Prague.

Beginning from the reign of Emperor Joseph II (1741—1790), who closed down many churches and monasteries, only secular buildings were constructed in Prague. In the nineteenth century, industry and commerce took the initiative, embankments were constructed and the river was regulated.

Prague underwent no more building development until the beginning of the struggle for the Czech national revival in the late 18th—early 19th centuries. But this development was not halted even by the defeat of the rising of 1848. Important witnesses to the national revival movement include the National Museum, which dominates Wenceslas Square, and the National Theatre, built, and again re-built after a fire, from the voluntary contributions of the people. In its foundations there are blocks of stone from the country's various important mountains. What is now the House of Artists also dates from about the same time. Somewhat later, magnificent exhibition grounds were constructed in Prague and on Petřín Hill an imitation of the Eiffel Tower was erected.

With the development of the modern city which required banks, railway stations, hotels and department stores, the expansive present frequently vied with the defenceless past. Many valuable historic buildings were pulled down, although the protests of artists succeeded in saving from destruction the most unique parts of Prague, the Old Town and the Lesser Town. The purely modern housing estates have found their setting in the suburbs where the new Prague is being built today. The historic centre of the city has been declared an urban reservation and great care is being devoted to the preservation of ancient buildings. Bethlehem Chapel, where John Huss used to preach, of which only the foundations and some of the outer walls remained intact, has been

34. The Emmaus Church of Our Lady and the Slav Patron-saints, Prague, with its modern spire-like construction

rebuilt in its original form. The Carolinum, the oldest part of Charles University, and many other valuable buildings have also been restored.

Prague still contains many unhappy reminders of the Second World War. They include the prison, torture chamber and execution cell in the former headquarters of the Gestapo in the Petschke Palace, as well as the Church of St. Cyril and Methodius, in the crypt of which the parachutists who assassinated the Nazi Reichsprotektor Heydrich hid and perished.

Little memorial plaques scattered throughout the city recall the liberation struggle of the people of Prague and those who fell during the uprising against the Nazis in May 1945. At Olšany Cemetery are the graves of soldiers and airmen of the Soviet Army and the other Allied forces who laid down their lives in the fight for victory over the common enemy.

Considerable damage, much of it irreparable, was caused to the city by air-raids during the Second World War. The Emmaus Monastery, where the Slavonic liturgy was fostered, was burnt down. Now its reconstruction is nearing completion. Special attention is being paid to the restoration of a unique cycle of murals, which are among the masterpieces of Czech Gothic painting. The towers of Emmaus Monastery have been topped with new spires and thus architecture of a past age has been combined with the artistic expression of our own times.

When freedom was won again and Prague Castle became the seat of the President of the Republic, it was restored and its underground precincts were investigated and opened to the public. Hradčany Castle bears eloquent witness to vital periods of the country's history and is, at the same time, a symbol of state sovereignty.

The blending of modern Prague with the ancient city, the skyscrapers in the vicinity of the four hundred towers and spires of historic Prague, all contribute to the fact that the city is so admired and venerated. From time immemorial it has been possessed of a special charm to which many great personalities have succumbed.

At the court of Charles IV, Petrarch declared that Prague's hills reminded him of the setting of Rome and at the time of the Counter-Reformation Prague was described as the "Rome of the North". René Descartes came here with the military forces which subjugated the country, but for him it was the interest of the scholar that prevailed. Chateaubriand expressed regret that such a lovely city did not lie beside the sea. Joachim Barrande made his home here and devoted his entire life to the study of Czech rock formations and the hill above the River Vltava where the main film studios are situated bears his name to this day. Rodin considered Prague — mainly because of the beauty of its women — to be "Dante's Paradise", and Paul Valéry regretted that Victor Hugo had never visited a city which could provide so many fascinating themes.

35. The Czechoslovak Television Centre at Kavčí Hory, Prague ▶

Music has always reigned supreme in Prague and many famous names in the world of music are closely connected with this city. The Estates Theatre, now known as the Tyl Theatre, was the scene of the glorious première of Mozart's *Don Giovanni* in 1787. The Bertramka Villa in the Smíchov district of Prague retains memories of Mozart's visit there and in particular of that October evening when the overture is said to have been written in such a hurry that the orchestra had to perform it from scores on which the ink was not yet dry. Prague has always felt the honour of having given Mozart some degree of happiness and guides to the Loreto Church and Strahov Monastery will proudly show you an organ on which the great composer played. Ludwig van Beethoven also had his time of enchantment in Prague, reflected in works for the mandolin which he composed for the Countess Clara. He, too, appreciated the understanding shown him by the people of Prague. Carl Maria Weber willingly learned the Czech language so that he could conduct in a Prague theatre. Hector Berlioz described the beauty of the city in poetic language and when he departed he sighed: "Oh Prague, when shall I set

eyes on you again?" Franz Liszt, who was loved by the people of the city as a wonderful pianist and composer, frequently stopped for a glass of Mělník wine at a wineshop which existed for a time in the old church of St. Martin-in-the-Wall. It was in Prague that Saint-Saëns composed his *Dying Swan*. Richard Wagner trecked here on foot from Dresden and shed tears when he left the city. Piotr Ilyich Tchaikovsky, who conducted a concert here, noted in his diary: "A minute of absolute happiness!" Edvard Grieg was in Prague. Gustave Charpentier came here to hear his *Louise* performed and was enraptured by the love songs Moravian students sang and danced for him in Prague inns.

Musicians, writers and artists have all found in Prague a lover, a sister and an intimate friend. The atmosphere in which for centuries artistic currents have met and intermingled is heightened by a peculiar inner tension. The Czech art historian V. V. Štech once put into words what many artists and ordinary folk have always felt when he said: "Prague is indeed a fateful city."

36. Panorama of Prague Castle with Petřín Hill

CENTRAL BOHEMIA

Central Bohemia forms a ring with a radius of a hundred kilometres, encircling the jewel that is the Czechoslovak capital city, Prague. It is an ancient land and the events that have taken place here go back into the most distant history of the Czech Lands.

The natural axes of Central Bohemia are formed by two great rivers which flow down into the centre of Bohemia from frontier mountains to the south and north: the middle and lower reaches of the Vltava and its tributaries, the Berounka and Sázava and the great River Elbe with its main tributary, the Jizera.

While the regions around the Berounka and the middle reaches of the Vltava and Sázava are full of hills and dales, forests and groves, the northern part of Central Bohemia, along the Elbe and the lower reaches of the Vltava, forms an extensive plain. Here is some of the most fertile soil in the whole country and so from ancient times this area has been referred to as the "Golden Belt" of the Czech Lands. Here are waving fields of wheat and barley and great green stretches of sugar beet fading into the distance and on the sunny slopes around Mělník are vineyards, blossoming orchards and market gardens where every type of vegetable is cultivated.

This was no doubt the picture of the fertile Czech landscape — a land flowing with milk and honey — which forefather Czech saw in his mind's eye when, as old chronicles tell, he gazed at it from Říp Hill — that strange hummock of clay, shaped like a bell or a helmet, rising in the midst of the flat blue-green landscape close to the confluence of Bohemia's two greatest rivers.

When you stand on the summit of Říp by one of the oldest Romanesque rotundas, you are struck by the gracious sweetness of the natural surroundings. The green of the woods and the gold of the cornfields are streaked

37. Great and Little Blaník, Central Bohemia

with the steel-grey surface of the Vltava and Elbe rivers. It breathes peace and echoes memories of a thousand years of history.

But long ago, in the distant mythical past, Central Bohemia was far different from how medieval chroniclers described it. It was actually covered with dense woods and marshlands through which streams and rivers fought their way. And rivers represented life. It was they that tempted the first settlers. Like geological layers, one above the other, the cultures of Europe's history intertwined, from the ancient hunters, via the Celts, Germanic tribes and Huns, to the Slavs, whose arrival in this part of the world began in the fifth century A.D. Various western Slavonic tribes settled close to the Vltava. This period, whose history is evidenced only by fragments of vessels, is deeply veiled in myths. Long and complicated developments had to take place before the Slav tribes united and before the Czechs assumed their leadership. The Latin name for the lands of the Czechs, Bohemia, which is used in West European languages to describe this area, comes from the name of one of the Celtic tribes, the Boii, who were the inhabitants long before the coming of the Slavs.

It is not surprising that life became concentrated in the heart of the Central Bohemian basin. It was not only a region full of rivers, but also a crossroads of trade routes. It was here, close to the Vltava and the Elbe, in this fertile, advantageously placed setting, that the first Slav fortified settlements were built and, with the coming of Christianity, the first stone churches. From here, too, beginning in the 10th century, came the glorious era of the Czech princely line of Přemyslids, whom Bohemia has to thank for four centuries of flourishing life and the laying of the foundations of towns which exist to this day. Even before Prague was founded, the Přemyslid princes built their seats on the left bank of the Vltava. At Budeč, we can find a reminder of the 10th century in the ancient and picturesque Rotunda of St. Peter and not far off, beneath the Gothic church of St. Clement at Levý Hradec, the foundations of a still older rotunda, dating from the 9th century, which was built by Prince Bořivoj.

The silent beauty of these historical structures is brought to life by old legends. The names of many great personalities of Czech history are linked with these spots: Princess Ludmila, Prince Wenceslas, Bishop Adalbert from the slaughtered line of Slavníks who had their seat at the Castle of Libice on the right bank of the Elbe. Connected with them, too, are the first steps towards creating a Czech culture in the monasteries established in Prague, at Sázava, Zbraslav and Ostrov, at the confluence of the Vltava and the Sázava rivers. More than ninety Romanesque churches still to be found in the wider environment of Prague are witness to the life that went on in the ninth and tenth centuries.

The thirteenth and fourteenth centuries gave Central Bohemia Gothic architecture in all its phases, from early Gothic castles and fortified seats to the construction of an extensive network of towns which today still dominate the region.

The culminating phase of this period began to shape the cultural landscape of Central Bohemia. The mysticism of the Gothic was humanized and adapted to the character of the countryside and the artistic sensitivity of the Czech people. The Přemyslid era, followed by the no less fruitful age of King and Emperor Charles IV impressed this part of the country with a heroic and romantic atmosphere. The Bohemia of Romanesque and Gothic mingles with Renaissance and Hussite architecture and the elaborate Baroque of the Counter-Reformation, Czech Rococo, Empire and Art Nouveau.

The valley of the River Berounka, which snakes its way through dense woodlands, has kept its romantic character to this day. The wealth of old castles in their beautiful setting scarcely touched by modern civilization enchant everyone who sets foot in this region. All of them, from the ruined Gothic castles of Žebrák and Týřov to the ancient Castle of Točník, carry within them a tiny piece of Czech history, like Krakovec Castle, where John Huss stayed before his fateful journey to face the Council of Constance.

There are two castles which must be mentioned, not only because they are in an excellent state of preservation, but chiefly because the splendour of their architecture and the wealth of art treasures they contain means that they rank among the jewels of medieval culture. One is the Castle of Křivoklát, founded in the thirteenth century, situated in the midst of dense forests. Its slender round tower surmounts the triangular forecourt and a complex of many different buildings gradually added in successive centuries. Where the stone castle now stands there used to be a wooden hunting lodge built by the first Přemyslids. Křivoklát was the scene of secret diplomatic negotiations and discussions among medieval scholars. The most powerful of the Přemyslid rulers, Přemysl Otakar II and his son Wenceslas II, were frequent visitors. Charles IV was forced to spend part of his childhood there. After completing his education in France and returning to Bohemia, he spent some time at Křivoklát with his first wife, Blanche de Valois. It is said of him that he had song birds and nightingales trapped and brought to Křivoklát wood where they were released so that their song would gladden the sad heart of his wife. A later king, Vladislav Jagiello, had Křivoklát rebuilt and, with a few small changes, it has been preserved in that form till now. At the same time, Křivoklát served as a stronghold guarding the western approaches to

Prague. The castle contains examples of every phase of Gothic architecture. Inside there is the Gothic altar, wonderful wood-carvings, and the building itself perched on a rocky promontory over the valley of the Rakovník stream produces a tremendous effect on the observer.

Central Bohemia can boast of yet another castle which apart from its historical significance and its magnificence has become symbolic of Czech sovereignty. This is the Castle of Karlštejn. It is one of the many outstanding works of architecture with which Charles IV, regarded as the "Father of the Country" enriched the Kingdom of Bohemia. This wise ruler, although educated abroad, so completely assimilated with Bohemia that all he did to increase its architectural glory is regarded as the complete embodiment of Czechness. Karlštejn provides just one such example. It is no ordinary Gothic castle, designed as a demonstration of power and to protect the kingdom against its enemies. Charles IV gave his architects an exact idea of what he wanted. Karlštejn was intended to be a state repository for holy relics and a symbolic and tangible proof of the divine origin of rulers and, at the same time, a repository for the Imperial crown jewels. The very choice of the castle's site showed considerable foresight. It rises up in purposefully vertical articulation where it can be seen from several sides between the surrounding hilltops. It took only nine years to build and inside it was concentrated all the very best of European Gothic architecture, sculpture and painting. The Chapel of the Holy Rood, situated in the main tower, remains almost untouched just as it was when the Czech king kept his vigil in the midst of all

38. The Royal Castle of Křivoklát

39. The chapel of Křivoklát Castle ▶

the wonderful panel paintings of saints and kings from the brush of the famous medieval painter Master Theodoric. Although the castle was restored and rebuilt in the course of the centuries, its original conception and the beauty of all it contains are virtually unchanged.

Similar in some ways, yet different in others, is the character of the landscape of the central reaches of the Vltava and Sázava rivers. The face of this area is perhaps more dramatic. The hilly broken surface of the land here made it impossible for any bigger towns to grow up and the poor little fields were far from generous to man. Since the Middle Ages, timber was floated down the Vltava from the Šumava Mountains and goods were sent down on rafts. Along the banks of the Vltava were the cottages of the raftsmen who knew all the tricks of the rapids and could guide their rafts along the treacherous rapids between the rocky banks. Little old villages and inns, frequented by the raftsmen, which grew up here in a natural way, add to the enchantment of the setting. The Vltava cascades of today, with their system of dams and power stations and great artificial reservoirs, tamed the river and transformed part of the Vltava valley into huge recreation areas like that around the Slapy dam.

The scenery along both banks of the Sázava has lost nothing of its romantic character. This region of stone-masons and cottagers is a paradise for those who want to ply their craft along swift waters between ancient weirs and find refuge in these lovely, almost forgotten spots.

But again, it is not nature alone that has shaped the landscape. Here, too, we find reminders of the earliest history of the Czech people. Sázava Monastery is among the rare national cultural treasures that bear witness to the distant Slav past. It was to this monastery that, in the 11th century, the Slavonic liturgy was brought from the Great Moravian Empire, making it the cradle of Czech literature. Not far off are other reminders of the Middle Ages, including the nearby Gothic Castle of Český Šternberk and the Romanesque Church in the village of Poříčí-on-Sázava.

One castle proudly dominates the region around Benešov, its tall cylindrical tower providing a clear land-

◄ *40. The Prague Gate at Rakovník*　　　　　　*41. The ruins of Krakovec Castle, Central Bohemia*

42. *Confluence of the rivers Elbe and Vltava at Mělník*

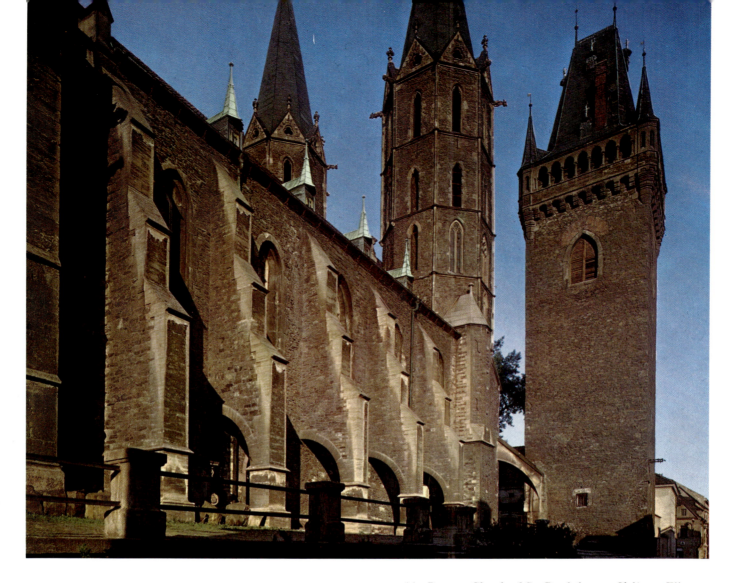

44. *Deanery Church of St. Bartholomew, Kolín-on-Elbe*

◄ *43. Gothic stained glass window from Slivenec Church. Applied Arts Museum, Prague*   *45. The medieval fortifications of the royal town of Nymburk*

46. *Miniature from a copy of the Kutná Hora Mining Charter. State Library of Czechoslovakia, Prague*

47. *Gothic Church of St. Barbara and the early Baroque Jesuit College at Kutná Hora*

48. *Italian Court at Kutná Hora*

mark. This is Konopiště Castle, originally built in Gothic style and standing on a wooded hill amidst a beautiful English-style park with a huge fishpond and rose gardens, ancient oak trees and a great deal of statuary.

The area around the left bank of the River Vltava gets its intimate character from the deeply wooded Brdy Hills. To the south lies the old mining town of Příbram. Three times since the Middle Ages this town has had a taste of its former glory. The last occasion was after 1945, when at the site of the original silver and lead mines, a still more precious ore — uranium — began to be mined. On the fringe of the original town of Příbram, new housing estates were built after 1948. Above it all, the once famous place of pilgrimage, Svatá Hora (Holy Hill), the setting of bitter campaigns in the days of the Counter-Reformation, with its glorious Baroque architecture, is somewhat of an anachronism. Not far away, on the fringe of the small town of the same name, is the Castle of Dobříš, built according to a design by the French architect Jules Robert de Cotte in the middle of the 18th century, in the setting of an extensive French- and English- style park.

The last interesting historic treasure before you reach Prague is the Castle of Zbraslav. A castle built by Přemysl Otakar II stood here. His son, Wenceslas II, founded a Cistercian monastery here in 1292. The original Gothic buildings were destroyed during the Hussite wars and at the beginning of the eighteenth century the castle was again rebuilt, this time in Baroque style.

The Elbe basin and that of the Vltava forming the northern part of the Central Bohemian region is for the most part flat. It cannot be said that this area has a dearth of royal castles, seats of the nobility and ancient towns. But the nature of the landscape provides more space for towns and the medieval cores of these towns exist unspoilt to this day. The golden cornfields of the fertile valley of the Elbe are criss-crossed with roads lined with avenues of trees and what might otherwise be a monotonous landscape is given variety of wooded hilltops, little birch groves, slender poplars, tiny patches of woodland and, from time to time, gleaming ponds and lakes.

The mist arising from the countryside brings back memories of past happenings which gave this place its character. In Stará Boleslav one can almost hear the footsteps of Prince Wenceslas, murdered here early in the tenth century on the orders of his brother Boleslav, ostensibly for his appeasement of the enemies of the growing powers of the Přemyslids. In Poděbrady one can almost hear the clatter of the hooves of King George of Podě-

◀ *49. Konopiště Castle near Benešov*　　　　　　　　　　　　　　　　　　　　*50. Interior of Konopiště Castle*

brady's horse — that same George of Poděbrady, the Hussite King, who had his seat in the local castle. Near the town of Kolín it is the hoof beats of the troops of the Austro-Prussian Imperial armies who shed their blood here in 1757.

One of the most picturesque towns to be found here is Kutná Hora. The town owes its glory to the silver mines which were sunk as long ago as the thirteenth century. It was the silver found here that at one time made Kutná Hora second only to Prague in its glory as a city. In the year 1300, the first Prague silver *groschen*, generally accepted as a means of payment, were minted here. Kutná Hora became the treasury of the kingdom and for a time it was even the seat of the Czech kings, one of whom, Vladislav Jagiello, came to the throne here in 1471. The valuable metal brought people here from all over the country. The architects and artists who came here were among those whom the town had to thank for its priceless historic buildings and all they contained. Among the finest of these is the Italian Court, originally the mint, attached to the royal palace. There are also many fine churches, the magnificent Cathedral of St. Barbara, dating from the fourteenth century, a number of beautifully preserved Gothic and Renaissance houses and the Jesuit College, built in Baroque style. In the sixteenth century, the silver mines were exhausted and the town existed only on its past glory. Today, Kutná Hora is a state urban reservation, its historic buildings have been restored and its medieval mines have been partially opened to the public.

51. Canyon carved by the River Berounka near Srbsko

52. Karlštejn Castle

Other towns in the Elbe valley which should not be missed include Kolín, once a royal town. Today it is a big industrial centre and yet, in the midst of its chemical and engineering factories, one can find the town's Gothic core with its lovely square, its Gothic church of St. Bartholomew with its presbytery which was the work of Peter Parler, the architect of St. Vitus's Cathedral at Prague Castle. Kouřim has a splendid early Gothic church, the Church of St. Stephen, a two-storey Gothic bell-tower and remnants of medieval ramparts. The royal town of Nymburk also has well-preserved medieval fortifications, linked with a moat, which are among the most interesting old fortifications to be found anywhere in Bohemia. At Lysá-on-Elbe, a Renaissance chateau and Baroque statuary stand in a lovely park. Brandýs-on-Elbe has its Renaissance chateau which was a favourite summer residence of Emperor Rudolph II, and Stará Boleslav contains the Romanesque Church of St. Clement, built in the twelfth century.

There are still a few more spots on the lower reaches of the Vltava where steamers from Prague ply their way, enabling the traveller to see the romantic beauty of both banks of the river. On the right bank, close to the village of Veltrusy, there is an interesting old building. At the beginning of the eighteenth century, the counts of Chotek built themselves a Baroque summer residence which was a frequent meeting place of the Czech nobility and Czech artists. As the time went by a big English-style park was laid out around the castle with a branch of the Vltava flowing through it, with an artificial irrigation system. In the park were small pavilions,

67

53. Master Theodoric: "St. Jerome". Gothic panel painting from the Chapel of the Holy Rood at Karlštejn Castle

54. Chapel of the Holy Rood in the main tower of Karlštejn Castle ▶

arbours and groups of statuary reflecting in the purest form the world of the Empire period and its delight in romantic nature. On the left bank is Nelahozeves with a chateau containing clear elements of the Czech Renaissance period. Nelahozeves is also remembered as the birthplace of the great Czech composer, Antonín Dvořák.

On a rocky promontory, rising out of an expanse of lowlands, is the slender tower of Mělník Castle. The present building is mainly in Renaissance style, though traces of the original Gothic architecture can still be found. Charles IV made Mělník a royal town and it was part of the dowry of Czech queens. Mělník has Charles to thank for the vineyards on its nearby sunny slopes. He brought the original vines from France and thus established the tradition of vine cultivation in Mělník which continues to this day. Mělník has all the charms typical of Czech towns. The view from the castle, so often painted by artists as the symbol of the Czech landscape, is unforgettable. Beneath the vineyard-covered slopes is the confluence of the Elbe and the Vltava, the two greatest Czech rivers. In the distance we can see only vast fields of wheat and rye stretching right to the foot of the legendary Říp Hill. Říp Hill, the very symbol of the Czech nation, is to this very day a magnet attracting every native of the land.

There are many interesting spots even in the close vicinity of Mělník. Kokořín valley — twenty kilometres long and carved out to a depth of a hundred metres — is lined with bizarre rock formations, caves and huge sandstone rocks. It was not surprising that this valley was chosen as the setting for a Gothic castle, built by the Luxembourgs with a tall cylindrical tower, a palace and battlements. The castle, destroyed several times in its

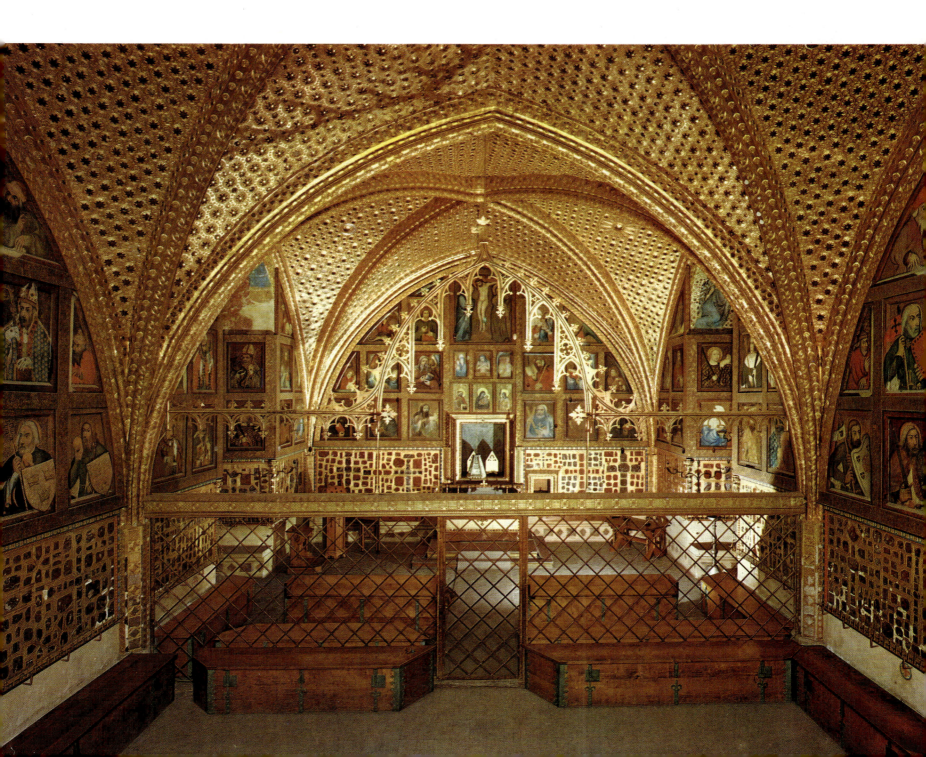

55. *Mill at Bláhova Lhota near Sedlčany*

history, was restored at the end of the nineteenth century. Today it rises out of the forests with the unreality of a stage setting and adds emphasis to the mysterious character of Kokořín Valley. There is also an interesting castle at Liběchov, originally Renaissance, but rebuilt in the first half of the eighteenth century in Baroque style. In the castle park are statues by the sculptor Matthias Braun and in the castle itself are paintings by two outstanding Czech artists, Václav Navrátil and Quido Mánes.

Thanks to the central situation of the region, an enormous amount of historic architectural and artistic treasures dating from all periods are concentrated in a small, extremely picturesque area in the close vicinity of the capital city. Most striking are the examples of Gothic and Baroque, which make a contribution going far beyond the borders of this region and the frontiers of the entire country. Today, carefully protected by the state, these historic treasures provide a real oasis in a land where, since the nineteenth century, industry has been developed apace, towns have rapidly expanded and life has been caught up in the tempo of the process of civilization.

Central Bohemia began to make great strides forward after 1945. This most densely populated and highly industrialized area in Czechoslovakia is now responsible for a fifth of Czechoslovakia's industrial production. Next to Prague, the biggest industrial centre of the region, are Kladno, a steel and mining town, Mladá Boleslav with its motor car works, the area around Králův Dvůr with its foundries and cement works, Kralupy, which is a centre of the petrochemical industry, and Neratovice, which is the site of important chemical works. The natural surroundings are changing, too. More and more dams and power stations are being constructed as part of what is known as the Vltava cascade.

A number of places exist in Central Bohemia closely connected with the glorious past of the Czech nation and with the nation's sufferings. In addition to Říp Hill must be mentioned another spot, just as closely linked with legends, Blaník, a rocky hill in whose depths knights are supposed to lie hidden, ready to come and aid the Czechs in their darkest hour. There is Lipany where the Hussite troops suffered a tragic defeat, and there, too, is Lidice, the Central Bohemian mining village razed to the ground by the Nazis in the Second World War, which became known throughout the world as a reminder of Nazi atrocities and the symbol of resistance to fascism. In the Rose Garden of Friendship, rose shrubs given by peacelovers from all continents bloom as a reminder of the need for friendship among the nations. And finally there are many places where stand memorials recalling the arrival of Soviet liberating forces in May 1945, when the centre of Bohemia was the last part of Europe where fighting was still going on when the rest of the continent was freed. It was here that the Second World War ended in Europe and where, on the ruins of the war, a start was made in building a new life.

56. Garden front of the Baroque Chateau of Dobříš

57. *The lake behind Orlík dam on the central reaches of the River Vltava*

South Bohemia is undoubtedly one of the best loved of Czech regions because of its unusual natural surroundings and the unusual historical atmosphere that pervades it. Sparkling fishponds alternate with dark patches of woodland, plains with rolling hills, mountain meadows with peat bogs and the melody of springs seems to answer the tinkling of the bells of sheep and cattle grazing on the mountain slopes. Lovers of historic buildings take pleasure in wandering through ancient towns whose architecture retains the beauty of the past — towns such as Tábor, Písek, Jindřichův Hradec, Třeboň, České Budějovice, Český Krumlov and Prachatice. They enjoy stopping a while on village greens, surrounded by solid little houses with their white-gabled façades which seem to have absorbed the soul of the South Bohemian country folk. This soul permeates the local folk songs, some slightly satirical, others wistful, but always marked by a slight melancholy which breathes from this landscape at all seasons of the year. In some villages beneath the Šumava Mountains, like Zechovice, Jiřetice, Čechtice and Němětice in the Volyně area, there are some of the loveliest examples of folk architecture built in the last century as an expression of the pride and confidence of the peasant farmers.

Go out on to the fields from the village and when you leave the last cottage behind you, there is a complete, almost mysterious silence. The waters of the ponds have a dual mirror-like quality, reflecting the heavens on their surface — the outer and the inner world, evoking in sensitive souls almost religious emotions. This deeply thoughtful land of farmers and fishermen has given birth, through the ages, to preachers, poets and thinkers. In the 15th century, religion had a decisive influence on the life of the people, who were determined to establish the Kingdom of God on Earth. To this end their armoured waggons rumbled over the field paths and their rampart-guns roared to the accompaniment of the Hussite chorale *Ye who are Warriors of God*. Let us cross this landscape from its northern border to its southernmost horizon formed by the Nové Hrady Hills and the Šumava Mountains.

Over the middle reaches of the River Vltava, two great royal castles, Orlík and Zvíkov, towered up on their rocky promontories. The latter, perched on a promontory over the confluence of the Vltava and Otava rivers was rightly called the "King of Czech Castles", because of its setting, its majesty and its strength. Even today, its great cylindrical tower with its ring of stone corbels and the Bulbous Tower, its massive walls marked with the marks of stonemasons, which romantic scholars of the past century regarded as Marcomannic script, creates a monumental impression. The frescoes of the castle chapel and the Gothic arcades around the courtyard are splendid examples of early Czech Gothic. The setting of both castles has changed out of all recognition in the recent past by the creation of a great lake, forty metres higher than the surface of the original rivers, so that the water now engulfs their foundations. The great Žďákov bridge that spans the Vltava in a single wide arc is another of the typical engineering feats of our time.

The royal town of Písek was founded in the thirteenth century close to a settlement where sand from the River Otava used to be washed for gold. Among the most interesting historic treasures in Písek is the stone bridge across the river, first recorded in 1351. It is the oldest bridge in all Bohemia, built simultaneously with the town and the royal castle. The Knights' Hall of the castle is decorated with Gothic frescoes; there are cross-vaulted arcades around the forecourt and the remains of the town fortifications.

On the north-western side lie the Blatná and Lnáře districts — an area of silent footpaths, little gamekeepers' cottages and mills and an old tradition of fishing. The vaulted tower hall of the Castle of Blatná contains Gothic frescoes depicting the faces of saints and knights. The town used to be famous for its rose gardens. A jewel of architecture is the Baroque church at Paštiky, one of the last works of the famous architect Kilián Ignác Dientzenhofer.

Strakonice Castle, founded at the beginning of the thirteenth century by Bavor of Strakonice, also used to be surrounded by water which formed part of its defences, as was the case at Blatná and Švihov. The Rumpál Tower, with its unique silhouette, has dominated Strakonice Castle throughout the centuries. For six hundred years the castle belonged to the Knights of Malta. The town, built nearby, at the confluence of the rivers Otava and Volyňka, was to become famous for the art of its bagpipers and later for the production of fezes which were exported to the entire Muslim world. Today it is also famous for the production of motorcycles.

Great meadows stretch along both banks of the Otava between Strakonice and Štěkeň. On the dyke of Škaredý fishpond near Sudoměř, the Hussite commander Jan Žižka of Trocnov defeated in 1420 the armies of the nobility. A stone statue of Žižka stands on the heights between the ponds to commemorate Žižka's first great victory.

The scenery between the towns of Písek, Strakonice and Vodňany is typically South Bohemian, with fishponds and dykes with mighty oak trees. Both small castles at Kestřany will enchant you with their ancient beauty as will the churches surrounded by small graveyards standing on village greens, the most interesting of which are at Putim, Dobev, Heřmaň and Myšenec. In Albrechtice church near Týn-on-Vltava, art experts place special value on the rare Romanesque frescoes and the local churchyard, which is surrounded on all sides by little stone-walled chapels.

The River Lužnice marks the landscape between Bechyně and Tábor and Tábor and Soběslav. From Týn we go up river to Bechyně, where the Franciscan church is famous for its diamond vaulting. The rooms in the castle contain reminders of the life of Petr Vok of Rožmberk. Bechyně Spa has a tradition dating back into the past and according to legend the mythical Princess Libuše came here to be cured of an illness. The local pottery school is known well beyond the frontiers of the country and international symposia on the art of pottery are held here. Less well-known is the old electric railway, linking Bechyně with Tábor. It was constructed in 1902 by František Křižík, the inventor of the arc lamp, who spent the last years of his life in the little Chateau of Stádlec, not very far distant, and it was there that he died.

The situation of the Hussite town of Tábor makes it look like an eagle's nest set high upon a granite rock. At the end of March in 1420, the Hussite people came here after the town of Sezimovo Ústí was burnt down, in order to establish a firm defence post and to build a new religious and social order. No other Bohemian town had such a stormy origin, for people massed here to bring true their dream of the Kingdom of God on Earth and of a harmonious society in which all men were truly equal. Peasant farmers, journeymen, paid labourers and small yeomen farmers came from every direction to put their money and modest possessions into the common pool which priests and the people's leaders divided among the brothers and sisters according to their needs. To this day stone tables stand in the town square at which the fighting men had received communion in both kinds — the body and blood of our Lord in the form of bread and wine. The narrow winding streets of the old town were constructed for purposes of fortification, as was the labyrinth of underground passages together with cellars built at various levels. The council hall was originally a meeting place for the free community, composed of the domestic community concerned with agriculture and trades, and the community of "workers in the field", who protected the town militarily and took part in the struggle against the enemies of the Chalice. The defences of Tábor included a vast fishpond bearing the biblical name of Jordan, the Castle of Kotnov with the Bechyně Gate, the fortifications and their battlements.

Over the Lužnice valley a group of cupolas rise up marking Klokoty, a place of pilgrimage where Jan Žižka

◄ *58. Early Gothic Castle of Zvíkov*   *59. Žďákov Bridge over Orlík dam*

ordered the burning of the Adamites — members of the most radical section of the Táborites. The ruined castle of Kozí Hrádek, not far distant, recalls the residence there of Master John Huss when, because of his teaching, Prague came under papal interdict. Here he preached to the peasant farmers and it was here that he wrote his Czech sermons.

Pelhřimov, the centre of the region beneath the Czech-Moravian Highlands, has always been famous for its forest lands. There are Renaissance and Baroque houses round the town square, gateways and fragments of the old fortifications. Křemešník, a nearby place of pilgrimage, provides a wonderful view of the whole of the Czech-Moravian Highlands.

The surface of Vajgar pond and the River Nežárka mirror the architectural beauties of Jindřichův Hradec, crowned by the ancient castle and chateau with its cylindrical tower, and its circular pavilion and arcades dating from the Renaissance period. Walking by the river along the narrow streets beneath the castle we pass ancient houses, once the homes of drapers and tanners, with their wooden balconies and shingle roofs and we are reminded of the world depicted by the painter Hanuš Schwaiger, who was a native of this town. Among the town's greatest treasures are the vaulting of the provost church and the frescoes on the walls of St. John's Church, as well as the Red Tower and the legend of St. George depicted on the walls of the hall of the castle. Halting here on a journey to Prague, Wolfgang Amadeus Mozart once played on the ancient spinet, now housed in the museum. Another attraction in the museum is a collection of cribs carved by local woodcarvers which demonstrate the skill of the folk artists.

The wooded surroundings interspersed with fishponds exude a quietude and freshness of nature which has a soothing effect on townsfolk and brings them back, at least for a moment, into the arms of Nature. An archi-

60. The ancient town of Písek on the River Otava

61. *The town of Tábor, the centre of the Hussite revolutionary movement*

62. *Bechyně Gate at Tábor and Kotnov castle tower*

63. *Rožmberk fishpond in South Bohemia*

◄ 64. *The town of Třeboň, a medieval historic urban reservation*

◄ 65. *The Castle of Jindřichův Hradec*

66. *Diamond vaulting in a burgher's house at Slavonice, close to the Austrian frontier*

67. *Gothic and Renaissance town of Slavonice on the old provincial frontier route*

tectural jewel set in the deep woods is Jemčina hunting lodge. The great Czech opera singer, Emma Destinn, used to stay at the castle at Stráž-on-Nežárka.

The flat countryside around Třeboň, with its vast fishponds, contains far more than just interesting scenery. For centuries its face has been changed and altered by man's hand, for it was man who constructed the great system of ponds. Two outstanding designers and constructors of these ponds lived the better part of their lives in this region. One was the economist and designer of water projects, Jakub Krčín of Jelčany (c. 1535—1604), and the other Josef Šusta (1835—1914), founder of modern methods of fish-breeding.

On chilly autumn days one can catch the smell of fish and the pungent odour rising from the dark bed of the ponds on which the deep imprints of the fishermen's boots remain after the ponds have been drained for the big catch. The first rain transforms these footprints into silver mirrors. The sights, sounds and smells of this region of water and vast pine woods evoke a sense of secret poetry, deep thoughts and longings — and an overwhelming nostalgia.

Beneath the high vaulted roof of Třeboň church we are reminded of the work of the anonymous Gothic painter, known simply as the Master of Třeboň, who opened the way for a new era of art in the whole of central Europe. His pictures are now in the National Gallery in Prague. A tremendous wealth of historical sources exists in the archives established in the days of the Lords of Rožmberk. The last of these lords, Peter Vok, who died in 1611, possessed one of the greatest libraries in Central Europe, but during the Thirty Years' War it was plundered by the Swedes. He also wanted to establish a university in Soběslav for the whole of South Bohemia. The

Sviny Gate with its beautifully decorated gabled front, the old hangman's house, the castle and the ancient arcaded houses all combine to produce the typical and unique beauty of Třeboň.

On the southern horizon rise the three ridges of the Nové Hrady Hills. In Nové Hrady itself, a fortified castle was established in the Middle Ages to protect the trade route leading from Bohemia to Austria. The town also possesses its new chateau, surrounded by a park, its ancient town hall and abbey church, and ecclesiastical residences on the square. Around the little manor house of Žofín there is a virgin forest which has been declared a protected nature reservation. Over the River Malše rise the grey outlines of the castles of Louzek and Pořešín and beneath the Nové Hrady Hills the place of pilgrimage, Dobrá Voda, with its cupolas, has a ruddy glow. The Rožmberks treated their ailments with the healing waters of its springs.

Between Soběslav and the Třeboň plain lies the vast expanse of Blata Moor with its peat which was used as fuel for stoves, and which today is used as a fertilizer. It is usually known as Pšenice or Soběslav Moor. From Protivín to Hluboká stretches Zbudov Moor with its silvery fishponds, green meadows, deep brown ploughed fields and stretches of ripening corn. The white gables reflected in the surface of the village ponds and the now silent forge on the green are reminders of the quiet peace of days gone by.

One of the oldest Slav fortified settlements, Netolice, has foundations which go deep into the earliest history of the Czech state and groves with mounds in the neighbourhood go back still further into the past. The town used to be famous for its horse market, where heavy farm horses, bred in the locality, used to be bought and sold.

68. Zbudov Moor in South Bohemia

Close to the little town, situated in the midst of gardens, stands the Renaissance mansion of Kratochvíle with rare stucco decorations in its chambers and halls.

The Blata villages of Plástovice and Opatovice, Zbudov, Olešník and Munice are famed for the wealth and variety of the lovely gabled houses around their village greens. Towering over the flat meadowlands and over the River Vltava, stands the castle of Hluboká which was restored in the last century in pseudo-Tudor style. Its rooms are full of fine furniture, tapestries, pictures and valuable collections. The riding hall of this former princely residence has been turned into the Mikuláš Aleš South Bohemian Picture Gallery. Its most valuable collection is what is known as the "Suite of Gothic Ladies", containing smiling and pensive female saints, which alone makes a visit to the gallery well worth while. Also worth a visit are the old and new game preserves where stag, deer and wild boar live in complete freedom, and we should make a point of visiting Ohrada Manor and its zoological collections. We should also see the green plain which extends to the foot of Kleť Hill, from whose summit on a clear autumn day we can see the snowy peaks of the Alps, stretching along the horizon like a fairytale belt. On the broad surface of Bezdrev pond, the biggest in South Bohemia next to Rožmberk, we can catch a glimpse of the sails of little boats and yachts.

In the plain where the Rivers Vltava and Malše meet, the Czech King Přemysl Otakar II, in the middle of the thirteenth century, founded the fortified town of České Budějovice to help withstand the attacks on his royal power by the Vítkovci. Around the square, the sides of which are equal in length and face the points of the compass, we can stroll beneath the vaulted arcades and admire the frescoes in the Baroque town hall, painted by J. Adam Schöpf in 1730 and representing the Judgment of Solomon, and a tapestry depicting the panorama of the town designed by the contemporary artist Cyril Bouda. It is said that whoever steps over the witching stone finds himself in a magic circle from which it is hard to get back into the world of reality. This stone is set in the paving beneath the fountain topped by a statue of Samson. Through the traceries of the Dominican monastery's arcaded passages one gazes out on a beautiful cloister. The battlemented gable of the armoury could tell many a story of the distant past of this fascinating town. Walking along Česká ulice (Czech Street) to the Rook Tower and Mill Drain, around which extends a park full of ancient trees, we come to the old Butchers' Shops and find ourselves in a world of medieval yards belonging to the old tradesmen's workshops and stalls. On the banks of

◄ *69. Hluboká Castle near České Budějovice*

70. Reception hall at Hluboká Castle

71. Unknown master: Virgin and Child of České Budějovice. Mikoláš Aleš Gallery, Hluboká

72. Late Gothic armoury, České Budějovice ▶

the Vltava, close to the Long Bridge, are the former shipyards. These were established by Vojtěch Lanna, who laid the foundations for České Budějovice's industry in the days when salt used to be transported downstream to Prague. The visitor with an interest in technology can find the spot where the first horsedrawn railway from České Budějovice to Linz used to start. This was the very first railway on the continent of Europe. Two of the most typical industries in České Budějovice today are the pencil factory and the brewery, where the famous Budvar (or Budweiser) beer, second only to Pilsner Urquel as an export, is brewed. Of architectural treasures in the neighbourhood the finest is the Church of Our Lady of Sorrows at Dobrá Voda, built between the years 1733 and 1739 by Kilián Ignác Dientzenhofer. The stucco decorations were by John the Baptist de Allio from Vienna and the frescoes were painted by the famous Czech Baroque artist, Václav Vavřinec Reiner. At Rudolfov there are filled in pit shafts, a relic of the former mining industry. Not far off is the spa of Libnič.

South-east of Budějovice is an area known as Doudleby, where a Slav tribe of that name built a fortified settlement. The Doudlebs settled in the region between the Rivers Stropnice and Malše and left a whole system of fortified settlements here. At the Trocnov yeoman farmer's seat, the most famous of all Czech warriors, Jan Žižka, was born and grew up. It was said of him that "he engaged in many battles against powerful

73. *Square at České Budějovice*

74. *Český Krumlov*

75. *Zlatá Koruna (Golden Crown) Abbey by the upper reaches of the River Vltava*

76. *Monastery library at Vyšší Brod*

77. *"Missale pro prelatis pontificantibus", originally from Vyšší Brod, now in the National Museum, Prague*

*78. Pilgrimage Church of Our Lady
at Kájov*

enemies, but never lost the field". The foundations of the house in which he was born are still there, and so are the dykes of the fishponds which already existed here in his day. Close by there is a statue of Žižka by the sculptor Malejovský. Another memorial to this great warrior can be found in neighbouring Borovany where, immediately after Žižka's death, a monastery was built. The Abbots of Borovany did their best, though quite in vain, to erase the memory of the great "Warrior of God". Besides the castle and the Baroque town hall, a stone pillory stands in the square. Several other little towns in South Bohemia have similar "pillars of shame", which remind us of the ancient rights which towns used to possess. They can be found at Přídolí, Rožmitál in the Šumava, Hořice (famous for its Passion Plays), as well as Dolní Vltavice, Frymburk and Vyšší Brod. Římov, a place of pilgrimage, is famous for its twenty-five little chapels representing the stations of the cross from the seventeenth century. This example of folk Baroque art, which fits in perfectly with the landscape, is unique in Bohemia.

In the quiet valley of the Vltava, King Přemysl Otakar II built a monastery after his victory over the Magyars at Kressenbrunn in 1263. He endowed it with a great deal of property and entrusted the Cistercian monks with the colonization and administration of this outlying region. Besides presenting the monastery with worldly goods, he gave it a single thorn, said to be from Christ's crown of thorns, a gift of the King of France. Thus the monastery was given the name Trnová Koruna — meaning "Crown of Thorns" — though later it was renamed Zlatá Koruna (Aurea Corona) — "Golden Crown". The monastery's church is in Gothic style, as is the chapter-house with its columns with splendid capitals.

The "Region of the Five-Petalled Rose" is a name that could be given to the whole of South Bohemia. On its castles and mansions, its towns and churches, we frequently come across the emblem of the Lords of the Rose, whose power for several centuries rivalled that of the crown in this part of the country. The founder of the line

91

79. *The lake of Lipno Dam on the upper reaches of the Vltava*

80. *Late Gothic Church of St. Mary Magdalene at Chvalšiny*

81. *Prachatice, an ancient town on the Golden Route*

82. Farm house at Volary

was Vítek of Prčice, whose personality and times were described by the German writer, Adalbert Stifter, who was born in the Šumava area, in his historical novel *Witiko*. The first seat of the South Bohemian family of Vít-kovci was the castle of Rožmberk, built on the heights above the township of the same name. But from there their estates expanded to cover the whole of South Bohemia. All that remains of the original castle is a solitary cylindrical tower. In the newer parts of the building we find magnificent rooms with coffered ceilings, armoury, many beautiful art treasures and even a picture of the ghostly White Lady (Perchta of Rožmberk), the guardian angel of the family, who according to a legend appeared as a white shadow, presaging happy and sad events, at all the Rožmberk castles.

The most splendid of the Rožmberk family seats was that at Český Krumlov, towering over a triple bend in the River Vltava and over the fortified town. Before crossing the three-storey "Na Plášti" bridge to be guided through all the courtyards, halls and chambers, we should take a look at the Baroque castle theatre and study all the original stage settings which are unique in Europe. The ballroom, too, attracts attention by its murals painted by Josef Lederer in the middle of the eighteenth century. In the castle garden there are fascinating Rococo statues, charming little cupids, archways of trees and linden avenues. Beneath the castle, shadows fall on the narrow little streets of the old town with its high-roofed little houses built in different styles, each of which is unique.

There are several exceptionally lovely Gothic churches in the neighbourhood, such as the Church of St. Mary Magdalene at Chvalšiny with its rare vaults, the Church of the Assumption of the Virgin Mary at Kájov, a place of pilgrimage which contains wonderful wood-carvings as well as splendid architecture, and the Church of St. Nicholas at Boletice with its unusual Romanesque tower.

Where a bridge now stands facing the old abbey at Vyšší Brod, there used to be just a single ford. According to an old legend, Lord Vok of Rožmberk was miraculously saved here from a sudden flood by the Virgin Mary

94

and in his gratitude he built a church to her on this very spot. The founder's descendants richly endowed the monastery and he himself entered the Cistercian Order. The monastery's library contains 70,000 volumes.

Between Lipno and Želnava stretch the waters of a great new artificial lake behind Lipno dam and power station. It is forty kilometres long and in some places as much as ten kilometres wide. The waters spilling out into the surrounding countryside have formed fascinating new fjords and gulfs. Ash and willow trees grow along the banks. The lake has completely covered vast peat bogs and the graphite mines at Černá and the entire landscape has been changed beyond all recognition.

From Plešné Lake to Volary and on to Kvilda there is a deep belt of frontier forests, meadows and marshes whose brown surface reflects the twisted dwarf pines, miniature birch trees and violet-blue gentian. The typical Šumava village of Volary was always famous for its German population's love of antiquities and for its wooden cottages with carved balconies and roofs weighted down by stones as in the Alps. Nearby Lenora is renowned for the manufacture of Bohemian crystal glass, which is exported to many countries, and the town of Vimperk, in addition to producing glass, is known for its prayer books and almanacs printed in many different languages.

Along the Golden Path — the trade route leading from Passau to Prague via the Šumava Mountains — salt used to be transported into Bohemia by pack mules. The main warehouse for storing this salt belonged by special right to the burghers of Prachatice. Trade in salt was the source of the town's riches and this was reflected in the costly construction of the town hall, the parish church, the town's fortifications, its gateways and its grammar school. To this school came young John Huss, born in the nearby village of Husinec.

South Bohemia and the South Bohemian landscape are particularly dear to the Czech people for the memories of history they evoke and for the dreamy atmosphere of the pine forests, mountain meadows, rivers, ponds and lakes, overhung with low grey clouds.

83. Boubín in the Šumava range

Advancing from the flat lowlands of Central Bohemia in a westerly direction you mount a long and gradually rising staircase composed of hills and wooded ridges. The rivers show you the way. You proceed upstream towards their springs among steep slopes, past their tributaries which converge and help to create those broad and venerable rivers lower down.

Whether you choose the road along the Berounka River via Pilsen and thence along the Úhlava towards the Gateway to the Šumava Mountains — as the town of Klatovy proudly calls itself — or whether you pass among the poles in the hop-fields of the Ohře River basin towards the Carlsbad area — your path will always eventually be obstructed by ranges of hills. They surround the entire western borderland like black ramparts, visible from the distance on the horizon. From time immemorial they have formed the natural boundary of this part of Bohemia. They are the Šumava Mountains, bordering on the Bohemian Forest in the area of the Všeruby Pass and, in a north-westerly direction, on the ridges of the Krušné (Ore) Mountains.

The rolling ranges of the borderland mountains are covered with deep woods. Their magnificent serenity, quiet lakes and "rock seas" seem to be the very personification of pagan natural beauty unaltered since Nature first shaped these highlands.

In addition to their melancholy beauty the borderland forests also have different characteristics. Their hills have always guarded the western approaches to Bohemia. This is what gives them their heroic pathos, frequently referred to by Czech poets. They have been fulfilling this mission since the dawn of history, when the land of Bohemia was still uncivilized and when nothing but trade routes traversed the virgin forests. On the rocky hills the kings of Bohemia eventually built dozens of strongholds, small fortresses, magnificent castles and bastions to protect the security of the country's frontiers and watch over the trade routes, fords, frontier crossings and mountain passes. One of the trade routes led via Pilsen to the Šumava Mountains and on to Passau in Bavaria. It was used for transporting salt to Bohemia. Another traversed the upper part of the region, starting in Prague and continuing via Stříbro and Přimda to Nuremberg, and yet another one led from Pilsen via Horšovský Týn and Klenčí to Waldmünchen. It was a specific feature of this area that, even in those ancient days, the rulers of Bohemia entrusted the villagers in the borderland with the task of watching over the security of the frontier and the frontier crossings, of arousing the king's soldiers when in danger, and of felling trees to obstruct roads in the event of enemy attack. In return for these services the local people were not subjected to the nobility and enjoyed privileges guaranteeing their status as yeomen owning the freehold of their land as early as the Middle Ages.

While the hilly areas are only sparsely populated, the lowlands, especially the spurs of the Šumava Mountains, have been densely populated since ancient times. The history of the area can be traced in the ruins of castles and strongholds and in well-preserved medieval fortresses, many of which were rebuilt at a later date, in old townships and towns, in the layout of villages dominated by small medieval churches and in freeholders' fortresses and mansions. Many of these localities originated in the Middle Ages because of the occurrence of iron ore, silver or gold, which were mined at Kašperské Hory and Hory Matky Boží. Iron ore was also extracted at Železná Ruda, the name of which is self-explanatory (iron = železo, ore = ruda).

The interior of the region of West Bohemia consists of the Pilsen basin on which all rivers, brooks and streams converge from the borderland hills and the hilly country of the surroundings. Pilsen (Plzeň) is the metropolis of this area. The city is situated at the confluence of four rivers — the Úslava, Úhlava, Radbuza and Mže, the latter flowing on towards Prague, eventually bearing the name Berounka. Up to the thirteenth century the area's economic development was determined by monasteries, especially those at Plasy, Kladruby, Chotěšov, Nepomuk and Manětín. Rapid development in the mid-nineteenth century was stimulated, above all, by the discovery of coal deposits, iron ore and kaolin. Those were also the days witnessing the initial stages of Pilsen's world-wide fame as a centre for the brewing and engineering industries. This part of Western Bohemia is now one of Czechoslovakia's most advanced industrial centres.

Another of the most important areas of West Bohemia is that of Carlsbad (Karlovy Vary). Its world-famous spas and watering places rank among the most outstanding natural resources of Czechoslovakia. Some 3,000 square kilometres of this undulating part of the country contain hundreds of mineral springs of varying chemical composition, taste and temperature.

Let us now take a closer look at the region's three main components — the Šumava Mountains and their foothills as well as the Pilsen and Carlsbad areas. Their main features tell their own tale of the past and present of the region, of its specific beauty which constitutes an important component of the Czechoslovak mosaic.

The main mountain-range lining the western boundary of Bohemia is called the Šumava. It is the continuation of part of the South Bohemian ridge, joining with the interior Šumava area to form a compact and specific part of the country. This area used to be occupied by the spurs of a glacier which left behind several fairyland-like lakes. The most beautiful are the Devil's Lake and the Black Lake (Čertovo jezero, Černé jezero). They are situated among precipitous rocks, their deep waters are of greenish-blue colour. These places have barely been touched by civilization. Serene silence reigns below the skies, a silence which has brought forth countless fables and legends about the two mountain lakes of the Šumava range.

The Šumava Mountains comprise two zones of broad and straight ridges with extensive valleys. Their special characteristic are high plateaus. While the slopes of the hills, soaring up to a height of over 1000 metres, decline steeply in Bavaria, the Bohemian hillsides descend gradually, traversed by a network of countless paths and tracks resembling a labyrinth. Nature abounds in original local plant-life. There are extensive areas without villages, interspersed only with lonely cottages or gamekeepers' houses. It is a kingdom of wild-life and trees. A genuine virgin forest is to be found on Boubín Hill; its area was declared a nature reserve as early as the middle of the last century, set aside as a sample of untouched woodland development. The original beauty of the Šumava is protected by the Czechoslovak State, the Šumava Mountains having been declared a Protected Landscape Area comprising ten nature reserves with the famous Šumava peat-bogs, whose waters supply the mountain sources of the river Vltava, in addition to the Boubín virgin forest and the two mountain lakes.

The Šumava is a romantic mountain-range where history and patriotism have left their traces. Standing guard over the homeland, it is the cradle of many Bohemian rivers. It is here, at the hills' lowest extremity, that the Vltava and all its tributaries rise, converging in a fan-like fashion and combining into a single magnificent river.

One of the most fascinating areas in the central Šumava area is that of the rapid mountain-torrent, the Vydra. It makes its way through a mountain valley, tumbling over gigantic boulders in which the water has created large tunnels, rearing and foaming, but calming down when leaving the hilly area and falling into the gold-bearing River Otava. The Vydra Valley ascends into the interior of the mountains via the mountain villages of Srní, Antigl, and two villages called Kvilda, as far as the community of Modrava. Up there the scenery turns into a magnificent plateau with unique flora, wild trees and shrubs and extensive peat-bogs.

The Vydra basin provides no less picturesque scenery. It can be reached via the royal town of Sušice which

85. Basalt rocks in the River Vydra

86. *Renaissance town hall, Kašperské Hory*

was founded in the 12th century. It was a place where salt imported from Bavaria was reshipped and it was the scene of a goldrush when the sands of the River Otava yielded gold. A beautiful main square with Renaissance houses, a Gothic church, preserved parts of the town's fortifications — all this makes Sušice one of the gems of the Šumava area. One of the present-day traditions of Sušice is represented by a large match-factory which has been turning out its produce for over a hundred years.

The second centre of this part of the Šumava area is Železná Ruda, a mountain township established in the seventeenth century near blast-furnaces. The glass-making trade began to develop after the mining of iron ore had stopped. The small town, with its Baroque church with onion-shaped tower, was linked with the interior of the country by a railway constructed in the mid-nineteenth century, making its way to Železná Ruda through an almost two kilometres long tunnel. Present-day Železná Ruda is a tourist and winter sports centre.

While the Šumava Mountains have their protected oases of silence and tranquillity, their torrents, their mysterious twilight, their legends, the area at the foot of the hills can be compared to a song sung by many voices. The number of villages and towns increases, the gently sloping ridges drop down to the lowlands and instead of small hillside fields there are vast expanses of agricultural land, where life pulsates more rapidly than up in the hills.

Here Bohemia opens up into a wide land, criss-crossed by roads, adorned with ancient towns and ancient witnesses of days long gone-by. Among them are the ruins of medieval castles, scattered all over the Šumava foothills and combining into a powerful system of strongholds. The largest, and one comparatively well-preserved, is Rábí Castle. It is perched on a rocky hill, overlooking meadows and spots where gold was washed. During the Hussite Wars its owners took sides with the gentry. The Hussite leader Jan Žižka twice penetrated its powerful walls and it was while besieging the castle for the second time that he lost his second eye. The fortifications of

99

Rábí were ingeniously constructed and were frequently extended, but the castle began to dilapidate after the Thirty Years' War. As late as the seventeenth century it was considered an important fortress and, by order of the Habsburg emperors, it was not repaired. Then it gradually fell into an imposing ruin.

The ruins of the castle of Velhartice are situated near Sušice. The castle was founded in the early fourteenth century to protect the border and a trade route. The Gothic bridge, which is ten metres high and used to connect the tower with the palace, is of unique construction and has been preserved. Kašperk is another of the Šumava area's ruined castles. It was founded in the midst of deep woods to guard the local silver mines. Kašperské Hory, a royal town nearby, derived its wealth, its numerous architectural monuments, magnificent town hall and two Gothic churches from extensive silver-mining in the Middle Ages.

Another two castles, differing considerably in their natural setting, attract the visitor's attention in the Klatovy area. The medieval noblemen's residence of Klenová is perched on a wooded cone-shaped hill over-looking the surrounding countryside. It used to guard the open valley of the river Úhlava at the edge of the borderland forest. The ruins of its original Gothic walls have been preserved, together with a more recent Renaissance palace which now serves as a picture gallery. The late Gothic Castle of Švihov is situated on the flat banks of the Úhlava. It was constructed by Benedikt Ried, one of the most outstanding Czech builders. Being situated in flat country, the castle was protected by its own fortifications and by moats filled with the water of the River Úhlava.

Domažlice and Klatovy are the centres of two typical regions of the Šumava area, the former being the capital of the Chodsko district. The royal town of Domažlice, founded in the year 1260 by Přemysl Otakar II to protect the border and neighbouring area constantly threatened by German raids, abounds in historic relics. The Lower Gate, which used to be part of the town's medieval fortifications, is the imposing gateway to the rectangular square surrounded by ancient houses with arcades. The only remnant of the original royal castle is a round tower overlooking the town, but everywhere you will find traces of numerous historic styles and,

87. Ruined Castle of Kašperk

above all, historic monuments reminiscent of the glorious past of the Chodsko area. The people of Domažlice cherish the memory of the defeat of a several hundred thousand-strong Imperial army in the first half of the fifteenth century, and they are particularly proud to possess a hat discarded by Cardinal Cesarini who was put to flight by the thundering chorale of Hussite soldiers. The people of Chodsko are proud of their hero Jan Kozina, leader of the Chodsko peasants. Eleven free villages of frontier guards — the renowned Dogs' Heads, who enjoyed privileges granted to them for centuries by the kings of Bohemia in return for their services rose, in the seventeenth century, against the new owners of the estate, who wanted to deprive them of these privileges. After a fierce struggle the rebellion was quelled. Jan Kozina was executed in Pilsen.

Chodsko is a district with a highly original folk culture of merry and boisterous songs and colourful national costumes. A stick, a stylized axe, a cape and a broad hat are the most marked symbols of their authority, together with a wolfhound's head. Tens of thousands of inhabitants of Chodsko, clad in their national costumes, meet on Vavřineček Hill every year to take part in a local folklore festival resounding with the music of village bands with bagpipes. Folklore and folk art are still very much alive in this area, together with the broad local dialect. A stroll through some of the Chodsko villages — such as Stráž, Trhanov, Újezd, Draženov, Lhota, Pec, Chodov and Tlumačov — leaves an unforgettable impression. One of the most picturesque places is the small town of Klenčí which is still known for the production of Chodsko folk pottery, embroideries and lacework. Many a Czech artist, whose works enriched the nation's culture, was born and lived there. Let us mention at least one of them — Jindřich Šimon Baar. His larger-than-life-size statue stands at the foot of Čerchov Hill, commanding one of the most fascinating views.

The rolling hills descend like rippled water into the interior of Bohemia and its villages and towns. Roads and paths criss-cross the country in every direction, and every crossroads or stop-over has something to attract the visitor — the yew tree grove near the Chodsko village of Kanice, for example, whose thousand-year-old trunks have witnessed many stormy events of the past, or the ancient township of Horšovský Týn with its castle,

88. Albrechtice near Sušice, a village in the Šumava foothills

in the vicinity of which toll-money was collected for crossing the River Radbuza. The castle and the town used to be the property of the Archbishops of Prague.

The town of Klatovy stretches along the right bank of the River Úhlava. It was founded 700 years ago, and has retained its original chessboard-like layout, remnants of the city-walls with circular bastions, a square with ancient houses, a town hall, a church, underground catacombs — and its slim symbolic landmark, the Black Tower. It is one of the Czech towns whose annals include all the historical epochs of the Czech state, all architectural styles and a varied cultural tradition. The synthesis of the scenic frame and the town with its seven spires even today creates a peculiar emotional atmosphere which has not been deleted by modern times, which have turned the town and its surroundings into an industrial and agricultural area. Roaming through this south-western tip of Bohemia you must make a point of visiting Horažďovice, a town with a well-preserved medieval centre, typical of the Šumava area. You will find charming places among the hills and hillocks — such as Chudenice, embedded in a scenery resembling a huge park, or Lužany, the castle of which was a favourite resort of many outstanding personalities of Czech cultural life in the nineteenth century.

We next proceed towards the Pilsen basin where the traces of ancient times are less tangible as a result of the industrial development of the area. And yet even there we can find remnants of ancient Slav settlements and proofs of the fact that the origin of the towns in this area can be traced back to the Middle Ages. Starý Plzenec in the vicinity of present-day Pilsen is the site of a Romanesque stone rotunda which ranks among the oldest in Bohemia. It was there that a fortified settlement, belonging to the oldest members of the Přemyslid dynasty, was situated. The development of trade relations induced medieval kings to found the new city of Pilsen (Plzeň) on the confluence of the four chief rivers of the area, where the most important trade routes met. The Gothic core of the thirteenth-century city, with its large square and church, has retained its medieval layout. After a number of conflagrations Gothic Pilsen developed into a Renaissance city. It was there that the first Czech printed book, the *Trojan Chronicle*, was published in 1468. The present-day city, with its Škoda Engineering Works and a huge brewery, is Czechoslovakia's fifth largest town. Its near and more distant surroundings abound in historic relics. A typical landmark of the Pilsen area is the ruin of the Gothic Castle of Radyně, overlooking the

89. The square at Sušice

102

90. Ruins of the Gothic Castle of Rábí

entire area. Near the city is the oft-visited Kozel Mansion, a Neo-Classical structure housing eighteenth-century period furniture.

The ruins of Přimda Castle, which used to be an important borderland stronghold, are perched on a ridge of the Bohemian Forest. Only the walls of its Romanesque tower have been preserved. Other borderland towns and communities, such as Tachov, Stříbro and Bor near Tachov, or Nepomuk, Chotěšov, Dobřany and Plasy at the opposite end of the Pilsen area, are steeped in history.

The northern part of West Bohemia borders on the Bohemian Forest, which touches the Ore Mountains further north. The River Ohře, flowing through a broad valley and eventually falling into the River Vltava, is the central axis of this area. Fortified settlements, and towns at a later date, were established on its banks early in history. One of the most typical reflections of the past is the town of Cheb, situated close to the border. It grew out of an ancient Slav settlement which was later colonized by German inhabitants; in the early 14th century, however, it was joined with the Kingdom of Bohemia. There are few towns which can boast such an abundance of historic relics, ranging from the Romanesque to the Baroque styles. The charm of the completely preserved historic centre of the town is enhanced by its superbly renovated square, the Romanesque residence of Frederick Barbarossa, the famous Black Tower, churches, monasteries and burghers' houses with high roofs and bay-windows, by picturesque lanes and nooks and on the square, the group of ancient houses, known as "Špalíček".

Loket is another town on the River Ohře. The romantic nature of this town is created by an arm of the river and its three loops, which embrace the medieval royal Castle of Loket, perched on a steep rock. The castle used to guard an important trade route leading from Nuremberg via Cheb to Prague. One single gate gave access to the town — this being the reason why neither the town, nor the castle were ever conquered. Loket Castle played

103

91. Panorama of the Šumava Mountains from the summit of Mount Pančíř

an important part in the history of Bohemia. Young Charles IV — the future king and emperor — was held prisoner there by his father John of Luxembourg who feared that Charles and his mother, Elizabeth of the Přemyslid dynasty, might depose him. Charles IV bore his former prison no ill-will. He frequently visited Loket Castle, hunting in the deep forests surrounding it. According to an ancient legend it was thanks to this fact that the famous healing springs, bearing his name to this day, were discovered (Carlsbad, Karlovy Vary).

In the Market Colonnade of Carlsbad there is a commemorative sculpture depicting Charles IV stopping in front of a hot spring which had scalded one of his hounds chasing a stag. Be that as it may — the emblem of Carlsbad bears the picture of a chamois and a stag, and the spa itself cherishes the memory of its founder, who built a castle there and raised the settlement to the status of royal town. The history of Carlsbad as a watering-place goes as far back as the fifteenth century. Ancient pictures show the original buildings, most of them timber houses, with private baths where the patients took the waters. The springs of Carlsbad are hot, the most prolific of them — the world-famous Vřídlo (Sprudel) — constantly soars up to an altitude of 15 metres from the thousand-metre-deep bowels of the earth. The old centre of the town lies huddled in the narrow valley of the small River Teplá, which flows into the Ohře on the outskirts of the town. The two chief colonnades were erected in the vicinity of the spa's twelve most important springs — a century-old meeting place of patients from all over the world. In addition to these springs, each having its own name, some eighty nameless springs are scattered over the area. This subterranean "factory" of medicinal waters is gigantic. Its daily output is over three

92. Železná Ruda in the western part of the Šumava Mountains. The Church of Our Lady of Assistance

93. *The royal town of Klatovy*

million litres of thermal water. It is saturated with aragonit, which turns budding roses into brown stone flowers. The healing powers of the water have attracted many generations of people intent on restoring their health — among them maharajahs, sultans, kings, emperors and czars as well as other outstanding personalities from all over Europe. This accounts for the varied cultural history of Carlsbad. The great German poet Johann Wolfgang Goethe visited Carlsbad thirteen times, devoting numerous treatises to the mineralogical composition of the area. Moreover, nearby Loket was the scene of his passionate adoration for his last great love — young Ulrike von Lewetzow — to whom he devoted one of his most beautiful poems. Among noted guests to visit Carlsbad were such celebrities as Bach, Beethoven, Schiller, Brahms, Gogol, Liszt, Marx, Mickiewicz, Chopin, Dvořák, Čapek and Sholokhov.

The cultural traditions of Carlsbad have been further expanded since 1945, with the spa retaining its world-wide reputation. The town is growing, and it ranks among the largest in this northern part of the region. It can boast the most up-to-date balneological and therapeutical facilities and model medical care. It has, at the same time, all the assets of a metropolis, such as modern hotels, a varied cultural life, picture galleries, a theatre, and a symphony orchestra. The view of Carlsbad, embedded among wooded hills, is unforgettable in its beauty.

The spa district of the town has frequently been compared to a cake, elaborately decorated by a confectioner. Most of its present-day buildings of Rococo or Empire-style character date back to the 18th century.

94. Domažlice, a town established on the old provincial route leading into Bavaria

95. Pilsen, Square of the Republic

96. Interior of Kozel Castle near Šťáhlavy in West Bohemia

Bygone days are recalled to mind by the renovated tower of Charles's former medieval castle. In addition to a Baroque church there is a specially noteworthy picturesque Orthodox church, which was built in commemoration of a visit of the Russian Czar, Peter the Great, to Carlsbad. Many statues, busts and commemorative plaques recall the visits of great artists who took the waters there. Carlsbad ranks among Europe's most famous spas, its international character enhancing its charm and unique beauty.

The town proper is separated from the spa, the former being a centre of the production of local porcelain and glassware. Glass services of the Moser trade-mark represent the quintessence of the renowned art of Czech glass-making. Nearby Horní Slavkov is the site of Bohemia's oldest porcelain factory. The historic centre of this township, with its late Gothic and Renaissance buildings, is a historic urban reservation.

Carlsbad is the most famous, but by no means the only, watering-place in West Bohemia. This part of Bohemia boasts 230 mineral springs, only about ninety of which are utilized. Waters of the most varied composition, taste and healing properties constitute the immense natural wealth of this area, which is ideal for restoring health. Seven spas were founded in the vicinity of these springs. Next to Carlsbad the most famous are Marienbad, Franzensbad and Joachimsthal (Mariánské Lázně, Františkovy Lázně and Jáchymov).

A picturesque road, snaking its way through a valley, takes us to Marienbad. Let us stop for a while at least at Kynžvart Spa, which specializes in the treatment of children. The local Empire mansion, furnished in the original style, houses extensive collections relating to Goethe, Dumas, Stifter and other outstanding exponents of cultural life. These collections were accumulated by the Austrian Chancellor Metternich, who had this

110

97. Late Neo-Classical Castle of Kynžvart, near Marienbad

mansion built on the site of a Baroque structure of earlier origin. This area is also steeped in ancient history, which is recalled by the ruins of a thirteenth-century castle overlooking the town.

Marienbad is a town of parks and gardens, situated at an altitude of 600 metres above sea level. This spa, surrounded by deep forests, which is a veritable gem among Europe's watering-places, is Czechoslovakia's second largest. The territory of the present-day spa was hidden in impenetrable woodland until the 18th century. It used to belong to the domain of the Premonstratensian abbey of Teplá, one of Bohemia's oldest monasteries. Teplá Abbey and its extensive library have been preserved to this day. Several of the forty springs of Marienbad have been known since ancient times. The kings of Bohemia tried to exploit them for the production of salt, which had to be imported from abroad. But it was only at the beginning of the nineteenth century that the Premonstratensians of Teplá founded a spa here. The town was laid out in magnificent style and, thanks to the ingenuity of the Czech landscape gardener Skalník, the wilderness was soon converted into a colourful park, extending over an expanse of 110 hectares, adorned with Empire-style spa buildings, a colonnade with the famous Cross Spring, hotels and other structures attracting our attention. Most of the springs are situated in natural surroundings on the outskirts of the town, hidden in romantic pavilions resembling small antique temples.

The charming scenery, the carbonic waters of varying chemical composition, the spa-centre which is completely separated from the town, the local cultural points of interest — all these assets have always been of great attraction to visitors from abroad. That is why Marienbad, too, has a rich cultural tradition. Goethe and

111

98. *Group of ancient houses in the centre of the main square at Cheb, known as the "Špalíček"*

Turgenev, Chopin and Gogol, Wagner and Gorky used to take walks through the spa parks. These cultural traditions are being preserved and further developed by present-day cultural life, which is of international character.

Franzensbad is a spa of a different kind. Set in the soothing scenery of a highland plateau, its parks — occupying an area of 228 hectares — are situated next to deep forests. A total of thirty kilometres of well-tended paths through birch coppices and spruce forests form romantic and idyllic natural surroundings — created since the late 18th century by generations of gardeners, architects and artists. The healing properties of the twenty-four local springs have been known since the Middle Ages. The spa developed rapidly during the nineteenth century. Today it is popular with visitors both from Czechoslovakia and abroad.

The extremely interesting nature reserve of Soos is situated on the outskirts of Franzensbad. Its extensive peat-bog, with "active volcanoes" of bubbling mud, raised by thermal mineral waters and carbon dioxide, is a unique European natural phenomenon. It also has its own specific flora, thriving in saliferous surroundings. Soos is a state nature reserve like nearby Komorní Hůrka, the youngest extinct volcano, the crater of which still contains boulders of cooled lava and volcanic ashes which were used in older times as building material for the city walls of Cheb.

Joachimsthal is another West Bohemian spa which should not be omitted from our list. This ancient town is situated in a romantic valley of the Ore Mountains at an altitude of 650 metres. It originated as one of the numerous mining towns of the Ore Mountain area, where a variety of metals had been extracted since the Middle Ages. Of these, Joachimsthal has had the most dramatic history. In the Middle Ages it was one of Europe's most important silver-mining areas. It was then that the town developed rapidly, this development being reflected by its existing historic relics, such as ancient houses in the square, a Renaissance mint, a town hall and a church. After the exhaustion of the silver mines and a prolonged period of deterioration, another dramatic phase took place. Tons of Joachimsthal uranium ore were sent to the Paris laboratory of Pierre and Marie Curie at the beginning of this century — and in the year 1903 they succeeded in extracting the first grams of radium from this ore. Heaps of black uranium ore, existing for centuries as waste material from the silver mines, had become precious overnight. The fame of Joachimsthal was eventually restored and, after the year 1945, the Joachimsthal uranium mines ranked third on the world list. And finally there was a third milestone. When the ore deposits were exhausted, Joachimsthal became the world's first radioactive spa. The waters of its radioactive thermal springs are applied for baths and drinking cures. Joachimsthal's world renown is enhanced by its extremely beautiful sur-

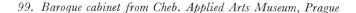

99. Baroque cabinet from Cheb. Applied Arts Museum, Prague

100. *Colonnade of the Ferdinand Spring at Marienbad*

101. *Soos Moor, state nature reserve in the valley of Vonšovský Brook*

roundings as well. Boží Dar, the highest community in Bohemia, situated at an altitude of 1015 metres above sea-level, is a popular tourist resort in the vicinity.

A quarter of a century of socialism has also left its mark on this area. The state's attitude to Nature has been reflected in the establishment of nature reserves and protected areas for the benefit of its citizens, who find rest and recreation there. Many new hotels have been constructed in the Šumava area and in the West Bohemian towns in the Ore Mountains. The conservation of architectural treasures of the past is taken good care of by the state. West Bohemia boasts several thousand historic points of interest, including castles, mansions and whole towns. The best preserved relics of the past have been converted into museums and picture galleries, others are recreation centres for working people. Industry has also further developed in the midst of this beauty — coal and kaolin mines have been expanded, new factories have come into being, together with new housing estates. Every visitor to this region can see the sweeping changes brought about by socialism in this formerly poor region. It is a region which is beautiful at all times of the year, a region with a heroic past, a dynamic present and a great future.

102. Royal Castle of Loket on the River Ohře

104. *The world famous spa of Carlsbad* 117

◄ *103. Porcelain vase from the late Rococo period from Stará Role near Carlsbad. Applied Arts Museum, Prague*

105. *Baroque Castle of Libochovice*

North Bohemia forms a belt, some fifty kilometres wide, lining several ranges of borderland mountains known as Krušné hory (Ore Mountains), Děčínské stěny (Děčín Walls), Lužické hory (Lužice Mountains) and Jizerské hory (Jizera Mountains) as far as the Krkonoše (Giant Mountains). The River Labe (Elbe), flowing through the Děčín Walls into Saxony, divides the region into two parts of about equal size. North Bohemia is largely a mountainous and wooded country. Mountains were the natural boundary of the ancient Kingdom of Bohemia. For thousands of years they were practically impenetrable. The basalt zone of the Central Bohemian Range, situated between the rivers Bílina and Ohře, consists of cone-shaped solitary peaks, dominated by Milešovka Hill. To gaze down on this area in the hours of dawn or dusk from the Milešovka, Hazmburk or Lovoš is a memorable experience. The beauty of the extinct volcanoes is unique.

The greatest wealth of North Bohemia is hidden underground. Lead, tin, cobalt and, above all, silver used to be mined in the Ore Mountains. The silver mines were so prolific that the members of the Schlick family, who owned the domain, were entitled to mint their own silver coins called "Joachimsthaler". Uranium ore was mined there at a later date, but the most precious treasure is brown coal. The first coal deposits were found at Most as early as 1613, but in those days it was only used by blacksmiths. It was not until the last century that coal was mined on a large scale.

The Děčín Walls, lining both banks of the Elbe River, are sandstone formations shaped by water and the ages which have given them strange and bizarre forms. The most interesting part is known as Pravčická brána (Pravčice Gate). A gigantic boulder resting on two magnificent pillars at a height of twenty metres forms the gate giving access to a maze of rock formations called Bohemian Switzerland.

The nearby Lužické hory (Lužice Mountains) are of a different kind, their typical feature being deep valleys. The highest peak is Ještěd Hill overlooking the area called Poještědí. It was once topped by an outlook tower which was destroyed by fire several years ago. Its site is now occupied by a structure designed by the architects K. Hubáček and Z. Patrman, comprising a television tower and a hotel — a masterpiece of modern Czech architecture. There is an excellent road leading across Ještěd, its hairpin bends commanding a breathtaking view as far as the Central Bohemian Range and the Liberec valley to the east. In addition to the road there is a cableway, enabling tourists in the summer, and skiers in the winter, to reach the top of Ještěd Hill.

Further east there are the Jizerské hory (Jizera Mountains) which combine into an extensive nature reserve. These hills are lower than the Giant Mountains, but all the more romantic with their pine and mixed woods, special flora, black peat-bogs and an abundance of game. There were silver, lead and copper mines, together with deposits of sapphires, garnets, emeralds, rubies and amethysts. Italians from Venice and Florence used to go as far as the sources of the River Jizera in search of precious stones, and Albrecht of Wallenstein sent his prospectors to the Jizera Mountains. Even the famous chapel at Karlštejn Castle is supposed to be decorated with semi-precious stones from the Jizera Mountains. The sources of the Jizera River are high up in the mountains, their waters, and those of Jizera's tributaries, feeding the old Souš River Dam, which is a traditional bathing place. This artificial lake with transparent water, situated in the midst of woods high up in the mountains, resembles a small part of Canada transplanted into the Bohemian landscape.

Each part of North Bohemia has its own surprisingly different features. The cone-shaped elevations of the Central Bohemian Range, the fantastic formations of Bohemian Switzerland, the "Basalt Organ" near Kamenický Šenov, deep St. Christopher's Valley in the Lužice Mountains, which reminds the visitor of an American canyon, ancient castles in ruins, ancient towns, magnificent mansions, lakes and rivers — the Elbe, the largest of them all, taking all the waters of Bohemia to Germany and the North Sea. "Variety is the main feature of this land, graceful charm and majestic dignity are combined in it as in the face of the youthful lad whose eyes now sadly gaze upon it" is how the scenery was described by the young poet Karel Hynek Mácha, the founder of modern-age Czech poetry, whose immortal poem "May" was inspired by this landscape.

But even the most charming scenery remains mere stage-setting unless we perceive it along with its people, its inhabitants, whose work has shaped it throughout the centuries. It is only the material adapted to man's requirements by man's own skill which is capable of creating cultural treasures. Mountains, lonely hills, lakes, rivers, woods, strange rock formations — all these were created by Nature without human interference. But it was man who cleared the woods, turning them into fields and pasture land, man built dykes for fishponds, regulated rivers, planted orchards and vineyards, constructed towns, railways, roads, bridges, as well as castles and mansions surrounded by magnificent parks with exotic trees and shrubs. All this has combined to shape the present-day North Bohemian scenery.

North Bohemia ranks among Bohemia's most densely populated areas. Mining predominates in its western half, together with the chemical, iron and steel, engineering and glass-making industries and large power-plants, while in the region's eastern half textile and glass production prevails. And yet it cannot be said that these advanced industries deprive the area of its scenic beauty.

119

The original ancient Slav settlements in this region must have been sparse and restricted to the more fertile parts, to the valleys of rivers and streams, rather than the hilly areas. It was not until the 12th century that settlements grew denser, especially those of the colonists who had arrived from the over-populated areas of central and western Germany. Most of them were artisans, miners and peasants. In these days the rulers of Bohemia also founded many new towns yielding substantial revenue. They encouraged foreign colonists to settle in those towns, with numerous monasteries following suit in their own domains. The example set by the sovereign was followed by the local gentry, such as the Markvart, Ronovec, Vartenberk and Hazmburk families and the Lords of Zvířetice, Lipá, Dubá and others. In addition to towns, both the royal towns and those subject to noblemen, several trade routes were established, the most important ones connecting Česká Lípa with Zittau, Frýdlant with Görlitz and Ústí on the Elbe with the Meissen area in Saxony. By the fifteenth century large-scale colonization had resulted in the Germanization of the greater part of the region. During the Hussite Revolution the German population took sides with the Catholic camp. Towns, monasteries and the gentry supported the crusaders and afforded shelter to Catholic refugees. This, of course, did not protect the area from becoming the scene of fierce fighting and frequent visits by soldiers. Many villages were destroyed at that time.

A hundred years later, on the other hand, the population of this area willingly accepted Protestantism. Lutheran teachings were accepted by the nobles, such as the Salhausens of Děčín, the Biebersteins of Frýdlant, the Räderns, the Thuns, Schlicks and others, but the burghers and villagers, too, welcomed Protestant preachers and teachers. Well-to-do people used to send their sons to the universities in Leipzig or Wittenberg. By the time

106. The valley of the River Ohře

107. *Interior of St. Nicholas's Church, Louny*

108. *Romanesque crypt of the Premonstratensian Church at Doksany*

109. *Mount Říp, where Czech history was born*

110. *The Master of the Litoměřice Altarpiece: "Christ before Caiaphas". Regional Gallery at Litoměřice*

of the Thirty Years' War, in the seventeenth century, the overwhelming majority of the area's population was Protestant. In those days the profit yielded by agriculture was not enough for the feudal lords, and they sought new sources of revenue in handicraft and industrial production. Those were the early days of the North Bohemian weaving, drapers' and glass-making trades. These industrial branches soon acquired great renown.

The Thirty Years' War, which ravaged and impoverished the country, resulted in forced mass Catholicization. Some 30,000 families from the area emigrated, among them the most skilful craftsmen and peasants. The war brought enormous gains to the nobility and the Catholic church. Well-known Albrecht of Wallenstein, the Commander of Imperial armies, acquired the extensive Frýdlant, Liberec and Jičín domains for next to nothing, combining them into one gigantic domain. As a duke he was entitled to mint his own coins and knight his subjects. The minting of Bohemian coins brought him enormous profits. In addition to his Prague palace, the sumptuousness and size of which was to compete with the Castle of Prague, he built a similar palace in the town of Jičín, which he had chosen to be the residential centre of the Duchy of Frýdlant. His building expenses were as much as 22,000 florins a month, and each of his subjects had to pay his share of four kreutzers a week. However, the Emperor had his Commander murdered at Cheb in the year 1634 — before he was able to put his ambitious plans into effect. Wallenstein's estates were divided among those who had engineered his murder.

The nobility, having acquired new riches, began to build magnificent chateaux, along with parks and game preserves. The more sumptuous their way of life, the more oppressed were their subjects. A cavalier's hound or horse were valued higher than one of his subjects. This unbearable oppression resulted in an uprising of the North Bohemian peasantry in the year 1680. Its developments were particularly dramatic in the Děčín, Litoměřice, Kamenice, Šluknov, Liberec and Frýdlant districts where the insurgents were headed by Ondřej Stelzig, a blacksmith of Řasnice. The rebellion was brutally quelled by the Imperial generals, Piccolomini and Harrant,

111. Litoměřice

but in the end the Emperor himself was forced to give in to some of the rebels' demands and issue a decree moderating some of the subjects' duties. Even so, serfdom as such was not abolished until a century later by Emperor Joseph II. The uprising of 1680 was the first great social struggle in North Bohemia, waged jointly by the Czech and German sections of the population.

The new era, commencing in the late eighteenth century, brought a rapid growth of handicraft and industrial production. This poor area, abounding in water and fuel from the nearby forests, was also a prolific source of cheap labour. North Bohemia was to become industrially the most advanced area of the whole of the former Austro-Hungarian Empire. Almost its entire textile and glass-making industries were concentrated here.

Relentless working class exploitation soon resulted in fierce social struggles, with the workmen destroying machinery like the Luddites in England — as if the machines had been to blame for their misery. But soon the ideas of socialism — as advocated, above all, by Ferdinand Lasalle — began to take root here. Social democratic organizations originated in Liberec sooner than in Prague. Next to Vienna and Brno, Liberec was the strongest centre of the social democratic movement in the Habsburg Empire. The working class organizations and their ideas took the edge off the increasingly intense national struggle. The memorable mass meeting at Pláně below Ještěd was attended by some 30,000 Czechs and Germans jointly demanding universal suffrage and a rise of the working people's living standard. The authorities, the press and, above all, the patriotic organizations of both nationalities constantly increased the tension. The nationality problem was not even satisfactorily settled by the establishment of the Czechoslovak Republic in 1918. Before World War II the majority of the German population succumbed to Nazi propaganda spread by Hitler's Third Reich. Instead of a sensible co-existence between both nationalities, nationalist passions were constantly instigated. Adolf Hitler found his North Bohemian counterparts in Konrad Henlein and K. H. Frank. With the Munich dictate of 1938, a large piece of the territory which had once offered the colonists its hospitality was illegally annexed to Germany. Following Adolf

112. Milešovka, the highest hill of the Central Bohemian Highlands

113. M. B. Braun: Holy Trinity column, Teplice in Bohemia ▶

114. *Pravčická Gate, sandstone rock formation close to Hřensko*

Hitler's defeat and the removal of the German population, the area became markedly under-populated, but new inhabitants soon arrived from the interior of Bohemia, finding new homes and jobs.

History, recording the political, social and cultural changes taking place in this area, should be a lesson, a warning and inspiration at the same time. We must proceed from historical developments to be able to understand the present and foresee future developments. We have devoted considerable attention to history — and now the time has come for a trip round about the region of North Bohemia.

In addition to the magnificent Labe (Elbe) River, North Bohemia is irrigated by the moderate flow of the Ohře River. The River Bílina flows parallel with the Ohře along the spurs of the Ore Mountains. The Jizera, rising in the swamps of the Jizera Mountains, is the most important river of the eastern part. It makes its way through the foothills and a romantic valley, turning southwards near Turnov in the direction of Prague and joining the Elbe River near Toušeň. The Jizera is one of Bohemia's most charming rivers which has so far retained its pure, clean water.

As a state began to take shape under the rule of the Přemyslids, the rulers built castles for administrative and defence purposes, and settlements originated at the foot of these castles. Many fortresses and castles were built throughout this region. Some remain as ruins, usually situated on steep hills and high rocks, others were later converted into comfortable chateaux, many of which have been preserved to this day. Two steep cylinder-shaped hills — Great and Little Bezděz — soar up from the flat surrounding country. The higher of the two hills is the site of a royal castle which was constructed in the 13th century, and was practically impregnable at the time. It was the permanent residence of a royal burgrave who was the administrator of the surrounding country. The

◄ *115. Ruined Gothic Castle of Bezděz*

116. Television tower on the summit of Mount Ještěd, near Liberec

castle was also used as a prison. Following the death of King Přemysl Otakar II (reigned 1253—1278), Otto of Brandenburg, the Administrator of Bohemia, held Queen Cunegunda and her son — future King Wenceslas II — prisoners at Bezděz Castle. A monastery of the Benedictine order was established at Bezděz in the eighteenth century. The castle began to fall into decay after the monastery was abolished in 1785, and today it is in ruins. These ruins, however, visible from a distance and dominating the entire area, are still a most imposing sight.

In the eastern part of North Bohemia alone a number of similar castles have been preserved, such as Bernštejn, Jestřebí, Tolštejn, Lemberk, Sloup, Střekov — to name just a few. Lemberk, above the community of Lvová, is well worth a visit. It was founded in the thirteenth century and converted into a chateau in the 17th century; its owner was the notorious Count Breda who inhumanly exploited his subjects. A Museum of Urban Dwellings is now accommodated in the extensive halls of the castle. Another point of interest is the rock castle of Sloup near Nový Bor. The fortress was hewn into a gigantic sandstone rock. There used to be wooden structures above the rock chambers, but after the castle had ceased to serve its purpose it became the abode of hermits who constructed an extensive chapel in the interior of the sandstone rock. Today it is hard to believe that people contented themselves with such a dwelling.

Numerous chateaux, former seats of feudal lords, have been preserved in North Bohemia. Frýdlant chateau, perched high above the small River Směda, is one of the most magnificent. It originated from a watch-tower guarding the trade route leading from Bohemia to Görlitz. It then developed into a stronghold belonging to the Berkas of Dubá, later on into a castle of the Biebersteins, and eventually into a chateau owned by the Rädern, Wallenstein and Gallas families. It now houses extensive collections of weapons and armoury as well as exhibits relating to Albrecht of Wallenstein.

Present-day towns and cities originated at the same time as the local castles; Kadaň was established on the River Ohře, as well as Žatec and Louny, Chomutov on the River Bílina, Duchcov and Ústí on the Elbe. The Hussite revolution swept away German superiority in the towns. However, the Czech element would have pre-

117. Valley of the River Jizera near Spálov above Železný Brod

vailed in these towns even without the Hussite Revolution. There was a steady influx of the Czechs which was much stronger than that of the German colonizers.

The city of Ústí nad Labem (on the Elbe), which has some 70,000 inhabitants, is the picturesque administrative and cultural centre of the area, situated on the banks of the River Elbe at its confluence with the Bílina River. It is of ancient origin but today its character is predominantly modern. It is an important centre of the chemical, iron and steel and engineering industries, and an important pivot of communications. The village of Stadice, situated south-west of Ústí, is closely connected with a legend about the origin of Bohemia's first ruling dynasty. According to this legend Princess Libuše chose Přemysl, a ploughman of Stadice, as her husband. Even long after this, the rulers of Bohemia put on bast shoes before ascending the throne — to remind themselves of their predecessor's peasant origin. It was in 1426 that the united Hussite troups, led by the Taborite commander Prokop Holý, defeated a crusaders' army three times their own strength in a battle on Na Běhání Hill, killing 20,000 enemy soldiers, mostly armoured knights on horseback.

The visitor's attention is attracted by Střekov Castle, perched on a basalt rock on the right-hand bank of the Elbe. The sight of Střekov is said to have inspired Richard Wagner when he composed his opera *Tannhäuser*.

Teplice Spa, the oldest watering-place in Central Europe, is situated near Ústí. The healing properties of its waters have been known since the fifteenth century. Volf of Vřesovice had the first Teplice spa building constructed at great expense in the year 1500. Teplice was a meeting place of many noted guests; Czar Peter the Great visited the spa in 1712, Richard Wagner in 1842. In the year 1813 Teplice was the site of the headquarters of the allied armies of Czar Alexander of Russia, Emperor Franz of Austria and King Friedrich Wilhelm of Prussia. A noteworthy Baroque plague column, created by Matthias Braun in the year 1751, stands in front of the local castle.

The city of Most is the centre of Central Europe's most prolific lignite deposits. Coal has been mined in the surroundings of Most since the middle of the last century. With the influx of miners' families the city grew rapidly

118. The orangery at Sychrov Chateau near Turnov

119. North Bohemian landscape near Česká Lípa

in size, but not in beauty. But soon it will disappear altogether as large deposits of high quality coal have been found below it. A new and modern city is now developing near the old city of Most. Only the ancient sixteenth-century Gothic church, constructed by Jacob Heilmann, a disciple of Benedict Ried, will be moved to the new city.

The town of Duchcov — allegedly the birthplace of the medieval poet Walter von der Vogelweide — lies farther east. The town boasts a beautiful castle which used to belong to the Wallenstein family. The famous adventurer and writer Giovanni Casanova (1725—1798) worked as librarian at Duchcov Castle. His twelve-volume memoirs provide an outstanding document of his era. Casanova is buried in the former cemetery near St. Barbara's Chapel. The German poet Friedrich Schiller visited Duchcov in 1791 in pursuit of studies for his great Wallenstein Trilogy.

Ancient Kadaň is situated at the Ohře River basin which is a friendly and tranquil area, protected by the Central Bohemian Range and famous for its hop fields. The town has retained its ancient character and many historic monuments, such as the Žatec and Mikulovice gates, parts of the former fortifications, the Gothic tower of its town hall on the extensive main square and a former Capuchin monastery with noteworthy diamond vaulting.

Žatec, which is also a town of ancient origin, has been the centre of Bohemia's hop-growing district and hop trade since the sixteenth century. The extensive green belts of hop fields are a characteristic feature of the area.

Nearby Louny is renowned for its Gothic church built in the first quarter of the sixteenth century. The town is the birthplace of Jaroslav Vrchlický, known as the "Prince of Czech Poets".

The small town of Doksany, and its Premonstratensian monastery, are situated farther down on the River Ohře. The crypt of the monastery, with a cross-vault supported by seventeen columns with interesting capitals and bases, ranks among the area's most outstanding architectural monuments.

At Libochovice the local Baroque chateau is well worth a visit. It was built on the site of an ancient strong-

120. Lord's Rock in the Central Bohemian Highlands

hold according to designs by the architect Antonio Porta. The rooms are furnished with highly interesting stoves created by the Dresden master Georg Fischl. The room where Jan Evangelista Purkyně — the famous Czech physiologist — was born is situated on the ground floor. His father was the administrator of the Dietrichstein domain of Libochovice.

From Libochovice it is not far to Roudnice-on-Elbe where there is a former chateau of the Lobkowicz family. Its highlight was a unique picture gallery and a library with 100,000 volumes, among them 1,200 early books and 600 manuscripts. The surroundings, dominated by the ruins of Hazmburk Castle and the memorable Říp Hill, abound with orchards, hop fields and vineyards.

The road to nearby Litoměřice leads via Terezín, a former citadel and prison. One of its prisoners was Gavrilo Princip, the Sarajevo assassin of Archduke Ferdinand d'Este and his wife. During the Nazi occupation Terezín was a Jewish ghetto and an ill-famed concentration camp which took a heavy toll of innocent victims. Everybody should pay a visit to the memorable cemetery at the Little Fortress — to realize what man is capable of perpetrating, regardless of how advanced his civilization may be.

Litoměřice lies on the opposite bank of the Elbe, guarded to the north by the cone-shaped Radobýl Hill. It is the centre of an area worthy of its epithet "Orchard of Bohemia". Litoměřice had been one of Bohemia's most important towns since the Middle Ages — and there were only a few towns enjoying the same privileges. All barges going up the Elbe with their cargoes of salt, salted fish, wool, grain, timber, tin, lead, fruit and hops had to call at Litoměřice river port either to exhibit their ware in the municipal market or to pay customs duties. It is therefore not surprising that the town grew very rich. Many architectural monuments have been preserved: the ancient Renaissance town hall, the Municipal House with its goblet-shaped roof, the house "At the Black Eagle" with graffito decoration, the episcopal residence and several churches. Another memorable object is the Litoměřice Hymn-book, dating back to 1510—1514, and weighing 50 kilogrammes. The broad Elbe River was first spanned in Litoměřice by a wooden bridge in the year 1452.

The natural centre of the eastern half of the region is the town of Liberec (70,000 inhabitants) which lies in a beautiful valley between the Lužice and Jizera Mountains. Liberec originated from a small settlement situated at the intersection of ancient roads linking Frýdlant with Görlitz and Hradec with Zittau. It was first mentioned in historical records in the reign of John of Luxembourg (1310—1346) when Liberec and Frýdlant drapers took their ware to the Prague market. Liberec was renowned for its drapers' trade especially in Wallenstein's days when the Commander provided his armies with uniforms from this city. By the year 1799 Liberec was turning out 38,000 bales of cloth which were sold throughout Austria and exported to Italy, Russia and other countries. In those days Liberec paid more taxes and duties than Prague. This otherwise poor area lived predominantly on the textile industry for several centuries. There are not many historic monuments in Liberec — the sumptuous town hall reflects wealth rather than good taste — but Liberec has a renowned theatre, a picture gallery, a museum, beautiful botanical and zoological gardens, many schools and, last but not least, surroundings of unique beauty. New housing estates, designed by noted architects, are mushrooming all over the town. Cultural activities are most varied. The annual Liberec Trade Fair has acquired world fame.

Nearby Jablonec-on-Nisa is known for its glass industry and the production of costume jewellery. Jablonec is a modern, neat and hospitable town. Its annual exhibitions of costume jewellery attract countless visitors from abroad. The local Glass and Bijouterie Museum is of world renown. The local glass-making traditions go as far back as the early eighteenth century. Zenker's Glassworks at Antonínov were constructed before 1712, and dozens of others were to follow. Throughout the Jablonec area there existed cottage industry producing glass beads and other trinkets which were exported to many parts of the world, especially to Asia and Africa.

Libverda Spa, one of the most beatiful parts of the Jizera Mountains, was known as early as the seventeenth century. Even the famed Commander Albrecht of Wallenstein used to have with him a barrel of health-giving Libverda mineral water during his campaigns. Like many other people in his days he suffered from gout — and the water obviously had a favourable influence on his ailments.

There are many other interesting towns and castles in the region, such as Zahrádky Castle which used to belong to the Kaunitz family, as well as Zákupy Castle, also known as Reichstadt, from which Napoleon's son derived his title of Duke of Reichstadt. There is also Starý Rohozec Castle and many others — but we shall only pay a fleeting visit to Sychrov. This magnificent chateau was built in the early nineteenth century by the Rohans, a noble family of French descent who emigrated to Austria after the French Revolution. The chateau bears many traces of the work of local artists and artisans, such as the wood-carvers Peter and Dominik Dušek, the stone-mason Smolík, the painter Kandler and the sculptor Max. Present-day Sychrov is a museum. It also pays tribute to the memory of the great Czech composer Antonín Dvořák who frequently visited this place, coming to see his friend who was administrator of the Sychrov domain. A separate small museum has been established in commemoration of Dvořák.

121. Frýdlant in Bohemia, the castle of Albrecht of Wallenstein

The most reliable guide to the East Bohemian region, a guide that will not get you lost in the labyrinth of magnificent scenery, mountain ranges and valleys, the bizarre fantasy of rock formations sculptured by nature, and in the vast plains over which gentle breezes blow, is the River Elbe. It rises in the Giant Mountains and its waters embrace the whole of East Bohemia, swelling as its tributaries rush swiftly down from the mountains to join it: the Orlice, Úpa, Metuje, Loučná, Cidlina and Jizera. East Bohemia, too, is bounded to the north by mountains which gradually descend in terraces of hills and hillocks towards the centre of the region to be transformed into fertile plains. It was not without reason that the ancient Czechs gave part of East Bohemia the name "Bohemian Paradise" because of its unparalleled natural beauty, nor was it by chance that they named the area around the Elbe River the "Golden Belt" of Bohemia. Finally it should be stressed that East Bohemia has unusually close links with the history of Czech culture, literature and music. The classic writers Božena Němcová and Alois Jirásek both loved this part of the country dearly and in their works described the past of the local people so convincingly that they imprinted it forever in the minds of the whole nation. Two great twentieth-century writers also had their roots here. Karel Čapek was born at Malé Svatoňovice and Jaroslav Hašek not only completed his famous book *The Good Soldier Schweik* at Lipnice, beneath the ruins of an ancient castle, but he also died in this little town in the Czech-Moravian Highlands.

From the mosaic that makes up the past and present of East Bohemia we can select only the clearest and purest of the stones like the gem-cutters who work the precious local stones.

To the north-east, East Bohemia is bounded by the Krkonoše (Giant) Mountains. This is the highest range in the Czech Lands and forms a natural frontier with Poland for a distance of forty kilometres. This continuous range of curving summits is dominated by the cone-like, bare stony peak of Mount Sněžka (1,603 metres). Although these are high mountains, the Krkonoše are neither wild nor inaccessible. Side by side with broad stretches of pine forests and zones of dwarf pines, we also find treeless summits covered with boulders, deep crevices and abysses cleft centuries ago by glacial moraines. Because of their beauty and unique flora, mountain meadows brightened by the bells of blue gentian and golden lilies, other alpine flowers, ancient plants and shrubs and natural rock formations, the Giant Mountains have been proclaimed a national park and there are many nature reserves in the area. The Krkonoše, which, according to legend, are guarded by the Giant of the Mountains, Krakonoš, have their admirers in summer and winter alike. The main starting points for expeditions into the range are three popular little resorts: Špindlerův Mlýn, at an altitude of 700 metres, is the starting point for walks to the sources of the Elbe; Pec, which has a cable railway up to the summit of Sněžka; and Harrachov, the centre of the western section of the range. There are chalets, boarding houses, hotels and holiday centres to be found scattered everywhere, on the slopes leading down to the valleys and high up on the mountain peaks. Cable lifts take you to the top of Sněžka, to Černá Hora (Black Mountain) and to Pláně. And countless ski-lifts enable winter sports enthusiasts to penetrate right into the heart of the mountains. On the slopes of the eastern part of the Giant Mountains lies the health resort of Janské Lázně whose medicinal springs have been known since the Middle Ages and where the first baths were constructed in 1675. The spa's patients are mainly children convalescing after poliomyelitis.

From the Krkonoše National Park we go down to the foot of the high mountains to a region known as Podkrkonoší (Foothills of the Giant Mountains) which has a peculiar character of its own. It used to be the home of many self-taught scholars, cottage weavers, glass-workers and woodcutters. We descend into scattered little villages and delightful towns, among the ruins of castles and charming chateaux on the hills. But here, too, industry is developing apace. Sawmills buzz, paper and cellulose works process the Krkonoše timber, textile mills turn out mile upon mile of cloth and engineering factories are bringing new pulsating life to these formerly idyllically peaceful spots.

Between Turnov, Železný Brod and Jičín lies the quiet region known as Český Ráj (the Bohemian Paradise). Nature here seems to have been a generously talented sculptor who carved out the sandstone rocks into strange shapes. The primeval sea created here an extensive city of rocks on its bed with weirdly shaped sandstone boulders.

The gateway to the city of rocks is the medieval town of Turnov. It lies beneath Mount Kozákov, on whose slopes, long before the birth of Christ, jaspers, chalcedonies and agates used to be found. Today chunks of dark red Bohemian garnet are quarried here which, in the hands of Turnov gem-cutters, are shaped for use in necklaces, rings, bracelets and brooches.

◄ *122. Ruined Gothic Castle of Trosky*

123. *Gothic Castle of Kost*

124. *Dlask farmstead, framed structure at Dolánky near Turnov*

125. *Prachovské Rocks* ▶

The Bohemian Paradise is dominated by two slim cones of volcanic origin. In the second half of the fourteenth century, a feudal lord built an inaccessible eagle's nest known as Trosky on their summits.

On the fringe of the City of Rocks, known as Prachovské Skály, lies the town of Jičín, founded by Queen Jitka, wife of Wenceslas II. Albrecht of Wallenstein, the Commander of Imperial forces, made it the headquarters of his estates where, at a much later date, European rulers were to meet and discuss how to proceed against Napoleon. In the close vicinity, on low rocky foundations, stands the splendid medieval castle of Kost. Its halls, which have been restored and renovated, contain a rare display of medieval panel painting and Gothic sculpture.

Between the Krkonoše (Giant Mountains) and the Orlické Hory (Eagle Mountains) is the massif of the Teplice and Adršpach Rocks, some seven kilometres long and covering an area of 20 square kilometres, which is a state reservation. The waters of the receding primeval ocean carved a gigantic gallery of abstract sculpture out of the sandy sea-bed.

Not far off, hidden behind wooded hills is Broumov Monastery, one of the richest and proudest of its kind, founded in the year 1322. The acquisitive abbots and the burghers of Broumov waged continual feuds against each other. The disputes culminated in the unwise decision to order the Protestant people of Broumov to close down their newly built church. The consequent revolt of the burghers was one of the sparks that set off the Thirty Years' War. The eighteenth century was a period of unprecedented glory for the monastery. Immense wealth, accumulated over the years, was invested in the construction of a new monastery. The famous Baroque

architect, Kilián Dientzenhofer, was at his most lavish. He adorned the abbey church with stucco, gold, towering altars and wrought iron gates of perfect craftsmanship, frescoes and painted vaulting, pictures by famous artists and statuary, everything producing a harmony of perfection. In Broumov cemetery there is an impressive Gothic wooden church which testifies to the deep religious feelings of the ordinary people and their skill.

Beyond Broumov, close to the ancient town of Náchod, the belt of frontier forests continues in a wavy range of rounded crests, forming an uninterrupted line up to the massif of Králický Sněžník. These are the Orlické (Eagle) Mountains. Their gentle, unobtrusive beauty is to be found rather in the valleys and the boulder-covered beds of rivers and streams, in the hollows and rocky ravines, the emerald green meadows and forest clearings filled with the scent of mountain herbs.

The foothills of the mountains, little touched by civilization, have preserved to this day the idyllic cosiness of the Czech countryside with its deep and peaceful dreaminess.

From whichever side one approaches Náchod, the town seems to play hide and seek. The proud and imposing aristocratic seat, built in Renaissance style, half castle, half chateau, was once the residence of the richest families of the nobility.

At the end of the eighteenth century, Náchod Castle was purchased by Petr of Kurland. The duke transformed this seat of the Piccolominis, full of pomp, into a charming centre, both noble and fragile. In this atmosphere, the arts flourished; at the ducal court an orchestra used to play and foreign singers came to perform. The castle's chambers, furnished in the style of the period, now contain a rich collection of old tapestries.

Not far from Náchod, in the lovely valley of the River Úpa, a little girl called Barunka Panklová, the daughter of a bailiff, grew up under the care of her grandmother, a simple old countrywoman. She was destined to become a beautiful and famous woman, for as Božena Němcová, she wrote a book which one Czech poet described as "the greatest celebration of the Czech spirit" — *Babička (Granny)*. It has appeared in Czechoslovakia in more than three hundred editions. Two splendid memorials exist to the author and to her grandmother. One is provided by the book itself, the other was carved in stone by the modern Czech sculptor, Gutfreund.

127. *Allegory of "Slyness", one of Braun's sculptures in front of the Kuks hospital*

128. *Kuks, near Dvůr Králové, the hospital and Church of the Holy Trinity*

◄ 126. *The village of Ústí near Stará Paka*

In the Babiččino údolí (Granny's Valley), named after this old grandmother, in the middle of an English-style park, stands a small chateau that is more like a country manor house than the seat of nobility. It gained fame not so much from "Granny" as from its owner, Kateřina Benigna, Duchess of Zagan, daughter of Duke Petr of Kurland and mistress of the Austrian Minister Metternich. Here she sought rest after her adventurous travels and no less adventurous life. In 1813, she offered her chateau to the heads of the "Holy Alliance at Opočno" for the first of the two secret meetings where the alliance against Napoleon was forged and where his fate was sealed.

On the way from Ratibořice, which is where the Duchess's chateau is situated, it is worth stopping at the nearby town of Nové Město, often called the "Czech Bethlehem". Complete with its Renaissance castle, the town perches skilfully on the terraces of a rocky headland. Beneath the town, the River Metuje winds its way among the meadows and above it rise the towers of the castle from a circle of ramparts and the smooth ridge of the gables of the houses. The visitor cannot fail to be enchanted by the sun-lit square surrounded by arcades. On the northern side of the square, the Renaissance gables of the burghers' houses, which have been restored, present a picture of the original appearance of the town at the beginning of the sixteenth century. The entire old part of the town is a jewel of Czech Renaissance, even though many of the later arcades violate its unity. The interior of the graffito-covered castle testifies to the sensitive linking of the original and modern decoration.

129. Bethlehem, near Kuks, with M. B. Braun's sandstone sculptures   *130. Baroque glass goblet from East Bohemia. Applied Arts Museum, Prague* ▶

131. *The Krkonoše (Giant) Mountains — view from the summit of Snĕžka (Snow Peak) towards Obří (Giant's) Chalet*

From Nové Město it is only a step or two to the little village of Slavoňov. On a hilltop above the rest of the buildings, a small wooden church is situated, and close by is a tower with walls of wooden planks and a shingle roof. The church is a typical example of folk architecture.

At the junction of two roads in the square of the nearby town of Dobruška rises the lofty Renaissance tower of the town hall. Opposite, in an ordinary apartment house, the painter František Kupka, world-famous as one of the founders of abstract art, made himself a simple wooden studio while he was still a student in the 1890's. He spent his youth in Dobruška and some of his best early works can be seen in the local museum.

It is hard to understand just why Count Sporck, son of an adventurer in the Thirty Years' War, picked such a remote and melancholy spot as the village of Kuks in the upper part of the Elbe valley as the site for his magnificent and noble residence. On a steep slope above the River Elbe, where springs of curative water gush up from the ground, he had a spa constructed as well as a splendid castle. He promoted a lively social life to dispel his guests' boredom and to dazzle them with the luxury around them, at the same time gaining glory and social consequence for himself. As the spa centre was completed, it was adorned with magnificent Baroque statuary unparalleled in Europe. The world-famous sculptor Matthias Bernard Braun had a hand in this grandiose work. During the season, Count Sporck would invite the Italian opera company from Venice to his court and would arrange costly revelries in the castle and its surroundings, accompanied by music and artillery fire and in autumn he would stage great hunting parties for his friends.

F. A. Sporck was a nobleman full of contradictions, inconsistent in his behaviour, always dissatisfied and prone to litigation. At the same time he was a loyal supporter of Jansenism and of religious tolerance and was often involved in conflicts with the Church and, in particular, with the Jesuits from neighbouring Žírec. All Sporck's personal characteristics are reflected in the work of Matthias Braun. The choice of subjects, their conception and presentation tallies with the views and ideas of his patron. This should be borne in mind when one strolls along the pathways lined with figures symbolizing the human virtues and vices, religious statues and mythological statues, saints and dwarfs. No less interesting are works of statuary by Braun in the nearby forest in a spot known as Bethlehem. Among ferns, banks of moss and fallen pine needles, he carved in sandstone boulders monumental reliefs representing Biblical scenes.

The metropolis of Eastern Bohemia, Hradec Králové, and its rich history mirror the development, not only of this region, but of the whole nation. The town, which was intended as the residence of Czech queens should they be widowed, was given the grandiose title in the fourteenth century of "Royal Dowry Town". But Hradec made a much more honoured name for itself during the Hussite revolutionary movement, when Jan Žižka named it a "Lesser Tábor". Its fame died down somewhat in the 18th century, when it was converted into a fortress. The suburbs with their many churches, monasteries and craftsmen's workshops had to make way

◀ *132. Teplice Rocks near Broumov*   *133. O. Gutfreund: "Granny", Ratibořice near Česká Skalice*

136. *Little wooden church and bell-tower at Slavoňov near Nové Město-on-Metuje*

for the construction of powerful brick ramparts and the rest of the town was encircled by a system of moats, trenches and mounds. Hradec became a provincial town inhabited by troops, priests, bureaucrats and servants. Yet as far back as the fourteenth century it was, after Prague, the most densely populated and richest town in Bohemia. Close to the Royal Castle, towering above the roof-tops of the rich burghers' houses, the Gothic brick Church of the Holy Spirit was built. Beneath its vaulting, in front of the high altar, the Hussite commander Jan Žižka was buried in 1424, after he had guided the fate of the nation from Hradec for two years. In the sixteenth century, Hradec, like other towns, lived through a Golden Age. In the vicinity of the church, a new landmark, the White Tower, was erected. Of noble Renaissance form, it contains one of the biggest bells in the country. Entry into the town was provided by new Renaissance gateways.

After the Thirty Years' War, Hradec, along with the rest of the country, went through a time of deep depression. Less than one third of the original population remained in the town. A new wave of German burghers moved into the deserted houses and, together with the clergy, became masters of the town. The Jesuits settled within its walls. They built a powerful church and a college on the square and from there sent out their penal expeditions into the region. Hradec became the seat of the bishopric, which was transferred here from Litomyšl. The town underwent a new phase of development towards the end of the 19th century when it purchased from the state the land on which stood the fortifications and military buildings which had proved useless in the war of 1866. In the first decade of the present century, Hradec recruited outstanding architects to rebuild the town and give it a new look. The historic core of Hradec was left untouched while a great deal of building work was carried on in the outskirts.

To the south, on the River Elbe, lies Pardubice. This town, too, which today is a centre of the chemical industry, has many historic buildings and its core had been declared a protected urban reservation. Pardubice was given the status of a town in the year 1340 by the first Czech Archbishop, Ernest of Pardubice. In the six-

◀ *134. Náchod, the square and St. Lawrence's Church*

◀ *135. Nové Město-on-Metuje, with its wonderful examples of Renaissance architecture*

137. *The Church of the Holy Spirit at Hradec Králové*

138. *Hradec Králové, the square*

139. *The Castle of Kunětická Hora near Pardubice*

140. *The village of Kunvald near Žamberk in the Orlické (Eagle) Mountains*

teenth century, its new lord, William of Pernštejn, made it into a luxurious seat so that it well deserved the name "the town of the Czech Renaissance". Most impressive are the square with a row of houses decorated with stucco work of unusual artistic standard, the town hall and the "Green Gate" and, of course, the castle with its many Renaissance treasures. In the vicinity of the town, rising out of the Elbe plain, is an isolated basalt peak known as Kunětická Hora, crowned by a ruined Gothic castle. From its battlements one can admire the wealth of the "Golden Belt" of the Czech Lands, the most fertile stretch of Bohemia.

In the eastern part of the region bordered by the Czech-Moravian Highlands which divide Bohemia from Moravia, there are three towns that deserve mention. The first is Chrudim, a royal town founded by Přemysl Otakar II in 1260. It, too, can boast of many architectural treasures in the form of Gothic, Renaissance and Baroque houses. The annual festivals held at Chrudim have made it a centre of puppetry in Europe. The second is Havlíčkův Brod, founded in the middle of the 13th century close to the silver mines. Finally there is Litomyšl with its untouched beauty. The town, which became the seat of bishops in 1344, is dominated by a splendid Renaissance castle, built more to meet the needs of education and culture than to satisfy the pride of its owner. The castle's theatre, a unique masterpiece of Baroque, has been preserved to this day. It was at Litomyšl that the great Czech composer, Bedřich Smetana, was born.

Neither East Bohemia's historical profile nor its landscape can conceal the fundamental changes this part of the Czechoslovak Socialist Republic has undergone in recent decades. Here too, the state gives its protection to the natural beauties and historic treasures of the area. Tiny fields have been joined into huge co-operative farms which have completely transformed the character of the countryside and led to the rise of advanced agricultural production. From the little workshops of the handweavers in the foothills of the Giant Mountains, big textile mills have grown up. There are coal mines, large chemical plants, engineering factories and paper mills. New residential estates and towns have been built, too. It is not only a charming region, but it has become a wealthy one as well.

◀ *141. The town hall and plague column at Chrudim*

142. Litomyšl, the front of the castle

143. *Brno, Moravia's principal city*

Everywhere in the world the pattern of life on dry land is determined by water and this applies, perhaps more than anywhere else, to the Czech Lands and Moravia. The waters of the Czech basin flow by way of the Elbe towards the North Sea, Silesia's waters go by means of the Oder to the Baltic, and Moravia is drained by the Danube into the Panonian basin and the Black Sea. From time immemorial the way of life of the people and the life of the entire countryside has followed the course of the country's rivers and that perhaps explains the differences that have arisen despite the unity of the nation.

The city of Brno is built on several small hills which enclose the valleys of the Dyje and Svratka rivers; the South Moravian plains which are linked to the vineyards of Lower Austria and thus to the plains of Hungary actually begin in the town itself. In the Tertiary Era, the Miocene Panonian sea reached this point and from it the Pálava rose up on the Dyje like an island. In the time of the earliest Slav settlement of Moravia, life centred around the lower reaches of the Rivers Dyje and Morava, that is to say, around the two most powerful rivers, and Brno at the confluence of the Svratka and Svitava was only on the fringe of the main settlements. It was not yet Brno but rather Staré Zámky, the remains of which are still being uncovered close to Líšeň. The town of Brno itself came into being only in the days of the Přemyslids.

Brno's situation between plains and hills is a very advantageous one. It takes only a few minutes to get from the city centre to beautiful natural surroundings where you can roam at will through dense forests the whole day long.

But technology marches on and the Svratka — the Black River as poets call it — has been tamed and regulated. So has the River Svitava — once known as the White River — which flows round the opposite side of the city. Giant housing estates, like Lesná, have been built and others are growing up all the time. New hotels of an international standard are being built, the great trade fair grounds which are not only the site of the annual engineering trade fairs but of many other fairs and exhibitions, too, are being extended. On the city's outskirts factories are being enlarged. Besides new houses, administrative and public buildings, a new opera house has been built.

The old part of the city is like one great and splendid museum. A visitor should stroll through the quiet little streets between many monuments to the past. Among the sights well worth seeing are the Gothic Cathedral of St. Peter at Petrov Hill with its Baroque decorations, such as works of sculpture by Schweigel and paintings by Korompay, then the abbey church of the Minorites which was restored in Baroque style by the famous Brno architect, Maurice Grimm (1669—1757) with its Loreto and a triple Holy Stairway, frescoes by Etgens and paintings by Korompay. Then there is the Old Brno Abbey Church built by Queen Eliška Rejčka, which is a wonderful example of Czech Gothic (one of the abbots of this monastery until his death in 1884 was the founder of genetics, Jan Řehoř Mendel), and the parish church of St. James, built in the twelfth century under Margrave Vladislav Henry, which contains the tomb of Raduit de Souches, who defended Brno against the Swedes during the Thirty Years' War. Other places that should not be missed include Brno Castle on the summit of Špilberk Hill of which little of the original Gothic architecture has been preserved, and the Old Town Hall, especially its portal by Pilgram, the rare Pietà above the side altar and Maulbertsch's picture above the high altar in St. Thomas's Church and the Renaissance palace of Antonio Gabri. Finally every visitor should make a point of seeing the splendid courtyard of the Moravian Museum, where the winged god Mercury hovers over Neptune, Vulcan and Ceres and the space beside it is dominated by the spreading crown of an exotic paulownia. There is, too, Brno's only fountain, called Parnassus, the work of the sculptor Fischer of Erlach; the Baroque column dedicated to Our Lady on Svoboda (Freedom) Square, and the obelisk on Petrov Hill built to commemorate the end of the Napoleonic Wars. Gems of Gothic art in Brno, in addition to the stone Madonna of the Minorite Church, a wooden statue of an apostle and the later St. James's Altarpiece, include the cycle of panel paintings depicting the Passion of Christ on the Rajhrad Altarpiece.

Proof that splendid architecture is not only the privilege of past history can be found in modern buildings in Brno itself and its surroundings. For instance there is the modern altar in the church at Jedovnice which is the work of the Prague painter Mikuláš Medek and the sculptor Jan Koblasa from the year 1966.

Jedovnice is in the area covered by the Moravian Karst, a stretch of a hundred square kilometres of Devon limestone where water and time have transformed the inside of the hills into a maze of corridors, vaulted halls, stalagmite and stalactite caves and abysses. What most interests visitors are the central caves in the vicinity of the Punkva underground river. Through the great hall, easily negotiable passages and stairways lead us to the bottom of the Macocha abyss which is nearly 140 metres deep. There we find two lovely little turquoise-coloured lakes below steep rocky walls. Then there are the great Catherine Cave and the caverns of the Sloup group with the deepest of all underground abysses, the Nagel abyss, as well as the Kůlna and the Křížová caves where there have been many archeological finds bearing witness to the early presence of Paleolithic man. And there is the Balcarka cave with its Coral Lakes, the Hollow Tree, the Gallery, Cinderella and the Dome of Ruin.

In the romantic surroundings bordering on this territory we come upon Křtiny, a popular spot with tourists, dominated by the Church of Our Lady with its unusual cupola, close to the local castle. The church was founded in the middle of the eighteenth century, having been designed by the architect Giovanni Santini, and it is one of the purest examples of dynamic Baroque to be found in Moravia.

Not far off is Slavkov — Austerlitz — scene of one of the most famous battles of the Napoleonic Wars. Its Rococo castle, the gallery of which is full of rare masterpieces, contains many reminders of Napoleon. The surrounding countryside, beneath the Peace Mound, was the setting for the famous Battle of the Three Emperors. Here on December 2, 1805, as the sun rose through the morning mists, the battlefield on which Napoleon was to win his great victory was revealed. This was the setting of the "Soleil d'Austerlitz" painted by so many artists in the years to come.

What should follow Brno? Perhaps we should set out for the town of Kroměříž, with its trees, parks and lovely churches.

There are few towns that can boast such a perfect square. Seated firmly at the northern corner is the solid tower of the castle, like some dignified matron. Opposite, in the southern corner is the Renaissance town hall. A short distance away stands the twin-towered Gothic Church of St. Maurice. The fountain in the centre of the square and the marble column beside it are surrounded on all four sides by the fronts of predominantly Renaissance and early Baroque arcaded burghers' houses. Although the town can boast some Gothic architecture it is to Baroque that Kroměříž owes most. The first place to visit is the castle. Its courtyards, passageways and cellars were built in the years following 1643 by the skilful Italian architects, Filiberto Lucchese and Giovanni Pietro Tencalla. Works by Cranach, the Adoration of the Magi by Lucas van Leyden, Pordenone's Samson and Delilah, Van Dyck's portrait of Charles I and Henrietta Maria, Wouters' Diana and Callisto, landscapes by Vries, Johann Lyss's Vision of St. Jerome, and to crown them all, Titian's The Flaying of Marsyas, in addition to many other treasures of European painting, make the Kroměříž castle collection truly outstanding.

There you will be able to savour Baroque beneath the ceiling of the Vassals' Hall with the brilliant frescoes

144. The courtyard of the Moravian Museum, Brno

145. The Master of the Rajhrad Altarpiece:
"Bearing of the Cross". Moravian Gallery, Brno ▶

146. *Golden pendant, culture of the Great Moravian Empire, unearthed at Mikulčice. Moravian Museum, Brno*

147. *Castle garden at Telč*

of F. A. Maulbertsch. From the castle your path leads you to the earlier Baroque masters, Etgens and Stern in St. John's Church, and to works of sculpture by Tencalla and Fontana.

As to parks, there is the Flower Garden with geometrically laid out avenues, its great colonnade, in the niches of which are statues of forty-four gods and goddesses, and finally the rotunda in the very centre of this charming little park. In the Castle Park one can walk down the shady Chropyň Lane and across the Silver Bridge to the Pompeii Colonnade or along the promenade around the Long Pond and Wild Lake.

The Kroměříž district is only partly in the plainland area known as the Haná. The southern part consists of hills and deep woods, the Chřiby Range and the Buchlov and Ždánské Hills. Within a stone's throw is Střílky, known as the "Moravian Kuks", after Kuks in Eastern Bohemia. Střílky churchyard contains some splendid examples of Baroque art. The architect is unknown, but the churchyard was built in 1740—1750. The author of the sculptures is known. He was Bohumír Fritsch (1705—1750), who was sculptor to the Petřvalds in Tovačov.

In the midst of deep forests are the ruins of the powerful Hussite castle of Cimburk. All that remains of it are the bastions, a cylindrical tower, parts of the walls of the two-storey palace and the portal. The castle was deserted around the year 1700, long after the high commander, Ctibor Tovačovský of Cimburk (1438—1494) had successfully defended King George of Poděbrady against the Silesians. He was one of the most outstanding men in fifteenth-century Moravia and achieved fame for what was known as the "Tovačov Book" in which he wrote "Recollections of the Orders, Ancient Customs and the Administration of the Law in the Margravate of Moravia" (1481).

Past the long Koryčany reservoir, a path leads to Moravia's most ancient castle — Buchlov — which, unlike

148. The Gothic-Renaissance South Moravian town of Telč

149. *Residential palace of Pernštejn Castle*

150. *Gothic Cistercian Church at Žďár-on-Sázava*

151. *The Moravian Karst*

152. *Stalactite and stalagmite caves of the Moravian Karst*

153. Modern altar in the Church of St. Peter and St. Paul at Jedovnice near Blansko

154. Baroque Church of the Birth of Our Lady at Křtiny near Brno

155. *Minaret in the castle park at Lednice near Mikulov*

156. *Wine cellars at Petrov near Strážnice*

the last mentioned castle, has been preserved intact in all its architectural beauty. In its forecourt spreads the thousand-year-old "Lime Tree of Innocence", a reminder of the criminal court known as the "Hunter's Law", which from the fourteenth century used to sit here and pass judgment. Buchlov, as one of the best fortified of all castles on Czechoslovak territory, withstood even the attacks of the Swedes in the Thirty Years' War. Here reminders can be found of the enlightened Berchtold family. One of them, Leopold (1759—1809), a doctor and philanthropist, turned Buchlov into a hospital where all who needed it were given treatment. Bedřich Berchtold (1781—1876), along with Jan Svatopluk Presl and Jan Evangelista Purkyně, ranked among the most outstanding natural scientists. Their valuable library has been preserved to this day. Beneath Buchlov, at Buchlovice, the predecessors of the Berchtolds, the Petřvalds, built a charming chateau of the Italian type, standing in a lovely park.

The three little peaks, Buchlov, Holý Kopec (Bare Hill) and Modla (with the Berchtold mausoleum on its summit), all visible from a great distance, dominate the valley of the Morava, a valley which was the cradle

of Slavonic culture. From Velehrad via the Staré Město section of Uherské Hradiště, to Mikulčice and Pohansko close to Břeclav, the entire area is full of traces of the Great Moravian Empire dating from the ninth and tenth centuries, reminders of the greatness of the Mojmír line and the empire of Svatopluk, and of the founders of Slavonic literature, Cyril (Constantine) and Methodius. At Mikulčice, there is an exhibition of archaeological finds known as the National Memorial, where it is possible to see the results of the excavations made in this area. One has to admire the skill of the early Slavs: weapons, harnesses and other equipment, as well as enchantingly intricate and pure jewelry. On the other side of the valley of the River Morava, on the slopes of the White Carpathians, the town of Uherský Brod and the villages of Nivnice and Komná recall the memory of a great man of a later date, the "Teacher of the Nations", Jan Amos Komenský (Comenius, 1592—1670), who was a native of this area. Comenius's work as a philosopher and an educational reformer is of the same vital significance today as it was three hundred years ago.

157. Landscape with the River Dyje near Mušov

◄ *158. Windmill at Kuželov in Moravian Slovakia*

◄ *159. Baroque castle at Milotice near Kyjov*

160. Memorial to the Battle of the Three Emperors at Slavkov (Austerlitz) of 1805

161. Gothic Castle of Buchlov

162. Vassals' Hall of the Archbishop's Palace at Kroměříž

The lower part of the Morava basin, known as Moravian Slovakia, remains a cradle of folk art to this day. Folklore festivals at Strážnice, Tvrdovice, Velká and Hluk make it possible to see expressions of folk art of a very high standard. The songs and dances of this area, the rich folk costumes, the ornaments painted on the cottages, the hand-weaving and embroidery, the painted Easter eggs, the decorated entrances, the little huts in the vineyards and the fronts of the wine cellars, all aroused the admiration of the French sculptor, Rodin.

The White Carpathians cross into the Valašsko area with its picturesque little hills, to Lopeník, Bojkovice, Sidonie and the dignified summit of Makyta, full of deep woods, quiet corners and crystal brooks. Then comes the town of Gottwaldov, the metropolis of the southern part of Valašsko. In the Dřevnice valley, between Mladcov woods and Tlustá Hora (Plump Mountain) with Barabáš, the town of Zlín came into being in the 13th century as the result of colonization. It might have remained an insignificant little town with a few hundred houses to this day, but during the last century, shoe factories began to be established here. In 1894, the owner of one such factory, Tomáš Baťa, began to make slippers on a small scale. By 1913 he was exporting leather boots and shoes to Italy and when the First World War was over he had a world-wide market. The town grew with the factories. Kotěra's original plans for regulating building were far from sufficient, the extreme ideas of Le Corbusier who made a personal visit to Zlín could not be put into practice, and so it was Gahur's ideas for a Garden City that would blend in with the Valašsko landscape that were actually implemented. The final solution though, as in so many other places, was to build upwards and create tall buildings. In 1949, the nationalized boot and shoe concern was renamed SVIT and the town of Zlín was renamed Gottwaldov.

Not far off, set in deep forests, is the world-famous spa of Luhačovice, with its many alkaline springs, its parks and fountains, and its many pleasant hotels and villas. For more than two hundred years, disorders of the digestive system have been treated here, as well as diabetes and, more recently, attention has been concentrated particularly on the treatment of disorders of the upper respiratory tract.

Mountains to the east, mountains to the west — that is the picture of the South Moravian region. On the one side the younger system of the Carpathians which emerged in the Tertiary Era, on the other the ancient area that rose in the Primary Era, the dignified Czech-Moravian Highlands. The metropolis of the Highlands, Jihlava, seems to contemplate its glorious past. Founded in the twelfth century, Jihlava received a royal charter from King Wenceslas I in 1248 and, in addition, special mining rights — "ius regale montanorum". Mining has long since vanished from the area, but the town now throbs with industry and is rich in culture. A sister town of Jihlava is the nearby town of Třebíč which is a partner of Gottwaldov, for here fine boots and shoes are made. Třebíč is dominated by its castle and the Romanesque-Gothic Church of St. Procopius, built in the first half of the thirteenth century.

Perhaps there is no range of hills so tempting to the rambler as the Czech-Moravian Highlands. Little patches of pine woods hide countless small fishponds and flat meadows, and clearings of pastureland which offer an abundant wealth of mushrooms, wild strawberries, raspberries and bilberries, and the air is clean and fresh. In the southern part of the range lies the ancient town of Slavonice, close to the Austrian frontier. Telč, too, is one of the most lovely towns in Czechoslovakia, with its old castle and its arcades, and with a fine Gothic church. The long town square is edged by ancient houses with Renaissance façades and Baroque gables.

The northern part of the Highlands, the countryside around Žďár, is for the most part a protected area and its centre is dominated by the highest mountains of the range: Devět Skal (Nine Rocks) and Žákova hora with its surrounding virgin forest reservation. Beneath them is Velké Dářko, known as the "little sea" of the Highlands, and Ránsko Moor. Also well worth a visit are Vír Dam and Pernštejn, a fortified castle dating from the thirteenth century with well preserved architecture of all the later styles, from Gothic to late Baroque. Both the interior of the castle and the park are extremely pleasing. There are some very attractive towns in the neighbourhood, too: picturesque Svratka, Bystřice-below-Pernštýn and Nové Město na Moravě, an artists' centre adorned with statuary by the sculptors Jan Štursa and Vincenc Makovský, who were born here. A visitor may like to take a look at the beautiful castle of Žďár, or at the cemetery church at nearby Zelená Hora where Giovanni Santini left traces of his art, or the little churches at Zvole and Obyčtov.

In the centre of the South Moravian plain, in the valley of the River Dyje, there rises a floe of silver-like Jura limestone, unparalleled in this area — Pálava. It juts out from the vineyards and orchards where almonds, apricots, peaches, morellos, walnuts, apples and pears grow in profusion. The most striking example of the combination of the Karst nature of the surroundings and a town is provided by Mikulov. Dietrichstein Castle which seems to grow imposingly from its rocky foundations, the watch-tower on its rocky peak, the princely mausoleum, the churches, chapter-house, the Jewish cemetery, countless statues, and above all Svatý Kopec (Holy Mount) with stations of the cross and a chapel on the summit, are all extremely attractive to visitors. Great expanses of vineyards, spreading out in all directions as far as the eye can see, add to this impression.

163. Baroque cemetery at Střílky near Kroměříž

The fertility of the Pálava hillsides has been known to man from time immemorial. Karel Absolon, the discoverer of the Venus of Věstonice, an ancient statuette, in Dolní Věstonice, deduced from finds made close to the Baroque village of Pavlov that the Věstonice mammoth hunters must have had a high level of civilization — a culture similar to that of the people of Cro-Magnon and of the hunters of Předmostí. Podivín, just a little further on, is the oldest town in Czechoslovakia. Founded by the convert Podiva in the vicinity of the mysterious Sekyř church and mentioned in the 12th-century Chronicle of Cosmas, it is of great interest to historians.

The road from Valtice to Lednice is flanked by the vast areas of the Lednice fishponds, each of which is surrounded by lovely trees and delightful meadows and edged with rushes. Between the ponds are tiny lodges built by former owners of the estates. They are charming spots with attractive architecture, but are of comparatively recent origin, having been built in the first half of the nineteenth century. Where Hlohovec pond begins stands one of the largest of these buildings, Hraniční Chateau (1826—1827). Hranice means frontier and in the days of the Austro-Hungarian monarchy, the frontier between the Provinces of Moravia and Lower Austria, to which Valtice belonged, ran right through the middle of the pond. Close to the Mill Fishpond stands the Apollo Mansion, from the roof of which there is a splendid view of the surrounding countryside. The relief over the portal and the statues in the atrium are the work of the sculptor Klieber. It was he, too, who was the author of the Three Graces, charming statues standing in a small semi-circular woodland temple supported by twelve Ionic columns.

The quiet, neat little town of Valtice is full of examples of Baroque. Worth mentioning are the Monastery of the Brothers of Mercy — today a state hospital — and the abbey church, the plague column in the square, the work of the Viennese sculptor Gunst, and the imposing early Baroque church at the corner of the square, built from 1631 to 1671 and completed by the Brno architect, Ern, which has a small picture by Rubens over the altar. But most impressive is the huge square two-storey Liechtenstein castle which is wonderfully decorated and full of works of art.

Znojmo is often called the "White Metropolis". Its castle, going back to the times of the Přemyslids, places

172

the town well into the Romanesque period. Among its very oldest buildings is the rotunda with its frescoes depicting the genealogy of the Přemyslid Princes and an inscription dating from the year 1134, all of which was recently restored. There are several rare and well-preserved burghers' houses dating from the thirteenth century, which are fine examples of Gothic, and bear witness to the standard of building in this once royal town.

Znojmo suffered greatly at the close of the Second World War, and irreparable damage was done by bombardment. The surroundings of Znojmo are as interesting as those of Mikulov or Břeclav. A little to the north, in the midst of deep woods, lies the picturesque township of Jevišovice with its miniature dam, which is the oldest in Central Europe. The old castle, originally a Gothic fortress, the new chateau built in the style of Windsor Castle, the park with its ancient oak trees and statues by Lorenzo Mattielli, and the Hussite chalice (for Jevišovice was a bastion of the Moravian Hussite movement) are among the loveliest gems of the whole region. Count Raduit de Souches, whose tomb is in St. James's Church in Brno and who is known for his rather pompous portraits, used to live in Jevišovice Castle. Raduit de Souches, as an ordinary officer during the Thirty Years' War, succeeded in standing up to Torstenson's army and saving Brno from the fate suffered by many other towns at the hands of the Swedes and, in addition, he saved the Imperial capital, Vienna, from the northerners. He later became a marshal of the Imperial army.

The name of Znojmo is linked with that of Vranov-on-Dyje. On the site of the original castle known to have been in existence in 1210, stands a chateau perched on a rock like an eagle's nest. Inside are fascinating examples of pottery. Vranov Lake, which is another gem in the South Moravian landscape, is dotted with the white sails of little yachts and boats hurrying to and fro like worker bees. In addition it has a splendid beach and is good for swimming.

South Moravia, whether the plains of Haná, the Dyje Valley or the hilly regions of Horácko and Valašsko, evokes an ever-changing picture of the brightest sunshine and blackest clouds, gentle breezes and vicious storms, sweet-smelling wild strawberries and thyme, and threatening thunderbolts, rising to the skies, and nights as black as tombstones, all the colours of the rainbow and the emptiest of voids, the advent of the star that has already risen and that which is still to rise.

164. Gottwaldov, town of the footwear industry

165. The square at Olomouc

Moravia, the middle part of Czechoslovakia, has sometimes been compared to a maple leaf sketched in the rich colours of autumn. Lush green meadows and ochre-yellow belts of wheat alternate with patches of dark green and the russet colours of ploughed fields are interlaced with the veins formed by rivers and roads.

Moravia, contained by its historic borders, with Silesia left out, is indeed shaped like a maple leaf. Its stalk is formed by the River Morava, which flows from north to south from the Jeseníky Mountains, through broad dales into the Danube plain, making a wide arc round the Drahanské Highlands and the Chřiby Hills. The new administrative division of the Republic into regions has to a large extent eliminated Moravia's historic internal boundaries with Bohemia and Silesia and turned it into two of the seven regions of the Czech Lands.

Archaeological finds provide reminders of this land's turbulent and glorious past from the first to the tenth centuries A.D., when out of the misty past emerged the Great Moravian Empire of the Mojmír dynasty, which covered not only Moravia, Bohemia and parts of Slovakia, but also sections of what are today Hungary, Austria, Germany and Poland. There is concrete and tangible evidence of the existence of people of Slav origin in these areas and, in the Romanesque period, we have a great deal of solid evidence of their presence. The Moravians spread the reputation of their country throughout the civilized world: Jeroným Moravský (Hieronymous of Moravia) was one of the most outstanding musical scholars in Paris; Matyáš Moravský of Olomouc (Matthias Moravus) was one of the first printers in Naples and his compatriot Valentin Fernández de Moravia introduced book printing to Lisbon. Jan Amos Komenský (Comenius, 1592—1670), the last Bishop of the Unity of Bohemian Brethren, sought asylum for himself and those of his faith in many parts of Europe during the Thirty Years' War, and, like a voice crying from the wilderness, sought assistance for his suffering country among all opponents of the Habsburgs. He gave Europe a reformed system of education and made access to learning easier for generations to come.

When, after the Battle of the White Mountain, members of the Unity of Bohemian Brethren, the reformed church, had to flee the country to escape persecution, they founded a new Church abroad. It is still possible today to come across Moravian Brethren in Alaska, the Himalayas and South America.

Over the centuries, Moravia has given the world individuals whose importance has gone far beyond the frontiers of their country. Hynčice near Opava, in Silesia, was the birthplace of the founder of genetics, Jan Řehoř Mendel (1822—1884). The psychiatrist and neurologist, Sigmund Freud (1856—1939), founder of psychoanalysis, was born at Příbor near Ostrava. Prostějov was the birthplace of the philosopher Edmund Husserl (1859—1938), the founder of phenomenology, while the composer Leoš Janáček (1854—1928) was born at Hukvaldy in the Beskydy Mountains.

Approximately in the centre of Czechoslovakia, in the fertile plain of Haná, lies the third largest Moravian city, Olomouc. In the vicinity of this ancient capital of the Haná region, in the last wave of the Jeseníky mountain range, gleams the white church of Kopeček, a place of pilgrimage dating from the years 1669—1732. Still closer to the city, almost beneath its very ramparts, the left bank of the River Morava is graced by the splendid Baroque architecture of Hradisko Monastery, built in the mid-18th century on the site of a former fortified settlement dating from the Great Moravian Empire. Next comes something that makes an even deeper impression — the lush green of the flat countryside is dominated by the grey towers and spires of Olomouc itself. The three spires of the episcopal church of St. Wenceslas rise over the panorama of the city, together with the three cupolas of St. Michael's, the slim tower of the town hall, the dome of the Church of Our Lady of the Snows and the blunt angular tower of St. Maurice's Church. All are enclosed by a ring of fortifications, for Olomouc has always been a strategic town. Its history can be followed with certainty from the 11th century onwards. In 1063, it became the seat of a bishopric and in 1248 it was made a royal town. The well-preserved historic buildings give some idea of the size and importance of Olomouc. Most valuable from the artistic point of view is the late Gothic church of St. Maurice which possesses the largest organ in the country, built by Michael Engler of Wroclaw. The nearby church of St. Wenceslas contains the remains of a Romanesque palace which was the seat of the Olomouc Přemyslids. It was here, in 1306, that the last of the Přemyslids, King Wenceslas III, was murdered. The town hall, with a late Gothic bay to its chapel and a fine Renaissance staircase, can boast of a slender tower dating from the fourteenth century. But the highest point of this historic town is provided by the three Baroque towers of the originally Gothic, now Baroque church of St. Michael. Renaissance reconstruction, which is still preserved in several houses, was carried out on a large scale. Peculiar to Olomouc are the splendid Baroque group of statues of the Holy Trinity by Václav Render and a number of Baroque fountains. The metropolis of the Haná region grew in importance from the days of King John of Luxembourg (1296—1346), under whose rule it became the capital city of Moravia. In 1566 the Jesuits established a monastery and college here, which was soon raised to the level of a university, though later its significance declined. After the Second World War, Olomouc University was renewed and renamed Palacký University, after the well-known historian, František Palacký (1798—1876) who was born at Hodslavice in Moravia. In the years 1742—1754, after the loss of Silesia,

167. *Gothic Castle of Bouzov*

the Empress Maria Theresa fortified Olomouc to protect Vienna from Prussian attack, and did so to such an extent that it became the most powerful Baroque fortification on Czechoslovak territory. The fortress of Olomouc became a much dreaded prison in which the Habsburgs incarcerated chosen prisoners, such as the French General Lafayette (1794—1797) who had fought for the independence of the American people, the Russian anarchist Mikhail A. Bakunin, and the author of the libretto of Smetana's opera *The Bartered Bride*, Karel Sabina. In 1848 Olomouc was for a time proclaimed the seat of the Habsburg Court and so it was here that Franz Joseph I, at the age of eighteen, ascended the throne. On the spot where, according to legend, Jaroslav of Šternberk defeated the Tartar hordes, one of Olomouc's three big parks is situated. It is known as Bezruč Park after the Moravian poet Petr Bezruč and has wonderful flower beds and enormous green-houses. It is here that each summer the annual Flower and Landscape Gardening Show "Flora Olomouc" is held.

Before leaving Olomouc for the Jeseníky Mountains, we should stop at some of the castles and manor houses in the neighbourhood. Some did not stand up to the turbulence of their times; they were damaged in battle or lost their importance, some were deserted and fell into decay. But others were maintained by their owners in their full pride and often in their original style. We should mention at least Bouzov (west of Litovel) and Šternberk. Bouzov, built in Gothic style towards the end of the thirteenth or the beginning of the fourteenth century, was burnt down in the 16th century and suffered further great damage during the Thirty Years' War; at the turn of the twentieth century it was restored in a new style. Among the best preserved of Moravian castles is Šternberk. After the burning at the stake of John Huss, the Moravian Estates gathered here to protest against the perfidy of King Sigismund. During the Hussite Wars, the Taborites occupied Šternberk Castle for two years. Today, the castle's spacious halls are filled with unique collections of old art, especially Gothic sculpture and panel painting. Nearby Sovinec Castle, whose Lords supported the Hussite King George of Poděbrady, played a role in Czech history. After the Battle of the White Mountain it became the property of Teutonic knights, and during the Second World War it was partly burnt down.

◄ *166. The Master of the Torun Madonna: "The Šternberk Madonna". State Castle of Šternberk, Moravia*

The oldest town in Silesia, Bruntál, founded in 1223, has a fine Renaissance chateau which is the architectural highlight of the town. Today it houses the local museum. Žerotín manor house at Velké Losiny near Šumperk (built in 1580—1589) was notorious as the site of witch trials. It has an octagonal tower, a chapel, and charming open arcades. Other buildings of historical interest include the paper mill built at the beginning of the sixteenth century. It is one of the oldest mills in Central Europe for the hand manufacture of paper (it was actually founded in 1516).

At last we have reached the Jeseníky Mountains with their deep shady forests and wild valleys. Here there is a choice: either to ascend the majestic Praděd Peak (1492 metres) in the Hrubý Jeseník range, providing a magnificent view of the whole surrounding countryside, or to go by train from Olomouc to Krnov via Ramzovské Saddle, and to set out across Červenohorské Saddle to Jeseník Spa or Dolní Lipová, to take a rest at the sources of the River Morava, beneath the peak of Králický Sněžník (1424 metres) or under Vysoká Hole near the Moravice waterfall — the Moravice being the most romantic river of the Jeseníky Mountains. It has its source amidst heather and dwarf pines, winds its way through ferns and boulders, rushes through mountain passes, slows down as it reaches plains and floods the lowlands till it converges with the River Opava beneath the town of Opava. In the virgin forests on the slopes of Vozka, Keprník or Šerák, you can dream of days gone by, you can gaze at the five extinct volcanoes of the Low Jeseník or sit by Rejvízské Moors above the black waters of Mechová Jezera (Moss Lakes). Everywhere the air you breathe is crystal clear and filled with the scent of resin and forest flowers.

◄ *168. Velké Losiny, Renaissance chateau*

◄ *169. Courtyard of Velké Losiny Chateau*   *170. Červenohorské sedlo (Red Mountain Saddle) in the Jeseníky Mountains*

On the once much frequented trade route from Wroclaw to Olomouc, the town of Krnov was established. During the last century it gained fame on account of the work of organ builders from Wroclaw in Silesia. Today Krnov, which lies almost on the frontier with Poland, has the biggest and best known organ factory in Europe.

Silesia, which lies on the border between two states, has changed hands many times in the course of history and thus also changed its political structure and boundaries. After the fall of the Great Moravian Empire, the greater part of Silesia was seized by Poland. In the fifteenth century it became the property of the Czech King John of Luxembourg, who joined it to the Lands of the Czech Crown. In the sixteenth century it came under Habsburg rule, in the eighteenth century it was a source of discord between Austria and Prussia. Silesia formed an administrative unit within the Czech Lands and its provincial headquarters were in the town of Opava. It benefited considerably from its strategic position on an important route to Poland, and was given the status of a royal town in 1224. Silesia and the Opava area have found their place in the Czech literature through a collection of poems by Petr Bezruč, called *Silesian Songs*. Opava, which first found mention in the twelfth century, was almost completely destroyed towards the end of the Second World War.

To the south of Opava on what was once the Amber Route, in a romantic forest-covered region, lies Hradec which was the political and economic centre of Silesia before Opava took the lead. Hradec became the seat of the Přemyslids and remained the property of Czech kings until the middle of the sixteenth century. In 1428 it was taken by the Hussites and later various feudal families held the town, the last of them being the Lichnovskýs (from 1778). One of them, Karel Lichnovský, invited Ludwig van Beethoven to Hradec. The picturesque

171. Praděd, the highest mountain of the Jeseníky range

hilly countryside, with a chateau perched on a steep headland above the River Moravice, and with vast vistas reaching to beyond the last of the Oder Hills over the broad plain of Silesia, delighted the composer. Beethoven spent the whole summer and autumn of 1806 here and later returned for another visit. It was here that he composed his Fourth Symphony in B Flat Major and his Concerto for Violin and Orchestra in D Major. The atmosphere of the Empire chateau, set in an English-style park in the midst of romantic natural scenery was later (1846 and 1848) an inspiration to Franz Liszt; here he composed his symphonic poem *Hungaria*. Another famous visitor was the great Italian violinist Nicolò Paganini.

Part of the Upper Silesian coal basin extends into the northeastern part of Moravia. Coal began to be mined here in the 18th century, and this brought about profound changes both in the landscape and the life of the people. The easily accessible fuel led to the development of other industries, and so the centre of this region, Ostrava, rightly earned for itself the name "steel heart of the country". Head frames, slag tips, the cylindrically shaped blast furnaces and gas works and gas pipelines have all given this area beneath the Beskydy Mountains a bizarre appearance. The town itself is over five hundred years old, having been founded by Bruno, Bishop of Olomouc. It was fortified, captured by the Hussites and suffered raids by foreign mercenary armies and, like its surroundings, it was Germanized. In the nineteenth century, Ostrava experienced unprecedented industrial development, which continued into the twentieth century, until it became the third largest city in Czechoslovakia. Very few of the wooden buildings which used to be typical of this area still exist; there is the wooden

172. *The Castle of Hradec near Opava*

173. *The valley of the River Moravice*

174. *Ostrava, city of heavy industry*

175. *Little wooden Church of St. Catherine at Ostrava-Hrabová*

176. *The square at Nový Jičín*   177. *Štramberk, a town of Walachian timbered houses with a cylindrical watch-tower, once part of a medieval castle*

178. View of the Moravian-Silesian Beskydy Mountains

church of St. Catherine at Ostrava-Hrabová which dates from the sixteenth century, and there are some ancient windmills to be found in the area known as the Moravian Gate. This is situated at the dividing point between the Jeseníky and Beskydy Mountains, and has always been a place of contact between Silesia and the Haná region. Among the interesting spots in this area is Kopřivnice, which has concentrated on the production of motor vehicles and railway coaches. It was here that Austria-Hungary's first motor car was made in 1897. Nearby Nový Jičín can boast an urban reservation containing rare examples of architecture of early Renaissance period, as well as Gothic arcades. Today Nový Jičín is best known — well beyond the frontiers of this country — for the production of felt hats.

Now we come to the foothills of the Moravian-Silesian Beskydy range. From Hukvaldy Castle, records of which date back to the thirteenth century, the ecclesiastical authorities used to rule over the entire region beneath the Beskydy. At the time that the Chods of southwest Bohemia were in revolt, the serfs here rose up too in protest against forced labour and exploitation. But here too, the uprisings ended tragically. Hukvaldy Castle, the largest castle in Moravia, and one of the chain of fortified castles in the defence system of the Moravian Gate, was twice burnt down, and since 1820 has been in ruins. Beneath the castle with its big game preserve lies the village of the same name. It was here that the composer Leoš Janáček was born, and where he did much of his work. *The Cunning Little Vixen, Jenufa, From the House of the Dead* and the symphonic poem *The Danube* were all composed at Hukvaldy.

The small east-Moravian town of Štramberk is worth a visit, not so much for the remains of its fourteenth-century castle, as for the timber-framed houses of the Walachian type to be found on its outskirts. These little houses, some of which are two-storey buildings with supporting stone walls, create the special charm of Štramberk and its environs. Nearby Kotouč Hill, which is a limestone formation, is known for the rare fossils which have been found there, and in its Karst caves ancient skeletal finds have been unearthed. From the castle tower, known as "Štramberská trúba", there is a splendid view over the whole Beskydy range, which stretches from Valašské Meziříčí, over Rožnovské Saddle, via Radhošť with the chapel of St. Cyril and St. Methodius on its bare peak (1129 m), past Kněhyně, Smrk and Lysá Hora (1320 m), to the Polish frontier. As in the Jeseníky range, the steep slopes of the Beskydy are sometimes covered with the remains of primeval forests.

In addition to these "museums of nature", the region possesses some interesting conventional museums: at Třinec which lies on the ancient Copper Route, leading through Jablunkov Pass to join the Amber Route at the confluence of the Olše and the Oder, there is a special Museum of Metallurgy, at Kopřivnice a Museum of Motor Cars, in Nový Jičín the only Museum of Hat-Making in the world. Taking the Swedish Skansen as their example, the Museum Association at Rožnov on the suggestion of the Jaroněk brothers constructed the Walachian Open-Air Museum, which contains examples of the folk architecture of the area. Wooden structures were transferred here from various parts of the Valašsko area, ranging from wells, beehives and belfries to churches and inns. The buildings contain old furniture, utensils and equipment — everything the local people used to work their land, carry out their trades and so on.

Our wanderings have now brought us to the Valašsko (Walachian) area of Moravia. The word "Valach" (of Celtic derivation) originally meant a shepherd, a member of the nomadic tribes which moved with their herds from the Balkans along the Carpathian ranges. Later the name was given to the inhabitants of east Moravia. The geographical term Valašsko appears in the seventeenth century. The Walachians showed great courage in defending Moravia against Turkish and Tartar raids, against Hungarian rebels, the "kurucz", and against King Frederick II of Prussia, who invaded the country during the reign of Maria Theresa. During the Thirty Years' War they were notorious as rebels and joined the Swedes to fight against the Emperor.

Weaving, woodcutting, metallurgy, glass-making and cattle-breeding — these were the main occupations of the Walachian people. Today the most modern electro-technical and chemical industries have been added to the list.

By walking through the birch groves and juniper-covered slopes of the Bečva Valley, you reach the Javorníky Mountains which, from 1736, formed the border between Moravia and Slovakia. And from the Javorníky, further ranges of mountains and hills open up before your eyes and you find yourself gazing into Slovakia.

179. The Walachian Open-air Museum at Rožnov-under-Radhošť

180. *The High Tatras*

SLOVAKIA

How lovely is this land, towered over by the majestic Tatras, the land which gave birth to the romantic hero Juraj Jánošík, and the deeply thoughtful poet of Slavdom, Ján Kollár. Its turbulent history, extolled in odes to the bravery of the warriors who resisted the Turks, and laments on the suppression of peasant risings, is imbued with the love of generations who left neither ornamental tombstones nor magnificent castles, but simply mournful melodies of human sorrow and suffering.

How enchanting are the deciduous forests of the Small Carpathians, the rugged escarpments of the High Tatras, the virgin forests of the Slovak Ore Mountains, and the sunlit lowlands of Eastern Slovakia. The area has its special charms, with the peaceful mirror of the Zemplín Lake at Šírava, the cascades of the waters of the Velký and Malý Sokol in the Slovak Paradise, and the impressive confluence of the Morava and Danube rivers. In Slovakia's largest cities — ancient Bratislava and proud Nitra, Banská Bystrica and historic Košice life today is pulsing with a new rhythm reminding man, in the midst of all this wealth of nature, of his fruitful, life-giving work.

We can find traces of early man near Gánovce spring and in the Šariš Venus, in traces of Mesolithic fishermen at Sered, the encampment of hunters in the Domica cave, in the ruins of powerful strongholds dating from the Bronze Age and in examples of the artistry of Scythian iron workers. Retracing the footsteps of history we go back to the very beginnings of our era, when the Celts fought the Teutonic Marcomanni and Quadi, and battled against the Roman legions of Marcus Aurelius for possession of this land. It was at that time that the first Slavs penetrated into the territory of what is now Czechoslovakia from the region between the Oder and Dnieper rivers.

The Slav tribes lived by farming and cattle breeding as well as hunting and they engaged in such crafts as smelting, smithery, pottery and the making of jewelry. In addition to their villages, the Slavs built fortified settlements surrounded by deep moats. Trade flourished, especially along the Danube and Morava. Simultaneously with the transformation of the social order, efforts were made to bring all the Slav tribes together. First the Nitra principality was established in the first quarter of the ninth century, and at almost the same time, the Principality of Moravia was founded in the basin of the Morava and the Dyje. From the very beginning, these two state formations were subject to the pressure of the East Frankish German Empire, which they succeeded in withstanding with varying degrees of success. The feudal rulers of the Slavs were converted to Christianity by German missionaries. In about the year 833 A.D., the Archbishop of Salzburg consecrated the first church in Slovakia at Nitra, the seat of Prince Pribina. Shortly afterwards, Pribina was defeated at Nitra by the Moravian Prince, Mojmír I, founder of the Great Moravian Empire, which, as the first common state of the ancestors of the Czechs and Slovaks, withstood attacks by Frankish rulers until the end of the ninth century. During the reign of Rastislav the country became the cradle of old Slavonic literature. In recent years, archaeologists have uncovered interesting architectural relics in the former fortified settlements of Slovakia and Moravia, and many articles of everyday use, weapons and jewelry, which bear witness to the maturity of the culture of the time.

Nomad Magyar tribes, who penetrated into Slovakia from the steppes of southern Russia in the years 903—907, pushed a wedge between the western and southern Slavs, subjecting the settled Slav inhabitants and including them, for the next thousand years, in the feudal Hungarian state. The northern parts of Slovakia which in the tenth century still belonged to the Czech and Polish states also came under the power of Hungarian feudal lords. The Hungarian state was strengthened by the Magyar settlement of the Nitra region, and the settlement of Magyar and closely related Turko-Tartar tribes in south Slovakia, in the vicinity of the castles in the valleys of the rivers Ipeľ and Slaná. German colonization in the Poprad and Hnilec valleys, and in the mining centres, towards the end of the twelfth century violated the entity of the Slovak settlements. Many proofs remain from this period of the high standard of indigenous folk art — jewels from burial grounds, ornamental features of Romanesque buildings, and mural paintings, for instance at Žehra.

In the centuries that followed, Slovak history formed part of the general pattern of Hungarian history, though it did have certain features, personalities and events of its own. Among these were the Tartar raids, anti-feudal peasant risings on church estates, the development of trade and mining centres, the building of most of the castles and, at the beginning of the fourteenth century, the independent position of the Palatine Matúš Čák of Trenčany, the "Lord of the Váh and the Tatras" who, with the help of Czech mercenaries and the Slovak nobility, ruled over the greater part of Slovakia. A century later, Hussite ideas found fertile soil in Slovakia, especially among the town and village poor and the smaller yeomen farmers. Hussite garrisons (in Likava, Trnava and Topoľčany), the "Glorious Raids" (Spiš) and resistance to the feudal lords by the Hussites under the leadership of Peter Aksamit of Kosov, who took part in popular uprisings in the middle of the fifteenth century, once more strengthened the bonds between the Czech and Slovak people, and this, in turn, was reflected in the people's culture. The peasants' revolt in Zemplín in 1456 was an echo of these social changes. The peasants' uprising in 1514, led by Georgy Dózsa, and the powerful revolts of the miners in Central Slovakia in 1525 and 1526 were also staged to oppose the growing oppression of the ordinary people.

Following the Battle of Mohács in 1526, Slovakia, as part of Hungary, together with the Czech Lands, came under the rule of the Habsburgs, which was to last for 400 years. The country was torn by unrest. Southern and Central Slovakia were perpet-

190

ually ravaged by the Turks and by Tartar raiders who did not withdraw until 1685. The Slovak and Hungarian peasantry rose up with renewed vigour against feudal oppression in the years 1631—1632. Throughout the seventeenth and the beginning of the eighteenth century there were waves of resistance to the Habsburgs on the part of the nobility (Bocskay, Bethlen and Rákóczys). The resistance of the serfs often took the form of individual revolt and people fled to join the outlaw "mountain lads" who were the terror of the lords and their castles. The most famous of these outlaws who robbed the rich and gave to the poor was Juraj Jánošík of Terchová, executed at Mikuláš in 1713, whose memory lives on in folk poetry, songs, pictures and carvings.

In those stormy times, the torch of the common ideas of the Czech and Slovak nations was taken up by the Czech Protestant exiles. After the defeat at the Battle of the White Mountain, they found refuge from brutal Catholic persecution in Slovakia, where they helped to develop the educational system, and give strength to the national language and literature. In their songs, legends and folk plays, the people passed down from generation to generation their language, culture and their tradition of struggle against their overlords. In their literature, still written in biblical Czech, more and more elements of colloquial Slovak began to appear. Towards the end of the eighteenth century, the Slovak literary language started to develop, especially in the western parts of the country. Anton Bernolák, in 1787, first expressed the idea of establishing rules for literary Slovak, and in 1790 he carried this out. The writers of the age of Enlightenment, especially Jozef Ignác Bajza and Juraj Fándly, devoted increased attention to the life of the people and endeavoured to alleviate their lot. Although the reforms introduced by Joseph II did not greatly improve the position of the exploited strata of the rural population, they did at least give rise to hopes among the people and strengthened their resistance to their feudal masters. The ideas of the French bourgeois revolution spread among the intellectuals, who were cruelly persecuted by Viennese absolutism. The strongest expression of popular resistance to feudalism was the widespread peasant rising in East Slovakia in 1831, in which the urban poor and the mining population took part as well. The revolt was cruelly suppressed, but it showed the need for a democratic agrarian revolution.

The Slovak national movement continued to take shape, led in the first half of the nineteenth century by such outstanding figures as the poets Ján Kollár and Ján Hollý, and the historian Pavol Jozef Šafárik. In Kollár's poems and writings Slovak national consciousness is closely linked with the idea of Panslavism and co-operation.

This process culminated in the 1840's with Slovak intellectuals grouped around Ľudovít Štúr organizing broad foundations for the Slovak national movement. They propagated a progressive democratic programme in the Slovak National Newspaper, calling for the abolition of serfdom, and proposing to Hungarian liberals a national settlement in Hungary. The efforts of the group led by Štúr, however, were met with distrust on the part of the Czechs, who wrongly regarded their attempts to introduce a Slovak literary language as an endeavour to get away from the Czechs, and with persecution from the Hungarian authorities. In this atmosphere of youthful enthusiasm, Janko Matúška's song *Lightning flashes over the Tatras* (1844) was written, the first strophe of which was later to become part of the Czechoslovak National Anthem:

"Lightning flashes over the Tatras,
Thunder roars,
Rise up, brothers, arise,
Slovaks shall live again."

The writings of Štúr and his followers were based on realistic and democratic impulses arising from current social changes and folk literature. In poetry, the highlights were the epic poems *Marina* (1846) and *Detvan* (1853) by Andrej Sládkovič, the ballads of Ján Botto and the revolutionary verses of Janko Kráľ, and, in prose, the stories of Ján Kalinčiak. After the revolutionary upsurge in 1848 and 1849, when the followers of Štúr, together with Czech radicals, fought for the recognition of the rights of the Slovak nation, national life and culture in Slovakia developed more fully, especially in the 1860's when the Slovak cultural organization Matica Slovenská was set up (1863) and Štúr's literary Slovak language triumphed. Slovak secondary schools were opened and more newspapers and periodicals began to appear. This trend could not be halted even by increased attempts to Magyarize Slovakia following the Austro-Hungarian settlement of 1867, which did not recognize the Slovaks as a nation, and which created the conditions for cruel persecution.

From the 1860's, the working class, which was then rapidly increasing, began to play a more and more important part in the social struggle. The road from the foundation of the first workers' educational associations in Bratislava in 1869 to the establishment of a working class political party in 1890 and the journal *New Times* in 1897, was accompanied by struggles, which culminated in mass demonstrations and strikes at the beginning of the present century. The Czech and Slovak nations emerged together from the First World War. Under the influence of the October Socialist Revolution in Russia, the revolutionary endeavours of the people to establish their own state gathered momentum and the Czechoslovak Republic was established on the ruins of the Habsburg monarchy. In the period between the wars, and when the Nazis fell upon Czechoslovakia and broke it up, the working class, led by the Communist Party of Czechoslovakia, fought for a truly people's state. When the heroic Slovak National Uprising broke out in 1944, thousands of anti-fascist fighters took up arms to battle for the ideals of a social and national revolution which could only be achieved after the country's liberation in 1945 and particularly after the victory of the working class of February 1948. Today, as two equal nations, the Czechs and the Slovaks are building a new socialist society. During the short space of a quarter of a century of socialist construction, formerly backward Slovakia, once notorious for its poverty, unemployment and high rate of emigration, has turned into a land with advanced modern industry.

181. *The Danube below Bratislava Castle*

On the southern fringe of the Small Carpathians, washed by the waters of the Danube, lies the historic city of Bratislava, more than a thousand years old. This modern city with an ancient past stands on the site of Celtic settlements established in the fourth century B.C. At the beginning of the Christian era Roman garrisons of the XIVth and XVth legions were stationed there and the caravans of merchants and military expeditions used to pass through. Even in ancient times this was an important crossroad of the Danubian Route leading from east to west, with the AmberRoute going from north to south over a ford across the Danube. This strategic spot needed to be protected against raids and attacks. Archaeological research has established without any doubt that at the time of the Great Moravian Empire, founded in about the year 830 A.D., there was already a castle on the cliff overlooking the river, and that its walls enclosed a basilica and a burial place, where many valuable pieces of jewelry and articles of everyday use have been discovered.

The castle was then known as Pressalauspurch, and from this was later derived the German name of Pressburg, which the Slovaks turned into Prešporok. The Hungarians created the name Pozsony, from the Latin Posonium, and for a long time this was the official name of the city. Scholars attribute the origin of the new name to the Slovak Prince Božanov, to the Czech Břetislav and also to Svatopluk's youngest son, Predslav — but today the view prevails among historians that the name is derived from that of the Great Moravian Prince Braslav. The name used for the city today, Bratislava, was first employed by Ľudovít Štúr and his followers in the middle of the nineteenth century.

In tracing the history of Bratislava Castle, we find that as early as 1051 it already had brave defenders who succeeded for a period of two months in withstanding the superior forces of the German Emperor Henry III, which were, for their time, technically well equipped — having catapults to discharge stone balls. Moreover the defenders were able to drill holes by night in the ships of their besiegers, and sink them with a weight of their remaining stone ammunition. In the years 1073 and 1074, further fortifications were added to the clay mounds, in keeping with the significance of the town as a frontier stronghold and seat of the Hungarian district authorities. In 1169, Frederick I, known as Frederick Barbarossa, gathered the forces of the crusaders here for an expedition against the Turkish Sultan Saladin. But neither the King, nor the majority of his troops with which many citizens of Bratislava served, ever returned from the crusade. When fleeing from the Tartars in 1241, King Bela IV stopped at the castle, and when he left for Austria, Tartar horsemen invaded the unfortified villages around Bratislava, though they were unable to capture the castle or the settlements beneath it. Emperor Sigismund of Luxembourg wanted to make Bratislava the centre of his empire and turned it into a powerful fortress against the Hussites. In the years 1427 to 1432, a big two-storey Gothic palace was built here, protected by a moat. In about the year 1440, the imposing Corvinus Gate was added, and a further Gothic defence system. Many times the ramparts withstood Hussite attacks, and in 1529, the castle garrison fired on the fleet of Soliman II, who was intending to take Vienna, and managed to sink or capture several ships. After their unsuccessful attempt to seize Vienna, the returning Turkish forces preferred to avoid Bratislava. The increase of Turkish rule in Hungary tended to strengthen the importance of Bratislava for the whole country.

As far back as 1535, the Parliament decided that Bratislava should be the capital of Hungary, where its kings would be crowned, and the whole administration of the country concentrated. In the period between 1552 and 1560, the castle was rebuilt in Renaissance style, and two further wings were added to the palace, as well as frescoes in the interior and fine stucco work on the vaulting. The renovations carried out between 1635 and 1640 by the captain of the castle and hereditary district administrator, Pavol Pálffy, gave the building more or less the appearance it has today. From 1672 work was carried out on more modern anti-Turkish fortifications based on plans by Priami, though it was hardly necessary any longer since Turkish power was already on the decline. The last actual builder of the castle was the Empress Maria Theresa, who frequently stayed there. To the early eighteenth-century Vienna Gateway which forms the main entrance to the castle, she added a splendid new approach with a court of honour, watch-houses, a three-axled vestibule and a great staircase. After Joseph II transferred the highest offices to Buda in 1783, the castle began to fall into decline and only the barracks remained in it. During the Napoleonic Wars, while it was occupied by the French, a great fire broke out on May 30, 1811 in the riding hall, which destroyed the main palace and the adjacent buildings.

It was only when socialism was established that it was decided to save this rare historic building. Fifteen years were to pass before Bratislava Castle could be the setting of an event of great significance for both the Czechs and the Slovaks. On October 27, 1968 the President of the Republic, and other constitutional representatives, signed an act on the organization of federal relations between the Czechs and the Slovaks in their common state.

The town beneath the Castle developed quite independently from a small settlement which, from the very beginning, possessed its own system of fortifications, mainly on the northern side, while from the south the Danube helped to protect it. Together with the castle, Bratislava withstood the Tartar attacks of 1241, but during

◄ 182. Bratislava Castle

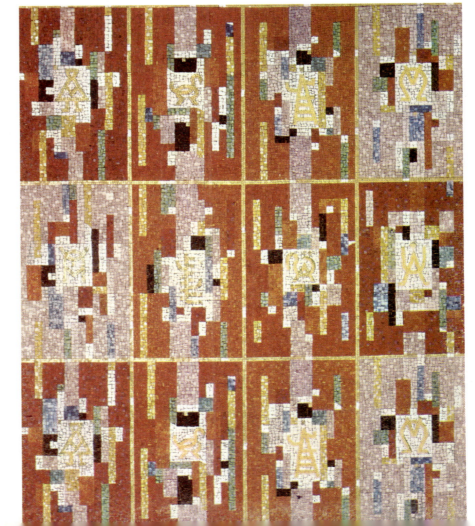

183. Lunette vaulting of the ceiling in the interior of Bratislava
     Castle

184. Ľudovít Fulla: Mosaic, 1968. Bratislava Castle

185. *South entrance to Bratislava Castle*

the disturbances of the 1280's it was set on fire and destroyed by Albrecht I. In 1291, King Andrew III of Hungary recalled its inhabitants who had fled and dispersed, and granted Bratislava the charter of a free royal town. In April 1429, King Sigismund had talks within its walls with the emissaries of the Hussites, led by Prokop Holý. Although the ideas of the Hussites gained many supporters among the poor of the city, the Hussites never succeeded in taking either the town or the castle.

The year 1465 was one of great importance for the city, for it was then that King Matthias Corvinus established Hungary's first university here. And on 20 July 1467, the Bratislava Academia Istropolitana was officially opened. Its first Chancellor was the famous Archbishop of Esztergom and well-known scholar, Ján Vitéz, while its professors included humanist scholars and writers from Bohemia, Germany, France, Italy, Greece and Poland. One of them was the outstanding astronomer, Johann Müller, known as Regiomontanus. After the King's death in 1490, the University disintegrated, but its building, in what is now Jirásek Street, has been preserved.

The face of Bratislava underwent considerable changes in 1529, when the city councillors, anticipating a Turkish raid, had a number of churches and public buildings standing behind the ramparts pulled down, and turned the city into a military garrison. Three decades later, in 1563, Bratislava again looked completely different, when the Hungarian King Maximilian was crowned here with all the civil and ecclesiastical pomp of the time. In 1619, Duke Gábor Bethlen of Transylvania entered Bratislava without firing a shot, when he went to the aid of the Czech nobility against the Habsburgs. After the defeat of the Czechs at the Battle of the White Mountain in 1620, he withdrew his forces and the people of Bratislava asked for Imperial protection. In August 1621, however, he tried once more to take the city, but in vain. In addition to wars, the greatest threat to the population was the Black Death. The worst epidemic was in 1679 when half of the city's twenty-five thousand inhabitants perished.

During the "kurucz" wars, Imre Thököly, who had rebelled against the Habsburgs, occupied Bratislava, but was driven out the following day by Charles of Lorraine. Among visitors to the city was the Czar Peter the Great, who went there in 1698 as a young man. He travelled incognito using the name of Piotr Mikhailovich, accompanied by two guides, to survey the shipyards, the Danube fleet, and everything connected with shipping on the River Danube.

196

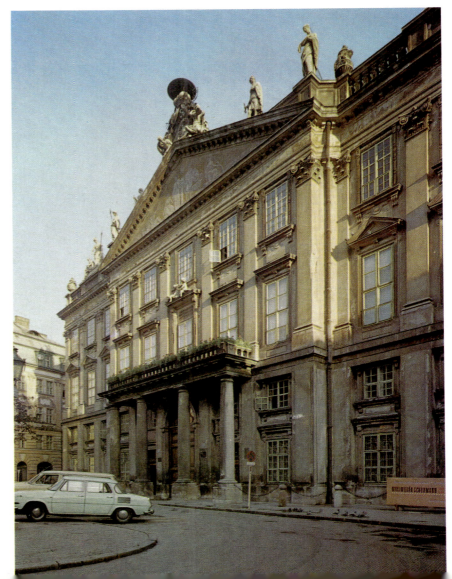

186. *Primate's Palace, Bratislava. 19th-century engraving*

187. *The façade of the Primate's Palace*

188. *Baroque vaulting in the Church of the Holy Trinity, Bratislava*

189. *The Michael Gate, Bratislava*

Among outstanding personalities connected with Bratislava, mention should be made of the Slovak scholar of the age of Enlightenment, Matěj Bel, a native of Očová, who was known as Magnum decus Hungariae (The Great Ornament of Hungary). It was here that he wrote all his works of history and geography, and in 1721 began to publish the first newspaper under the title *Nova Posoniensia*. A mysterious personality was that of the famous Bratislava-born physicist, Wolfgang Kempelen, who built the fountains of the Schönbrunn Palace in Vienna. He astounded the world by his automatic chess-player which overshadowed his other works, such as his pioneering studies of acoustics and the principles of human speech, which he tried to put into practice with a speaking mechanism. In 1776, Bratislava began to rid itself of its fortifications and bastions, and in their place splendid palaces and burghers' houses were built which still stand in the Old Town area of the city.

Among other disasters which frequently hit the town were fires. In 1798, a fire destroyed thirty-two houses and two years later there was a blaze so fierce that several streets and more than a hundred houses were burnt out. Another destructive element which often took its toll was water. Early in the year 1809, great blocks of ice diverted the River Danube towards people's houses — water flooded the palaces and the town hall to a depth of a metre, and only receded after three days.

The revolutionary events of the years 1848 and 1849 were also a flood whose waters carried away the hated system of serfdom and the privileges of the nobility. Unhappily the representatives of the Hungarian and Slovak camps in the Bratislava Assembly, Lajos Kossuth and Ľudovít Štúr, who passionately defended the rights of the people against the feudal lords, found themselves leading their followers in a fratricidal struggle which only harmed the revolutionary movement. In the years that followed, a new force took up the torch of the struggle for social and political justice, a force which swelled in the new factories on the outskirts of Bratislava.

The industrial development of Bratislava continued throughout the years of the independent Czechoslovak Republic prior to the Munich dictate, and with it grew the social struggle of the workers. Under the leadership of the then illegal Communist Party of Czechoslovakia, the struggle culminated during the Second World War in the anti-fascist movement. Socialist construction, which began after the country's liberation, gave Bratislava

190. *The Square of April 4 and the town hall, Bratislava*

many important new industrial plants, among which should be mentioned the Slovnaft chemical plant at the terminal of the oil pipeline from the Soviet Union.

Even while carrying out the exacting tasks of modern construction, the city is not neglecting its historical treasures. Mention should be made at least of the Primate's Palace, in Neo-Classical style, dating from 1777 to 1781, and the Baroque statue of St. George in its courtyard. It was in the Hall of Mirrors of that palace that the Peace of Bratislava was signed in 1805, between the Emperor Franz I of Austria and the French Emperor, Napoleon. Today the building houses the Municipal Art Gallery, possessing a rich collection of old paintings and works of sculpture. Most noteworthy is the collection of rare Renaissance tapestries from the royal workshops in Mortlake (1632), depicting the sad mythical love story of Hero and Leander.

The most interesting of Bratislava's churches is St. Martin's, the building of which was started on the site of a Romanesque church. The present Gothic church dates from the fourteenth and fifteenth centuries. It was actually a part of the city's system of fortifications. Between the years 1563 and 1830, eleven Hungarian kings and eight queens were crowned here — the most famous of whom was Maria Theresa. Among the splendid Gothic treasures of Bratislava is the Franciscan church, dating from the years 1278 to 1297, which was extended until the fifteenth century. The richly ornamented St. John's Chapel from the fourteenth century and the fifteenth-century Gothic tower of the church — a wonderful example of the craftsmanship of Bratislava stonemasons — deserve special attention. The thirteenth-century Clarissine Church with its fourteenth-century pentagonal Gothic tower is one of the most admired examples of ecclesiastical architecture. The Church of the Holy Trinity, built between 1717 and 1727, with its two towers and splendid interior, is among the very best examples of Slovak Baroque.

The Old Town Hall forms a picturesque complex with the Roland Fountain, which King Maximilian II had built in 1572 on what was once the city's main square.

Of the original fortifications of the city, all that remains today is the defence system of the Michael Gate, once one of the five gates of the city. Its present form dates from 1758 when it was restored. The spire is topped by a statue of St. Michael fighting the dragon. A moat has also been preserved with the remains of the city ramparts and the buildings outside the city walls.

On the outskirts of Bratislava lies Devín with the ruins of an ancient castle. Excavations here have brought to light many valuable objects from Celtic, Roman, Slav and medieval settlements.

191. Sanctuary in the Gothic Church of St. Martin, Bratislava

192. Watch-tower of Devín Castle, Bratislava ▶

193. *West Slovak landscape, on the slopes of the Small Carpathians*

Gentle, green-clad mountains with grapes ripening on their slopes from which isolated rocks spring up — that is the picture presented by the Small Carpathians.

To the west and east, they are bordered by a chain of ancient strongholds which from the thirteenth century protected the north-western frontiers of the Hungarian State. The first of these, Pajštún, rises from a rocky headland and overlooks the region around Stupava. Its present jagged appearance is a legacy from Napoleon's armies.

High on a peak above the village of Plavecké Podhradie towers Plavecký Castle, its name having been derived from a warlike tribe known as the Polovtsy. In the vicinity of this picturesque ruin close to Bratislava, on the summit of Pohanská Hill, an ancient settlement has been unearthed; and beneath the peak of nearby rocky Roštún, a splendid network of caves and underground caverns has been discovered. The ancient route from Moravia to Slovakia which goes from Břeclav to Trnava was well protected by Ostrý Kameň Castle, built on a steep rocky hill. Over the centuries this castle had many different owners and it was discord among them that led to its deterioration. Nearby Smolenice on the eastern slopes of the Small Carpathians was more fortunate. Although the original character of this thirteenth-century castle with its pentagonal keep was completely changed as a result of reconstructions in the Romantic style at the beginning of the present century, under the Pálffys, what actually resulted was one of the most remarkable works of architecture in Slovakia. Another castle, Červený Kameň (Red Stone) does not attract visitors for its bizarre tower or its fortifications so much as for its interior, which in 1537, under the Fuggers, was transformed into a fortified centre for the reloading of merchandise, with extensive cellars, and cleverly-planned sentry posts.

The cultural, industrial and commercial centre of the Small Carpathians is the university town of Trnava, situated in fertile lowlands. This is one of the oldest towns in Slovakia. Its advantageous position at a crossroads of trade routes enabled Trnava in 1238 to gain its charter as a royal town, at the same time making it the object of the aggressive designs of many conquerors. Přemysl Otakar II twice succeeded in occupying the town. The first time he sacked it after his victory at the Battle of Kressenbrunn, when he pursued the forces of Bela IV deep into Slovakia. The second time he marched into the well-fortified town in 1271 during fighting against Stephen I of the Arpads. When the Arpads had died out, the Czech King Wenceslas III, after being elected King of Hungary at Hodonín, marched through Trnava to Buda. Louis I of Anjou, Louis the Great, chose Trnava as his seat and it was here that in 1360 he received the Emperor Charles IV. The commander of the Hussite armies, Jan Žižka of Trocnov, passed through Trnava in 1423 during his famous expedition into Hungary, and, after that, up to 1432, four more Hussite expeditions came here. Under Jan Jiskra of Brandýs, the Hussites had a garrison here. In 1467, they suffered a terrible defeat near Kostolany, at the hands of Matthias Corvinus's forces, and this marked the end of their power. After the Battle of Mohács, when the Turks invaded Hungary, Trnava began to grow in importance. In 1541, the Primate, the Archbishop of Esztergom, moved to Trnava, which became a centre of Catholicism and culture. It was Archbishop Peter Pázmány who was the actual founder of the University, with faculties of theology and of the arts, in 1635; it continued to exist until 1777, when it was moved to Buda, but its Baroque buildings dating from the seventeenth and eighteenth centuries have remained, together with the University Church and the Jesuit Monastery. The university tradition of Trnava was not renewed until after the Second World War, when the socialist state established the Faculty of Education of the Comenius University here.

North of Trnava, in Dolná Krupá, in the Neo-Classical chateau of the Brunswicks, the melancholy notes of Beethoven's Moonlight Sonata and his Ninth Symphony used to be heard. For Beethoven stayed in the Baroque house close to the castle when he visited these parts between 1800 and 1810, composing some of his immortal works here. He also visited nearby Hlohovec in the valley of the River Váh at the foot of the Inovec Hills. Hlohovec is known as "the town of roses" and is overlooked by a Renaissance-Baroque chateau set in a big English-style park. The mother of the poet Heinrich Heine is buried here in the Jewish cemetery.

In our further journeys we shall follow the course of Slovakia's greatest and longest river, the Váh. Of the system of castles along the Váh, the best known is that of Čachtice, built in the thirteenth century on a bare hill above the village of Višňová. The castle gained ill-repute from the deeds of the terrible Lady of Čachtice, Elizabeth Báthory, who had many maidens from the surrounding area slain so that she could bathe in their blood in the vain hope of regaining her lost youth. In 1610, she was brought to justice, together with her helpers, and was imprisoned in the castle until her death in 1614. It was in the village of the same name, close to the castle, that in August 1847 the followers of Ľudovít Štúr had established the literary Slovak language.

We pass the town of Nové Mesto-on-Váh, the industrial and cultural centre of the area beneath the Javorina Hills where the White Carpathians dividing Slovakia from Moravia are close to the Váh. The isolated limestone rock formation on which stand the ruins of Beckov Castle recalls the romantic legend of Duke Ctibor, who had a mighty castle built on a rock for his court jester as a reward for entertaining his guests.

Many legends are also told about the most powerful of the castles on the Váh, Trenčín, which from time immemorial guarded access to the Váh valley. A Latin inscription on its rock, dating from the year 179 A.D., remains to this day to recall the victorious struggle of the Legions of Marcus Aurelius against the Barbarians, in what was then Laugaritium. In the fifth century, Slav tribes settled here and named their settlement, after its triple system of fortifications, Tri-týn, from which the name of Trenčín was later derived. It is more than probable that a castle already stood here at the time of the Great Moravian Empire, but the first historical records of its existence can be found in Czech and Hungarian chronicles dating from the eleventh century.

At the beginning of the eleventh century, Trenčín, with a part of Slovakia, came under the control of the Polish King Boleslav the Brave; however, before long, King Stephen I of Hungary added it to his Empire. At the turn of the eleventh and twelfth centuries, it was the scene of frequent struggles between the Hungarian and Czech kings. In 1116, the armies of Vladislav I won a great victory over Stephen II of Hungary here. Although at the time Trenčín Castle had no stone fortifications, it withstood the Tartar raids of 1241 which ravaged and burnt the town beneath the ramparts.

Trenčín experienced the most glorious period of its history towards the end of the thirteenth and beginning of the fourteenth century, when it was the seat of the Lord of the Váh and the Tatras, Matúš Čák. After the Arpád dynasty died out in 1301, he ruled over almost the whole of Slovakia, taking advantage of the disputes over the Hungarian throne to strengthen his own power. After the year 1302, he had a new palace built within the castle and subjected the residential tower and fortifications to considerable reconstruction. It was here, in 1335, that the reconciliation of the Czech King John of Luxembourg with King Kasimir III (Kasimir the Great) of Poland was celebrated. Also present was the future King of Bohemia and Holy Roman Emperor, Charles IV. A similar reconciliation also took place here in 1373 between Louis I (Louis the Great) of Hungary and Charles IV, in the presence of the Papal Legate Volteira. After reconstruction work carried out by Louis, the castle was further improved by Sigismund of Luxembourg, who used to stay here after 1401. Building work was speeded up when the approach of Hussite troops was feared, but they failed to take the castle.

In the middle of the fifteenth century, Jan Jiskra of Brandýs, protector of the interests of King Ladislaus

194. Plavecký Castle — medieval fortress in the Small Carpathians

195. *University Church of St. John the Baptist, Trnava*

Posthumous, ruled here. Jan Jiskra also perfected its defensive system. In 1461, Trenčín Castle was the scene of the official signing of the marriage contract between King Matthias Corvinus and the daughter of King George of Poděbrady. In 1476 the castle came into the possession of Stephen Zápolya. It was at that time that Trenčín acquired the appearance which it kept for centuries to come. In the fighting between Janos Zápolya and Ferdinand Habsburg for the Hungarian throne, the Imperial forces, after a prolonged siege, in 1528 set fire to the castle and eventually captured it. In the middle of the seventeenth century, it was still an important stronghold in the wars against the Turks. During the risings of the estates, the castle remained firmly in the hands of the Imperial forces, and it was near Trenčín that General Heister dealt the final blow to Ferencz Rákóczy in 1708. After a great fire in 1790, the castle was left to its fate. Not until the beginning of the present century was provisional reconstruction carried out on some of the buildings and, after the country's liberation in 1945, Trenčín Castle was proclaimed a national cultural monument.

196. Landscape in the Small Carpathians

In the northern part of the West Slovak region lies the well-known spa of Trenčianske Teplice with its rich thermal springs, one of the most popular health resorts in the country, not only for its therapeutic qualities but also for its lovely environment. Worth noting, too, are the ruins of the Skalka Benedictine monastery, which supplement the striking silhouette of Trenčín on the opposite bank of the Váh.

From Trenčín we move south-eastwards. Crossing the Tríbeč Hills we come down into the valley of the Žitava where another national cultural monument — the chateau of Topoľčianky — catches our eye. It was originally a moated castle and was captured by the Hussite forces in 1428. The Late Gothic building was re-constructed before 1662 by Count Lajos Rákóczy into a splendid Renaissance residence. In 1703 Ferencz Rákóczy settled there with his "kurucz" troops. A hundred years later, between 1818 and 1825, Ján Keglović gave the chateau — which had been restored in Baroque style by Karel Zichy in 1742 — its present appearance, by the addition of a wing in Neo-Classical style. In 1890 the chateau of Topoľčianky became the property of the Habs-

197. *The romantic castle of the Pálffys at Smolenice*

198. *Fortified Church of St. Ladislaus at Čachtice*

burg Archdukes, and in 1923 it became the summer residence of the Presidents of the Czechoslovak Republic. In 1949, President Klement Gottwald renounced his claim to the chateau, and it was transformed into a trade union holiday centre without changing the historic character of the building in any way.

Crossing the Tríbeč Hills we come down into the Nitra Valley beneath the memorable Zobor Hill. On the site of a former seat of princes, archaeologists have brought to light many valuable proofs of the advanced culture of the ancient Slavs who established their fortified settlements here and engaged in specialized craft production even before the time of the Great Moravian Empire. They must have come here in about the first half of the sixth century and they made Nitra — then known as Nitrava — into their principal centre. According to old legends, Nitra was ruled at the end of the 8th century by Prince Samoslav who is said to have surrendered to the Frankish King Charlemagne in 793 and adopted the Christian faith, together with his nation.

His successor was Pribina (or Privina), the first historical figure in Slovak history. He united the tribes of West, Central and Northern Slovakia early in the ninth century. Pribina's Slovak Princedom soon had to give way to a bigger state, which could guarantee protection against hostile pressure from without, particularly from the Eastern Frankish Empire. In the thirties of the ninth century, the Moravian ruler Mojmír I drove Pribina from Nitra and joined his Princedom to Moravia and a part of Austria.

Nitra remained the seat of the princes even within the Hungarian state until the Arpáds died out, and it was handed down in fief to the successors to the throne. Near to the former fortified settlement, a stone castle was built which, in 1241, withstood the Tartar attacks, but in 1271 it was heavily damaged while under siege by the forces of Přemysl Otakar II. In 1288, Nitra Castle became the seat of the Bishop, who was also the chief administrator. Early in the fourteenth century, Nitra was twice taken by Matúš Čák and in 1431 it was besieged

199. Gothic Castle of Trenčín

200. *The core of Trenčín Castle*

201. *Radvaň-on-Danube*

202. *Sandy beach at Kováčová in the Danubian lowlands* ▶

by the Hussites. In 1465, King Matthias Corvinus sacked the castle. The Turkish attacks reached their climax in 1663 and it was then that the castle fell to them, which happened again during heavy attacks by the "kurucz" forces under Ferencz II Rákóczy in 1703. The frequent battles for the castle, and the fact that it was frequently restored, have resulted in only individual elements of various styles of architecture being preserved intact.

The course of the River Nitra leads us to Nové Zámky, which was an important stronghold in the wars against the Turks. It had been built by Emperor Maximilian II in the period between 1571 and 1581 on low-lying marshland. The fortress was built in the form of a six-pointed star, with shooting galleries in each of the points, and with a deep and broad moat around the building filled with water from the River Nitra. The Imperial forces settled in the fortress with the task of guarding the whole Nitra basin. Soon, however, it was found that the fortress was by no means impregnable. After it had been captured several times, Emperor Charles VI had the walls of the fortress razed to the ground in 1725. All that remained was the town of Nové Zámky which is one of the cultural centres of southern Slovakia.

The south-eastern tip of Žitný (Grain) Island, at the confluence of the Váh and Danube, was, many centuries ago, of considerable importance as a Roman frontier stronghold. A castle (Castrum Komarniense) stood here in the early thirteenth century, and in 1307 became the property of Matúš Čák, who confirmed the charter of the town of Komárno. Matthias Corvinus extended the castle while Ferdinand I had a fortress built here which is now known as the Old Castle. In 1594, Turkish forces had to abandon their attempts to take it. Under Leopold I, between the years 1663 and 1673, the New Castle was established, linked by a bridge to the old system

204. Rococo iconostasis from the Orthodox Church at Komárno

205. Panorama of Nitra

215

of fortifications. The waters of the Váh and Danube gave Komárno the appearance of an island fortress — the most powerful in the empire. But nature achieved what the Turks and "kurucz" failed to do; in 1763 an earthquake damaged the castle and the town and a fresh earth tremor in 1783 completed the work of destruction. The fortress was not rebuilt until the Napoleonic Wars when, in 1810, it was reconstructed and extended. In this form it served the Hungarian rebels in the revolutionary struggles of 1848 and 1849, and the Imperial forces were unable to seize it until the agreement on capitulation was reached in October 1849.

210. "The Man of Sorrows". Folk sculpture from the neighbourhood of Topoľčany

◄ *208. Topoľčianky Castle*

◄ *209. The arboretum of Mlyňany Castle*

211. Ruined Gothic Castle of Strečno

Above the powerful and dignified chorus of the Danube's waves, and the gentle song of the fertile lowlands, rings the sharp, impetuous melody of the River Váh. Its upper reaches flow between mountain peaks and wind their way between the tall ruins of castles, but it is bordered, too, by towns and winding railway lines. From the river's surface, the mountains seem to rise more steeply, the castles appear still less accessible and the heavens still further off. The outlines of long-deserted robbers' hide-outs on the west bank give the valley of the River Váh a romantic atmosphere possessed by few other parts of the country. The legends and songs of this region combine human malice and greed with goodness and nobility of spirit. One of the most moving of Slovak legends is linked with Vršatec, whose ruins are difficult to distinguish from their rocky setting.

Nearby Lednica, surrounded by the peaks of the White Carpathians, was a place of fear. The band of the robber Bielek of Kornice commanded the route leading round the castle from Slovakia into Moravia. They used to rob merchants and other travellers and make raids into Moravia where they even plundered Vizovice Monastery. Bielek's grandsons, Janko and Rafael Podmanický, carried on in the same tradition and, together with their bands of thousands of robbers and outlaws, they spread terror throughout the region. In this case reality was very different from legends in which justice and goodness always win in the end. In 1542, the brothers fled to escape a strict sentence passed on them by the provincial assembly, but three years later, King Ferdinand I granted them pardon and returned to them castle and estates. The grandson of another owner of the castle, Michael Telekessy, crowned the robber tradition in most inglorious manner. After he had attacked the emissaries of Michael, Duke of Moldavia, when they were on their way to Prague with gifts for the Emperor Rudolph II, and after an abortive attack on Bytča Castle, he was executed in Bratislava as a criminal in 1611. Besides this aspect of its past, Lednica made a better name for itself in the seventeenth century. During the reign of Prince Rakoczy, persecuted Bohemian Brethren found refuge here and, in 1650, the great Czech educationalist and philosopher, Jan Amos Komenský (Comenius) spent some time here.

Another seat of the Podmanický family, who spread havoc and horror from Lednica, was Považský Castle. From Bystrica, as the castle was originally called, they could keep an eye on everything that was happening on the River Váh itself, and on the paths along its banks, and from there they launched attacks on rich travellers and on the surrounding villages and seats of the nobility. In popular legends they would certainly have been punished for their crimes. In actual fact, however, the king's pardon completely wiped out their guilt and in the parish church at Považská Bystrica you can still see the tomb of the proud bandit, Rafael Podmanický, who died — a good Christian — in the year of Our Lord 1558.

We come across the names of the Podmanický brothers once more in historical records concerning the unique Renaissance castle of Bytča. They received it as a gift from King Janos Zápolya in 1536. After the death of both brothers it became the property of the Thurzo family, and between 1571 and 1574, Ferencz Thurzo converted this lowland moated castle into a lordly manor, and his successor, the Hungarian Palatine, Juraj Thurzo, constructed a unique building — the Wedding Palace — close to the castle (1601—1606). His six daughters made good use of this palace, for their wedding celebrations continued till the birth of their first children. Until that time the newly-married couple would take up residence in a great hall, which covered one entire floor of the building, in which there was an alcove to hold a wide, elaborately decorated marriage bed and even a special place for musicians. There was no lack of revelry, food and drink. Records of the marriage of Judita Thurzo to the Lord of Vršatec Castle, Ondrej Jakušic, list the quantities of meat consumed by the wedding guests: 35 oxen, 117 calves, 156 lambs, 116 pigs, 27 deer, 188 hare, 526 partridge, 114 capon, 784 hens, 419 geese, 70 Danube salmon and 2300 trout. The horses which transported the guests to the wedding consumed 200 measures of oats and 36 waggon-loads of hay. The serfs could only gaze from the distance at the lordly revelry and feasting.

They thought up a wonderful story about a terrible dragon whose body was concealed in the Váh River and whose head dwelt in the well at Bytča Castle. They also invented a magician who wanted to cast a spell on the dragon, but the lords would not permit him to do so, for the lords were anxious to protect the dragon, precisely because the people hated it and because it harmed them. So the dragon stayed on in the Váh and every seven years it lifted the level of the water over the banks, so that it destroyed houses and tore down bridges, uprooted trees and broke up the rocks. For centuries the people waited for the destructive waters of the Váh to be tamed. It was only in recent decades that the Váh dragon was put in its place by the system of dams constructed on the river to drive the turbines of electric power stations.

A few kilometres beyond Bytča, the Váh begins to wind between mountain peaks and rocky escarpments. If we continued in a northerly direction we should come to the hilly Kysuca region, bordered by the mountains guarding the frontier with Poland and the isolated farmsteads of the Slovak Beskydy range. From this poor district, tinkers and other manual workers used to go out into the world to find at least a slightly better living. It was a severe region, with small cottages standing remote among the hills, and poor shabby little villages; a region where crops had to be scratched from the stony fields and where the misery of thousands of poor people found its reflection in folk songs which are both piteous and full of rebellion.

From the Kysuca of the past — a Kysuca which existed only half a century ago — all that remains today is the poetry which grew out of all that misery, a poetry which can still be admired at Budatín Castle at the confluence of the Kysuca and Váh rivers, where there is an exhibition illustrating the tinkers' art.

Budatín was once a fortress and a place where toll charges were collected. The old route from Silesia to Hungary crossed the Váh at this point by means of a ford. The original thirteenth-century fortified tower and the fourteenth-century ramparts had a Renaissance moated castle added to them in 1551 and this, in turn, was adapted in Baroque style in the eighteenth century. During the revolutionary struggles early in 1849, Budatín was captured by the Slovak volunteers and later it was burnt down by the Imperial forces. After the fire, the castle was restored in the Neo-Classical style, and then in 1922 and 1923 it received its present form. It is situated on the fringe of the North Slovak industrial and cultural centre of Žilina, which today is the seat of the university-levelled Transport School, and an important rail and road junction.

South of Žilina, going upstream along the river Rajčanka, we come to the foot of a great cliff on which stand the vast ruins of the Gothic castle of Lietava. One of the most lovely and picturesque of Slovakia's castles,

212. Vrátná Valley in the Small Fatra Mountains

it was first destroyed in 1241 by the Tartars. King Louis the Great had it rebuilt in 1360 and from then until 1770 it served as a royal fortress. Across the peaks of the Strážovské Highlands we reach the ridge of Súľovské Rocks and come to the romantic ruins of Súľov Castle. It is well worth to climb up to the castle for the wonderful view it provides of the wild beauty of the rock formations. But those who prefer an easier walk, and are satisfied with just gazing up at the heights, can continue along Rajčanka Valley to Rajecké Teplice, a delightful spa with warm mineral springs. At the very end of the valley, at the foot of Strážov and close to the source of the Rajčanka, lies the mountain village of Čičmany, famous for its folk architecture and unusual embroidery.

Further to the south, along the upper reaches of the River Nitra, we come to the mining centre of Prievidza, and the neighbouring spa of Bojnice. Towering over Bojnice and dominating the surrounding countryside stands the castle, which can be seen from very far off. The first historical mention of it can be found in documents dating from 1113. It was built on what was once the site of a primeval settlement and a Slav fortified settlement. Bojnice is one of the oldest castles in Slovakia, having probably been in existence since the beginning of the 11th century. Like Smolenice Castle, the Pálffy family had it rebuilt between 1899 and 1909 in the style of a French Gothic castle. It thus acquired a most romantic appearance and became a Mecca for tourists. Today it contains historic collections, galleries and archives. Part of the castle park has been turned into a zoological

213. Rajecké Teplice Spa

214—215. *The mountain village of Štefanová in Vrátná Valley, the native region of the popular hero, Jánošík*

garden. It is said that King Matthias Corvinus used to hold his parliament beneath the centuries' old lime tree in front of the castle.

But let us return to the River Váh at Žilina where we left it. Going upstream in an easterly direction we come to the Váh breach through the mountains which divides the northern and southern parts of the Small Fatra range. Raftsmen used to dread this spot; they were afraid of the Margita and Besná rocks which jutted out into the water, and of white fairies who were believed to bathe in the Váh at this point and to reach out their hands for hapless humans, who — once seized — were never released alive. They were afraid, too, of the whirlpools, which used to destroy rafts and devour careless raftsmen. On a rock over a bend in the river towered the threatening castle of Strečno about which many tales are told. These are linked with the name of Matúš Čák who is traditionally believed to have first built the castle, and the Palatine Ferencz Wesselényi who — so they say — lived a wild and profligate life within its walls. Only the legendary devotion of his wife tamed him. But it is a fact that from ancient times there was a fortress here guarding a crossing over the Váh. To the fourteenth-century prismatic tower which is the highest point of the ruins, further buildings were added at the end

of the fifteenth century, making it into a splendid feudal residence. In the seventeenth century it was the best fortified castle, serving well the Thököly rebels. For this reason Emperor Leopold I ordered it to be demolished. Unlike most other ruined castles, Strečno has its place in the modern history of Czechoslovakia, too. In the autumn of 1944, Slovak and French guerilla fighters succeeded here in throwing back attacks by superior Nazi forces. A stone pylon on neighbouring Zvonica Hill reminds younger generations of their heroic struggle.

On a rocky prominence in the Small Fatra mountains on the other side of the Váh breach stand the ruins of Varín Castle, today called Starý Hrad (Old Castle). Its strategic position in the Váh pass determined its defensive importance in wars from the thirteenth century onwards, and made it a spot where toll charges were collected in times of peace. The horseshoe-shaped tower with its eastern bastion was completed in the fifteenth century by further buildings, so that, together with Strečno, the Old Castle was one of the most powerful fortresses of the Upper Váh Valley.

A footpath leads direct from the castle to the ridge of the Small Fatras. The famous Vrátná Valley with its deep rocky canyons leads one to Terchová, the birthplace of the legendary outlaw leader, Juraj Jánošík. With

216. *Jánošík's band of outlaws. Folk painting on glass. Slovak National Museum, Martin*

his band of "mountain lads" he disturbed the peace of the feudal lords and the ecclesiastical hierarchy at the beginning of the eighteenth century, avenged the wrongs committed against the common people, robbed the rich and gave to the poor. It is for that reason that there are so many lovely Slovak folk songs and ballads about Jánošík, and why he gazes down on us from so many pictures on glass, and from so many little statues preserved in simple country cottages. In the Jánošík Memorial Hall in the village of Terchová we find a great deal of evidence about the real-life Jánošík, and about the later tradition connected with him, which gained new strength when the people were fighting against their Nazi oppressors.

The Oravská Magura mountains, which form a continuation of the Small Fatra range in a north-easterly direction towards the Polish frontier, bring us to the banks of the great Orava reservoir. A small island with a church perched upon it in the middle of the lake is all that remains of the submerged village of Slanica, the birthplace of the first codifier of the Slovak language, Anton Bernolák. The course of the River Orava beneath the dam wall, lined to the north by the Oravská Magura and the Small Fatra mountains and to the south by the Skorušinské Hills, is our guide through the region dominated by the lovely and historic castle of Orava. It began as a fortified settlement at the beginning of the Christian era. In the thirteenth century it became a stone castle, was rebuilt in Gothic style in the fifteenth and sixteenth centuries, and underwent complicated architectural developments up to 1611, when it received its present impressive appearance. Orava experienced stormy times, especially in the period of the risings of the estates and during the popular revolt of the year 1672, led by the squire of Liptov, Gašpar Pika, which ended with the execution of the rebels beneath the castle. The splendour of Orava Castle contrasted sharply with the dwellings of the local serfs who scratched the poorest living from their stony fields. "Orava, Orava, how sorrowful you are . . ." was the sad refrain of life round the Orava right up to the Second World War. Today evidence of its poverty can be found in the museum of local history in Orava Castle. Elsewhere the Orava region throbs with the rhythm of the machines working in the new factories at Nižná, Istebné, Námestovo and at Dolný Kubín, which has become the cultural centre of this once backward mountainous region.

From Vrútky, the centre of the Slovak revolutionary movement, of which we find reminders in the Klement Gottwald Revolutionary Press Museum in the town, we pass the memorial to Slovak, Czech, Soviet and French participants in the Slovak National Uprising above Priekopa, and come to the royal town of Martin, which from the middle of the last century became the Mecca of Slovak national life. A few dates in this connection are

217. Orava Castle, close to the Slovak-Polish border

218. Orava Dam on the upper reaches of the River Orava

worth mentioning: 1863 — the establishment of Matica slovenská — the supreme cultural association which published books and established museums, but was banned by the Hungarian government in 1875; 1893 — the founding of the Slovak Museum Society which, in 1906—1908, established the Slovak National Museum. These and other institutions and associations, as well as periodicals, helped to keep alive the national consciousness of the Slovak people at a period of greatest efforts to Magyarize Slovakia after the Austro-Hungarian settlement of 1867. The culmination of these endeavours came with the issuing of the Declaration of the Slovak Nation on October 30, 1918 at Martin, in which the Slovak nation, through their representatives, expressed their desire to join the Czech nation in the framework of the new Czechoslovak Republic.

In the spirit of this tradition, the town of Martin also played an important role in the anti-fascist struggle during the Second World War, and in the preparations for the national armed uprising of the Slovak people. A few days before the Slovak National Uprising broke out, workers from the local factories took up arms and

219. The little River Turiec beneath the Kremnica Hills

the local military garrison swore allegiance to the Czechoslovak Republic. The first shots of the uprising were fired here when soldiers, together with partisan fighters, put the German military mission of General Otto out of action. After this had happened orders were given for armed actions to begin, and from then, until the partisans withdrew into the mountains, the town remained a northern bastion of the uprising. The past of a nation and its culture are not only recalled by houses which bear memorial plaques or by exhibits in museums; in the cemetery at Martin, which has been declared a national cultural memorial, we can find gravestones and monuments recalling scores of writers, journalists, artists, musicians and educational workers who devoted their lives to the development of Slovakia and its culture.

South of the Turiec basin, our eye is caught by the ruins of the fourteenth-century Gothic castle of Blatnica, built in beautiful natural surroundings above a deep ravine. Still further to the south is the town of Mošovce, the birthplace of the famous Slovak poet, Ján Kollár, and in the mouth of the valley lies the spa and tourist

227

centre of Turčianske Teplice. On the western fringe of the basin we can find what remains of the old district administrator's castle of Turiec which — probably at the time of the Hussite Wars — was given the name of Zniev. The ruins stand on the site of a prehistoric fortified settlement beside the route leading from the Turiec to the Nitra Valley. The stone castle protected the population of the surroundings against Tartar attacks. Reconstructions carried out in the fifteenth and sixteenth centuries extended the castle and strengthened its fortifications. It was destroyed in 1681 when it was burnt down by Thököly's troops. In the middle of the fourteenth century, Zniev was replaced as district castle by the castle of Sklabiňa, which lies to the east of Martin. This castle was built in its final form during the fifteenth and sixteenth centuries. In its precincts a chateau with its own fortifications was later constructed. In the battles of the Slovak National Uprising, the fascist troops burnt down the chateau and the village of Sklabinský Podzámok.

North of the industrial town of Ružomberok stands the ruined castle of Likava. This probably originated in the fourteenth century. It served the Hussites for a time, and then became the Liptov district castle. It guarded the route between Orava and Liptov and from 1670, when it was conquered by the Imperial forces, it served as a barracks and jail. In 1707, Rákóczy II ordered it to be destroyed. Some popular legends say that Jánošík was imprisoned here, others tell of a tremendous treasure hidden away in its depths. From Ružomberok a main road runs southwards over the mountains, through the ancient little spa of Korytnica and the popular summer resort of Donovaly to Banská Bystrica.

The seat of the Liptov district administration, the town of Liptovský Mikuláš, gained a place in Slovakia's history as the birthplace of the romantic poet, Janko Král, the seat of the Slovak nationalist and publisher Gašpar Fejérpataky-Belopotocký, and the place where the Ľudovít Štúr Society for Slovak Enlightenment, known

◄ *220. Valley of the Smrečianka on the slopes of the Ostrý Roháč range*　　　　　　*221. Central Slovak village of Čičmany*

as Tatrín, was founded in 1844. The revolutionary efforts of Štúr's supporters culminated on 10 May 1848 with the proclamation of the Demands of the Slovak Nation at the first Slovak National Assembly held in the former spa town of Ondrašov. From the 1890's, Liptovský Mikuláš began to develop as an industrial centre, with textile mills, tanneries and timber processing and chemical works. At the May Day demonstration in 1918, the people of the town adopted what was known as the Mikuláš Resolution which expressed the demands of the Slovak people for self-determination and for joining the Czech nation in a common state.

One of the big advantages enjoyed by Liptov is its closeness to the most attractive tourist areas — the Western Tatras (Roháče Mountains), the popular High Tatras and the Low Tatras with the Demänová Caves and the recreation area of Jasná Valley to the south. A great tourist attraction is lovely scenery around Vrbické Lake and the Mikuláš Chalet, as well as the summits of the two highest mountains of the Low Tatras, Chopok and Ďumbier, which can both be reached by cable railway.

Neighbouring Liptovský Ján, which contains Renaissance and Baroque yeomen's seats, some of which are in a good state of preservation, gives an insight into the region's past. Svätojánska (St. John's) Valley is a very popular spot with its wealth of Karst formations and mineral springs which supply water to a swimming pool. It is the starting point for climbs to the summit of Ďumbier and other mountains of the Low Tatra range. Very attractive, too, is Liptovský Hrádok with its ruined Gothic castle and a Renaissance chateau within the castle's

222. *The square at Kremnica*

223. *Bojnice Castle which received its present form in recent times* ▶

224. *Banská Štiavnica, panorama of the town*

precincts. It is also worth while paying a visit to Kráľova Lehota, with yeomen's seats built in Neo-Classical style.

We move out of the Liptov area at a point where there are a number of typical mountain villages, one of which, Vyšná Boca, lies directly beneath the main ridge of the Low Tatras. We are reminded of the origin of this settlement by the mining symbol on the church tower. A comparatively easy road leads us to the saddle of Čertovica and from there along the side of Mount Ďumbier in a southerly direction to the Upper Hron Valley. The centre of this region, where beautiful national costumes are still worn and lovely folk songs are still sung, is Brezno.

On the road from Brezno to Banská Bystrica, our attention is caught by a white memorial in the village

232

225. Gothic Castle of Zvolen, rebuilt in Renaissance style

of Nemecká. It symbolizes a flame and beneath it a woman with outstretched arms. After the fighters of the Slovak National Uprising were pressed back into the mountains, the Nazis murdered hundreds of defenceless people and burnt their bodies in the Nemecká limekilns. A striking feature of this area that can be seen from a long way off is the well-preserved castle of Slovenská Ľupča which dates from the thirteenth century, and is one of the oldest castles in the whole of Slovakia.

We are now approaching Banská Bystrica, an ancient mining town on a bend in the River Hron, which received special privileges in the year 1255, and soon grew rich on the mining of silver and copper in the surroundings. Early fortifications which were strengthened at the turn of the fifteenth and sixteenth centuries by the construction of a municipal castle, made the town the flashpoint of one struggle after another against the

Habsburgs. The castle and the Renaissance Town Hall and splendid houses of the nobility and burghers, built mainly in the fifteenth and sixteenth centuries in the centre of the town, today constitute the core of a historic urban reservation, which contains as many as one hundred and ninety-five valuable examples of architecture, and is one of the largest of such reservations in Slovakia. Of great value and interest are the Renaissance houses on the square, which belonged to the Thurzo and Benický families. The great number of memorial plaques on the houses and the bold Memorial of the Slovak National Uprising recall the historic year of 1944 when Banská Bystrica was the heart of the Slovak struggle against fascism.

Passing round the memorial at Kremnička which recalls the fighting of the years 1944—1945, with a view of the outline of the spa buildings of the world-famous health resort of Sliač, set in the woods overlooking the River Hron, we reach the royal town of Zvolen, dominated by a fourteenth-century castle set on a low hill above it. This was a favourite residence of Louis I of Hungary, Sigismund I and Matthias Corvinus. Important meetings were held there, as well as weddings and coronations. It was from Zvolen Castle that Jan Jiskra of Brandýs controlled the whole of Slovakia, and its fortifications withstood Turkish attacks for more than a hundred years. Although the castle became the property of the state as long ago as 1805, it was not until 1956 that it was thoroughly restored. During the work of restoration, traces of adaptations were removed, and the castle is now used to house collections of medieval art belonging to the Slovak National Gallery. In the town beneath the castle, which came into being on the site of prehistoric settlements, a number of interesting Renaissance buildings and the remains of early fortifications have been preserved. Evidence of the strong national feelings

226. Memorial to the Slovak National Uprising, Banská Bystrica

of the people of Zvolen in the nineteenth century is provided by the fact that, in 1847, they elected Ľudovít Štúr as their deputy to the Hungarian Parliament. The vast nearby district castle, the ruins of which are now known as "Pustý Hrad" — meaning Deserted Castle — used to be the centre of the huge district of Zvolen which, in ancient days, reached right up to the Polish frontier. It comprises a whole system of fortifications and buildings; the Upper Castle, dating from the tenth to thirteenth century, and the Lower Castle from the following century. The two castles, about a kilometre apart, were joined by a defensive wall which — for strategic purposes — ran parallel to the ridge of the mountains. The whole large fortress, which provided sanctuary for the population of the entire surroundings, was abandoned in the fourteenth century and its material was used to build Zvolen Castle.

East of Zvolen in the Slatina River Valley, on the heights above the village of Vígľaš, stand the ruins of what was once the hunting lodge of King Matthias. When the defence system was strengthened it was one of the main points for withstanding Turkish attacks in Central Slovakia. The Turks failed to take the fortress both in 1577 and in the decades that followed. After the risings of the estates, in which the castle played a part, Vígľaš was rebuilt in Baroque style as a residence for the Eszterházy family in the middle of the eighteenth century. In 1891, the whole building was restored, but during the Second World War it was destroyed by fire.

From Vígľaš Castle, which provides a splendid view of the Zbojnická Poľana Mountains and Detva, we can cross the Kremnica Heights to the town of the same name — a name which in Czechoslovakia is synonymous with the minting of coins. Kremnica was built on a site where gold and silver used to be mined and, in 1328,

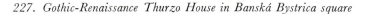

227. Gothic-Renaissance Thurzo House in Banská Bystrica square

228. *Low Tatra Mountains*

King Carobert conferred on it the rights of a free royal town. In the urban reservation in the centre of the town can be found the municipal castle, whose strong fortifications and bastions were linked with the outer fortifications of the whole town. The mint has attracted interest for centuries. Its gold ducats made it famous throughout Europe. The fortifications helped the town to withstand the attacks of the Turks, of anti-Habsburg rebels and bands of robbers. What harmed Kremnica far more than any enemy attacks was the decline of gold mining at a later time. Today its medieval beauty enchants tourists who should not fail to visit the interesting collection of coins and medals in the state mint.

The third great mining town in Central Slovakia, Banská Štiavnica, is hidden in the green of the Štiavnica Heights. This peaceful medieval town was known as early as the eleventh century. In the first half of the thirteenth century it gained its charter, but it was in the fifteenth and sixteenth centuries that it underwent its greatest expansion, thanks to the mining of extensive deposits of silver. Its Romanesque basilica, rebuilt into a Gothic fortified church, was converted between 1546 and 1559 into a well-equipped fortress intended to withstand Turkish attacks, with bastions, a drawbridge, and a forecourt which was originally the nave of the church. When the Turks approached the town, the richer citizens fled. The king refused to provide aid, but the courageous people, even in the worst moments, kept their heads, and sacrificed their lovely church which was their strongest point, in order to save the town. In addition they started to build the New Castle on a hill above the

229. Vyšná Boca, ancient mining village in the Low Tatras

town (1564—1572) and secured the town fortifications by building five gates. All these constructions did indeed help to withstand the Turkish raids, and they have given the characteristic outline to what is one of the most lovely of Slovak towns. Its historic urban reservation contains more than a hundred beautiful examples of architecture, including the *lycée* frequented both by Andrej Sládkovič and Alexander Petöfi. Many outstanding scholars used to teach at the mining and forestry academy as far back as the eighteenth century, and they did much research into the laws of nature. And those who created the foundations of Štiavnica's prosperity by the mining of gold, silver, copper and lead deep underground, for whom time was counted only by the beginning and ending of their work, and many of whom perished by the sword or the dreaded "Black Death", lived beyond the fortifications. History can provide many instances of the achievements of these self-sacrificing people. There were Matej Kornell Hell and his son Jozef Karol Hell who invented an ingenious pumping apparatus which in the eighteenth century saved the mines from destruction.

Along with the bare historical facts there are many lovely popular legends about the town and its surroundings, about a poor miner and a golden cave, about the gnomes of the rocks, King Rudník, the Red Knight and the founding of the Maidens' Castle, sometimes known as the New Castle. Nearby Sitno Hill has its place in these legends, too. Like Blaník Hill in Bohemia, it was said to shelter in its depths a regiment of hussars who, at their nation's hardest hour, would emerge and help the people to defend their existence.

230. Vrbické Lake in the neighbourhood of the Demänovská Valley

231. *The ridges of the High Tatra Mountains*

There is perhaps no other corner of Slovakia so often recalled in poems and songs as the peaks of the High Tatra Mountains. They form a stone-carved diadem for Slovakia, edged with the dark green of coniferous forests and dwarf pines, set with the sapphires of mountain lakes and veined by rapid silver streams. The origin of these mountains is veiled in legend: when God first made the earth, proud Kriváň was the highest mountain, but a careless angel sliced its peak with his wing and so the summit has a tortuous, lop-sided shape.

From time immemorial, nature was lavish here with her gifts, but life was not easy for the people. On the Tatra foothills there was poverty and hunger even after the First World War. There was unemployment and people emigrated on a mass scale.

Today the whole region has been declared the Tatra National Park, with a network of modern hotels and holiday resorts, sports facilities and good communications, and with advanced methods of the protection of flora and fauna, and a mountain rescue service to protect those thoughtless tourists who venture to climb the rocky slopes without sufficient experience or adequate equipment. The picturesque cemetery above Osterva, with its strange wooden crosses, tells the sad story of the annual toll taken by the steep slopes and deep abysses.

The centre of the western part of the range is Štrbské Pleso with a huge mountain lake of the same name. At Zelené Pleso (Green Lake) in Važecká Valley is the source of the stream Zlomisko, which joins up with the Furkota to form the White Váh; and from Kráľova Hoľa, in the Low Tatras, its partner, the Black Váh, rushes to meet it. The actual confluence of the two rivers is at Kráľova Lehota and from there the two join to form the powerful current of Slovakia's greatest river. For years tourists used to come here to admire Mlynica Valley and the Skok waterfall. Today it is a fairy land of ski jumps and tall hotels which dominate the mountain landscape.

As well as the sports enthusiasts and holiday-makers, patients come to the High Tatras, in winter and summer alike, who have to be satisfied with gazing from their windows or sitting on the terraces of sanatoria breathing in the clear, health-giving mountain air. Vyšné Hágy, at the foot of the King of the Tatras, majestic Mount Gerlach (2655 m) is one such centre where the battle for health is fought; at nearby Tatranská Polianka, half a century ago, the sensitive poet, Jiří Wolker, with his boyishly naive view of the world, wrote his last poems.

Starý Smokovec, the cultural centre of this mountain region, lies at a junction of roads and of the Tatra electric railway. It is the site of various festivals and the starting point of walks to the Great Cold Valley (Velká studená dolina), with its popular Brigands' Chalet (Zbojnická chata), and to the five Spiš lakes of the Little Cold Valley (Malá studená dolina). The gleaming beauty of the Cold Water Falls lines the way to Rocky Lake (Skalnaté Pleso), above which is situated the astronomical observatory of the Slovak Academy of Sciences. High above it, on Lomnický Peak, the staff of Europe's highest permanent meteorological station (2632 m) are on duty regardless of the weather. A cable railway goes up to the peak from Tatranská Lomnica, enabling thousands of visitors to experience the unique thrill of travelling in safety over a deep abyss to the peak of the second highest mountain in the Tatra range. A bend in the Velká Svišťovka conceals the magical beauty of Green Lake (Zelené pleso) Valley, which leads to White Water Valley (Bělovodská dolina), separating the central part of the High Tatras from the eastern part known as the Belanské Tatry.

These mountains are quite different from the peaks of the High Tatras. Their jagged summits seem to rise directly from the green carpet that covers the mountain slopes. From the health resort of Tatranské Matliare at the south-eastern foot of Kežmarský Peak, one can reach Tatranská Basin. Belanská Cave in its close vicinity is of enormous size, and visitors are attracted by the wealth of stalagmite and stalactite formations which grow out of its domes, halls and galleries. The road to the typical Tatra village of Ždiar, famous for its lovely folk costumes and richly ornamented folk architecture, offers splendid views of the Belanské Tatry and the wooded mountain valleys. Javorina, situated not far away in the northernmost tip of this region beneath the Tatras, lies directly on the Polish frontier.

The majority of visitors to the holiday resorts of the High Tatra range pass through the town of Poprad. This industrial, cultural and administrative centre of the region beneath the Tatra Mountains was in medieval times one of the twenty-four Spiš towns. Its economic development in the nineteenth century, together with the growing tourist trade, enabled Poprad to get so far ahead of the other small towns in the neighbourhood that, after 1945, some of them were absorbed into Greater Poprad. Most interesting from the architectural point of view is Spišská Sobota which also used to belong to the union of Spiš towns. Records of its history go back to the middle of the thirteenth century, but it really began to flourish in the sixteenth century. Quite a number of Renaissance burghers' houses dating from this period still exist along the sides of the spindle-shaped town square around the parish church and the former town hall. Today these houses form the core of a historic urban reservation. The most precious object in the church is the St. George's altar, dating from the year 1516, the work of the famous wood-carver Master Pavol of Levoča and his workshop. Most remarkable is the group of statuary representing the Last Supper, which is another version of the beautiful group of carvings in the church at Levoča.

The spa of Gánovce with mineral springs that were already known in the Middle Ages lies to the south-east of Poprad. Gánovce became famous when traces of Neanderthal man were found there — the travertine cast of a human skull dating from about 20,000 B.C., as well as finds of flora and the remains of the fauna of that period. Archaeological excavations have also brought to light many other finds dating from various periods of primeval settlement. Still further to the south-east, in the village of Betlanovce, there is a Renaissance chateau built between 1564 and 1568, which is one of the first such buildings to have had no fortifications and no towers at the corners. This was a noble residence with many portals, featuring richly articulated jambs with floral ornaments. It is a remarkably delicate work designed by sixteenth-century master builders. Next, the ruins of Kláštorisko open the door to the Slovak Paradise with its deep canyons and rock formations carved out of limestone by water: chimneys, shafts and walls — narrow and deep and in some cases almost closed from above, with waterfalls falling to a depth of forty metres, valleys edged with great expanses of woodland, and little farmsteads with their wooden cottages. The Slovak Paradise has a subterranean kingdom, too, where one can glimpse through a crevice of Bear's Cave, with its rare stalactites and stalagmites, or gaze through crystal curtains of the famous Dobšinská Ice Cave.

Going north-east from Poprad, the first stop is the ancient town of Kežmarok — a royal free town at the confluence of the River Poprad and Ľubický Brook, at what was an important strategic position on the road linking Poland and Hungary. The historic urban reservation of Kežmarok contains the remains of the medieval fortifications of the town, with a semi-circular bastion and parts of the defences of one of the town's four gates. As at Kremnica, the ramparts of the town were linked with the fortifications of the municipal castle which, according to some sources, is situated on the site where the church and burghers' houses used to stand. Others maintain that it is a rebuilt monastery. Among other buildings worth noting are the town hall dating from the mid-sixteenth century, which was restored in 1799, a late Gothic church with an enclosed belfry from the Renaissance period, and an interesting wooden church built in 1717 with a high pitched shingle roof. As for burghers' houses, a number of buildings in Gothic-Renaissance, Baroque and Neo-Classical style have been preserved in the town centre, including some craftsmen's houses dating from the end of the eighteenth century.

Following the course of the River Poprad, we reach the village of Strážky, founded in about the twelfth century, to protect Hungary's frontiers against Poland. On the site of a frontier watchtower, a U-shape Renaissance castle was built here from 1570 to 1590, with powerful bastions. After a fire in the early eighteenth century, a fourth wing was added, thus forming an enclosed courtyard, decorated with arcades. The picturesque appearance of the building was further enhanced by an English-style park, and a Gothic church with a Renaissance belfry nearby.

Close by is a small town of Spišská Belá, which has a remarkable thirteenth-century early Gothic church, which two hundred years later was converted into a church with two naves. There is a sixteenth-century Renaissance belfry and a number of double-storeyed gabled houses of the Spiš type. Across the peaks of the Spišská Magura we come to a northern frontier salient with Pieniny Three Crowns on the Polish side, the rapids of the Dunajec River, and a thirteenth-century fortified Carthusian monastery known as Červený Kláštor (Red Monastery). This rare historic monument was saved by considerable reconstruction carried out between 1952 and 1966. The original inhabitants, monks of the order of hermits, who lived in their cells with gardens where they dug their own graves before they died, would certainly not appreciate the crowds of tourists who visit this lovely spot, and float on narrow punt-like rafts down the waters of the Dunajec. Visitors are reminded of the figure of the Hussite commander, Peter Aksamit, in the Aksamitka Cave at the foot of a hill close to the neighbouring village of Haligovce.

Through the pine woods of the Spišská Magura we come once more to the valley of the Poprad, to the mountain spa of Vyšné Ružbachy with its modern buildings where international symposia on sculpture are traditionally held. A few kilometres further on, above the small medieval town of Stará Ľubovňa is a comparatively well-preserved castle on the summit of a small hill. It was built on Zlatá hora (Golden Mount) overlooking the River Poprad as part of the frontier fortifications and is one of the biggest and most lovely of Slovakia's castles. Dating from the thirteenth century, it used to belong to Matúš Čák, and from 1412 to 1772 it was the seat of Polish governors. Of these the family of the Princes of Lubomír did most to develop the castle, which they turned into a powerful Renaissance fortress, also completing the lower castle and its artillery bastion. From the end of the eighteenth century the castle was abandoned but the Zamoyski family, whose property it was between 1882 and 1945, carried out renovation work on parts of it. During the Slovak National Uprising, the Nazi Gestapo set up headquarters at Stará Ľubovňa Castle and made it a place of torture and execution for anti-fascist fighters.

The last of the castles of this frontier system — Plavecký, which lies further to the east — suffered an even sadder fate. It changed hands continually from the time it was built as a stone castle towards the end of the thirteenth century until the middle of the fifteenth century, when it became the seat of the commander of the Brethren and ally of Jan Jiskra, Peter Aksamit of Kosov. In 1456, when the peasants of north-eastern Slovakia rose up against feudal oppression, Aksamit was successful in helping them, but after his death at the Battle of Blatný Potok in 1458, their conditions once more deteriorated. In 1631, another peasant revolt broke out in the village beneath the castle, which was cruelly suppressed. Many who had taken part had to flee to Poland to escape punishment. The castle itself was an impregnable bastion during Rákóczy's uprising and withstood attacks by Imperial forces. Its fate was sealed, however, in the 1830's when its owner, Ferdinand Horvath, through lack of experience, made the castle uninhabitable. The past glory of Plavecký Castle is today only reflected in its crumbling walls.

Following the ridge of the Levoča Hills, we turn south-westward into the heart of historic Spiš. Beneath the mountains lies the pearl of all Spiš towns — Levoča. Levoča experienced every stage of settlement, from the Neolithic era to the Great Moravian Empire, and was settled by German colonizers in the thirteenth century.

232. Štrbské Pleso in the High Tatras

From having been the main centre of the Spiš Saxons, it became the free royal town which until the seventeenth century vied fiercely with neighbouring Kežmarok for supremacy in the area. According to old chronicles, this struggle developed in the first half of the sixteenth century into a life and death war, from which Levoča emerged triumphant. Although half the town's population consisted of peasants and there were many craftsmen, too, the town was ruled by rich German merchants. The famous Breuer Press was here which in 1685 produced Comenius's *Orbis Pictus* and which, in its 130 years of existence, brought out almost a thousand publications in Latin, Hungarian, German and Slovak. Among well known scholars and educationalists associated with the local school after 1520 was the English scholar, humanist and poet, Leonard Cox, who had been tutor to King Henry VIII. The school won such a name for itself that in the early seventeenth century it was to have been changed into a university. In that century, too, the town had its chronicler, Gašpar Hain, who, in great detail, recorded its history from earliest times. In 1654, the philosopher and educationalist Jan Amos Komenský (Comenius) stayed here. One of the most outstanding medieval artists whose life and work were connected with Levoča was

244

the remarkable Gothic wood-carver, Master Pavol, who established a workshop here and produced his great masterpieces for St. James's Church — the high altar with the group depicting the Last Supper (1508—1517), the altar of St. Nicholas (1507), the altar of St. Anne (after 1520), the group of figures on the altar of the Nativity and the equestrian statue of St. George in one of the chapels (1515). The mystery surrounding Master Pavol, about whose life very little evidence exists, has for long attracted the attention of art historians.

If Bratislava can be described as the treasure house of the history and culture of West Slovakia and Banská Štiavnica as the Central Slovak town with the most beautiful location, Levoča must certainly be ranked as the most striking urban unit in East Slovakia. This is also borne out by the fact that Levoča's historic reservation containing 288 rare buildings is the largest in the whole of Slovakia. Those who planned the town long ago chose the site with great care. The terrace on which the town was built is protected on two sides by a steep slope which, to-

233. Javorina Hunting Lodge beneath Ice Peak on the northern slopes of the Tatra range

gether with powerful ramparts from the fourteenth century, helped to ward off enemy attacks. The fortifications of the town consisted of three fortification walls and moats, and a number of bastions. In addition to the system of fortifications, two of the town gates have also been preserved to this day — the Košice Gate — also known as the Upper Gate — and the Menhardt Gate. The streets running off the large oblong town square used to lead to the various gates and bastions. On the site of an earlier church dating from 1280, a great Gothic church dedicated to St. James was built in the fourteenth century with a tall slender spire and rich interior furnishings in which Master Pavol played an important role. Close to the church, in the middle of the square, stands a Gothic town hall dating from the end of the 15th century, which was rebuilt following fires in 1550 and 1599 and again refurbished in Polish Renaissance style in 1895 by the addition of gabled dormer windows on the roof. The Levoča town hall is linked by a corridor to the Renaissance belfry which has been restored in Baroque style. Close to the town hall stands an iron cage in which slanderous women and unfaithful wives were pilloried. The Gothic, Renaissance and early Baroque burghers' houses with their arcaded courtyards form a picturesque unit round the square. Especially attractive to visitors is the Thurzo House with its well preserved Renaissance façade and rich graffito ornamentation.

Passing the peaceful little health resort of Sivá Brada with its sulphurous spring, we come to the valley where stands the ancient town of Spišské Podhradie which grew up in dependence on the great royal castle of Spiš. The town's inhabitants were mainly craftsmen and tradesmen (drapers), dyers and shoemakers, or peasant

235. Renaissance Chateau of Betlanovce

236. Bell-tower, Spišská Sobota

farmers. The well-preserved Gothic-Renaissance houses, together with later Baroque buildings, the old town hall, the Monastery of the Brothers of Mercy, rebuilt in Baroque style, and the enclosed parish church present an unusually interesting picture, as does Spišská Kapitula, situated on a slope above the town. This once great centre of Catholicism and seat of the bishopric was originally a small fortified settlement which was later enhanced by the late Romanesque church of St. Martin and by ecclesiastical palaces rebuilt in Baroque style. Today this smallest urban reservation in Slovakia, with well-preserved fortifications, a watchhouse, bastions, the Upper and Lower Gates and a prismatic clock-tower, is one of the most interesting historic towns in Eastern Slovakia.

On a nearby hill, Spiš Castle, which can be seen from a long way off, dominates the whole region. It is one of the oldest and largest of Slovakia's castles. First mention of it can be found in a Polish chronicle of the year 1113. At that time it was already an administrative centre, and later, in 1241, it withstood Tartar raids and saved the lives of many of the inhabitants of the surrounding area. The first parts of the new castle to be built were a three-storey Romanesque palace, an early Gothic cylindrical tower and an outer bailey to which a large enclosed area was added between 1370 and 1380. Jan Jiskra of Brandýs, who seized the castle in 1443, strengthened its defences by adding a strong stone wall and a moat and by building a huge outer bailey to the west of

248

237. Carthusian Red Monastery (Červený Kláštor) on the River Dunajec

the castle which was to serve as a military camp. The Zápolya family who lived here from 1465 added the late Gothic living quarters, as well as St. Elizabeth's Chapel, and modernized the system of fortifications. Finally, between 1558 and 1636, the Thurzos converted the castle into a comfortable Renaissance residence with buildings for the garrison in the outer bailey. At the height of its glory, the castle is said to have had five courtyards and altogether 135 chambers. After a fire in 1780, it was abandoned and work to conserve what remains of the castle — the best preserved parts in the Upper Castle being the palace, the cylindrical tower and the chapel — was not undertaken until recently when Spiš Castle was proclaimed a national cultural monument.

Dreveník, a travertine hill not far from the castle, is one of the richest sites where finds from ancient cultures have been uncovered. In the third millennium B.C. it was a fortified settlement and in the eleventh century a Slav fortified settlement. Here, too, a great treasure dating from the Bronze Age has been found. Within the hill is an ice cave and its summit is adorned with small geysers. In the valley beneath Spiš Castle lies the village of Žehra with its fortified early Gothic church — dedicated to the Holy Spirit. Visitors are attracted by the remarkable murals dating from the thirteenth to fifteenth centuries. Added to the village is the community of Hodkovce with a Baroque chateau containing rare antique furnishings from Spiš Castle. Close to Spiš is Branisko

249

238. *Dunajec Valley and the Three Crowns group of mountains*

240. *High altar of St. James the Greater in the parish church at Levoča, the work of the wood-carver Master Pavol of Levoča*

◄ 239. *Gothic-Renaissance Town Hall at Levoča*

241. Detail of the folding altar wing of St. James the Greater, Levoča

Pass, famous for the fighting that took place there in 1849. On the other side of the pass, in the valley by the road leading to Prešov, we come upon the Renaissance fortified castle of Fričovce, built between 1623 and 1630.

The southern route to the valley of the Hornád leads us to the ancient thirteenth-century mining community of Krompachy, where copper and iron used to be mined. Krompachy was also an important centre of the working class movement and the scene of many strikes. After 1945, it became one of the industrial centres of the East Slovak region.

Gelnica in the Hnilec Valley was a mining village back in the mid-twelfth century. Iron, copper, silver and mercury were all mined here and the economic growth of the community led to its acquiring a royal charter in the thirteenth century. A royal castle was built here which was destroyed in 1527. After a temporary economic decline, mining and metallurgy underwent further development in the middle of the eighteenth century and Gelnica was once more declared a free royal mining town in 1844.

Upstream along the River Hnilec and across the wooded ridge of the Slovak Ore Mountains we come upon yet another mining region in the valley of the Slaná. But first we should visit the chateau of Betliar, set in a large natural park, which used to belong to the Andrássy family. The chateau was rebuilt in the eighteenth and nineteenth centuries from a four-towered Renaissance structure into an edifice of uncertain style with luxuriously furnished chambers and rich collections from all over the world. Tourists usually visit another seat of the Andrássy family — Krásna Hôrka Castle. It was founded early in the 14th century by the Mariássy family and in 1352 it became the property of the Bebeks. From 1441 to 1461 Jan Jiskra took it over, after which, until 1566 it again

254

242. St. George, icon from the wooden church at Nová Sedlica. Slovak National Gallery, Bratislava

belonged to the Bebeks. They were ruthless feudal rulers who took an active part in quelling the Dózsa peasants' revolt of 1514 and who threatened the safety of the trade route beneath the castle. Therefore, at the request of the East Slovak towns, the castle was demolished and the new owner, Peter Andrássy, rebuilt it towards the end of the sixteenth century into a powerful fortress with bastions and artillery terraces. The castle was again reconstructed in the eighteenth century into a late Renaissance feudal residence. After a fire in 1817, the building fell into disrepair and was not restored until 1903, when reconstruction work began.

The mining town of Rožňava in the valley of the Slaná dates from the twelfth century when precious metals, iron and copper, were mined here. After the decline of the mining industry in the middle of the sixteenth century, crafts became the main source of livelihood of the inhabitants of Rožňava. Since the last century the town has been a centre of the region's working class movement. Interesting historic buildings in Rožňava include the remains of a fortress and of the town's ramparts, the two-storey Powder Tower, the town hall with its tower on the square, the Bishops' Palace and the burghers' houses, most of them rebuilt in Neo-Classical style. The Mining Museum contains documents and collections relating to the history of mining and of the guilds.

South of Rožňava, on Silica plain, close to the Hungarian border, is Domica Cave with its gigantic halls, its stalactite and stalagmite formations in all colours of the rainbow and the subterranean River Styx along which one can take a romantic trip by boat. Archaeological finds of stone tools, axes, daggers, awls, hoops and clay vessels, left here by the primeval inhabitants of five thousand years ago, are another interesting aspect of this subterranean world which continues on the Hungarian side of the frontier in the system of the Aggtelec caves.

Another attraction are the rocky passes of the limestone Zádiel and Háj Valleys, which are among the most beautiful in Slovakia, as well as the prehistoric fortified settlement with mounds above the village of Zádiel. The ruins of the Gothic castle of Turňa-on-Bodva, dating from the thirteenth century, enhance the picturesque beauty of the landscape by their wide silhouette. Our route leads us to Jasov, formerly a free royal town which attracts tourists by the peaceful expanse of its lake and the interesting Jasov Cave. From the Lower Palaeolithic Age it provided refuge for man who left tools and the bones of animals there.

Passing through the Slovak Ore Mountains we reach the metropolis of East Slovakia — Košice. Its favourable situation in the basin between the eastern side of the Slovak Ore Mountains and the Slanské Hills attracted settlers from time immemorial. Settlements of every period seem to have left their imprints here. The Slovak community, in which, after the Tartar raids, German merchants took up their abode, grew rapidly and assumed the character of a fortified town. Towards the end of the thirteenth century, markets were held here and Košice acquired certain privileges. In the fourteenth century, the town became an important trade centre which soon grew rich, and the forests in the vicinity were replaced by vineyards which filled the pockets of the burghers with valuable ducats. In 1347, Košice was already a free royal town through which trade was conducted between eastern Hungary and countries to the north. This found reflection in the town's appearance — in the fourteenth and fifteenth centuries it was encircled by double fortifications with four gates. Towards the end of the thirteenth century, the burghers' houses were added to by a Dominican monastery with its church and, a century later, the

243. Spišská Kapitula, formerly a fortified ecclesiastical settlement

244. *Ruins of Spiš Castle*

impressive Cathedral of St. Elizabeth, which art historians regard as the most valuable example of Gothic architecture in Slovakia, was built.

It is interesting to note that women had a considerable influence on the building of the Cathedral: the gold lilies of the Anjou and the black ravens of the Hunyady in its decoration are an indication that Queen Elizabeth, wife of Louis the Great, who used to pass through here when she went to visit her daughter, played an active part in the building of the Cathedral. After the death of Matthias Corvinus, it was again a woman who had the damaged church restored — his widow Queen Beatrix. Moreover, St. Elizabeth, to whom the Cathedral is dedicated, was actually born in Košice in 1208, the second daughter of King Andrew II of Hungary. Among the interesting features of the edifice, in addition to the loftiness of its overall appearance and its feminine charm, is the lovers' staircase on which two people may walk simultaneously without being able to see each other, and a memorial plaque which recalls that in 1440, on the instigation of Jan Jiskra of Brandýs, the citizens of Košice accepted Ladislaus the Posthumous as their King. There is also the crypt to which were brought in 1906, after two centuries in a foreign land, the remains of the anti-Habsburg rebel, Ferencz Rákóczy II and his associates who after the defeat of their uprising had sought refuge in Turkey. At the side of the Cathedral stands the Urban Tower, a Renaissance belfry, and to the south the thirteenth-century Gothic Chapel of St. Michael with its remarkable sculpture.

Among Košice's palaces, the late Gothic Levoča House is usually listed first. Close by we find the former Jesuit and later on Premonstratensian Monastery, which in 1657 housed Košice's first university with its Faculties of the Arts and of Theology (abolished in 1773, together with the Jesuit Monastery and Order). Rákóczy's Baroque Palace — originally a Gothic building — in the early seventeenth century housed a mint and from 1706 to 1707 it was the headquarters of Ferencz Rákóczy II, the leader of the anti-Habsburg uprising. On the main street, where the majority of Košice's historic buildings are to be found, an eighteenth-century Baroque-Neo-Classical building used to house the district administrative offices. In more recent times it gained fame from the fact that

257

on 5 April 1945, the Košice Government Programme was declared there — a document which provided the foundations for the building of a republic in which two nations — the Czechs and Slovaks — are equal partners. The Bishop's Palace, standing in the close vicinity, is in Rococo style and has rich stucco decorations. It bears witness to the power and pomp of the ecclesiastical hierarchy.

Košice's economic life is dominated by the giant East Slovak Steelworks at Šaca, the East Slovak Engineering Works and various other factories, power plants and transport undertakings in the town and its environs. The people of Košice have recreational facilities in nearby Črmel Valley, the slopes of Bankov, the ski slopes at Jahodná and at Herľany where there is a cold geyser at a spot where boring was carried out in the seventeenth century to a depth of 404 metres to find mineral springs.

In the deeply wooded Zemplín Hills to the south-east of Košice, the romantic ruins of Slanec Castle rise from a cone-shaped hill. It was founded in 1220, destroyed by Jan Jiskra in 1440 and afterwards rebuilt by its new owners. During the risings of the estates towards the end of the seventeenth century, Slanec was burnt down and again abandoned. Today only the high cylindrical tower reminds us of the legend about the scribe

245. Krásna Hôrka Castle in the Rožňava basin

258

246. *Protestant cemetery at Hrhov with carved wooden tombs*

248. *South front of St. Elizabeth's Cathedral*

who, for love of the lady of the castle, murdered his master but failed to win the lady's affections. Through vast vineyards, we move south-eastward to the Tokay region with wine-cellars that used to belong to the castle of Malá Tŕňa.

Crossing the entire area of the East Slovak lowlands split by the Rivers Ondava, Laborec, Latorica and Uh, we turn northward to the town of Michalovce in a fertile agricultural region. It was a prehistoric settlement and then between the tenth and twelfth centuries it was settled by Slavs. In 1418, Michalovce received its town charter. On the spot where a chateau now stands, there was a castle up to the seventeenth century. After various phases of restoration and reconstruction, the chateau gained its present Neo-Classical form in the early nineteenth century. It houses the History Museum of Zemplín, which contains rich collections of archaeological finds from the entire area of the East Slovak Lowlands and interesting evidence of the East Slovak peasants' revolt of 1831.

Northeast of Michalovce, at the foot of the Vihorlat Hills, lies the vast expanse of a reservoir known as Zemplínska Šírava. The picturesque appearance of the landscape is further enhanced by the romantic ruins of Vinné Castle on a hillock beneath the Vihorlat range. The chain of frontier castles in this region continues to the north with two ruined castles in the vicinity of Humenné — Jasenov and Brekov. Both date from the thirteenth century and belonged to the powerful family of Drugeth. During the anti-Habsburg risings of the estates, they

◀ 247. *St. Elizabeth's Cathedral, Košice*

were sacked by Rákóczy's forces. The town of Humenné also used to be one of the towns in the Laborec basin which were subject to the Drugeth family who, from the moated castle on the square used to administer the largest feudal estate in Slovakia. In the seventeenth century, when Gabriel Drugeth became Hungarian Palatine, the castle was rebuilt into a massive square chateau with towers at each corner. The official halls with rich interior decoration looked out on to a courtyard lined with arcades. After a fire in 1684 and yet another at the beginning of the twentieth century, the chateau was rebuilt in the style of a French Baroque residence.

In the Ondava Valley, near the town of Vranov and close to the pass known as the Polish Gate, the trade route was guarded from the thirteenth century by Čičava Castle. Its importance grew as a result of the Drugeths' holding Zemplín administrative assemblies here and lodging the district archives in the castle. Ever since 1711 when the Imperial forces destroyed it, only the ruins of this once busy castle remain. Around the Domaša reservoir in the Ondava basin which stretches between the southern promontories of the Low Beskydy range, many amenities for holiday-makers have been built, as they have round the great Zemplínska Šírava reservoir. It is only a short distance between these happy spots and Tokajík, the scene of one of the tragedies of the Second World War. To punish the villagers for helping the partisans, on 19 November 1944, the Nazis massacred thirty-one of the inhabitants and sacked and burnt down the village. The memorial built here as a reminder of these tragic happenings is called "Return to the Slaughtered Village" and shows the despair of a woman leaning over the body of her dead husband. The fate of Tokajík, like that of many other villages in Central and Eastern Slovakia, still serves as a warning today.

249. The Rákóczy House, Prešov

The proud castle of Kapušany which rises from a cone-shaped hill above the valley of the Sekčov is said to have been built by the Romans as a protection against the Sarmatians. Archaeological excavations have shown that there used to be a Slav fortified settlement here and that from the thirteenth century there was a stone castle which was destroyed in 1312 during fighting between Matúš Čák of Trenčín and King Carobert. In 1410, the Kapys replaced it with a powerful fortress with high ramparts and two towers, which was a hard nut for King Matthias and other rulers to crack. Emperor Charles VI, fearing further risings by the estates, eventually had the castle, together with other feudal seats in Slovakia, destroyed. All that remains are the ruins, old historical records and many legends.

Near the confluence of the Sekčov and Torysa rivers we come on the community of Solivary where salt has been mined from underground deposits since the Middle Ages. Old winding gear from the seventeenth century and salt warehouses dating from 1674 are among the tourist attractions today. Above the community are the ruins of the castle of Solnohrad which was destroyed at the same time as Kapušany Castle, in 1715.

Neighbouring Prešov, built on the southern spurs of the Čerchov Hills, stands on the site of an ancient settlement. The Slovak population of the area was joined in the twelfth century by Germans and later by Magyars. The oldest records of the town are from the year 1233, and Prešov became a free royal town in 1374. Its inhabitants were mainly artisans (chiefly shoemakers and weavers) and merchants. Towards the end of the fourteenth century, work was started on the building of the ramparts and up to the middle of the seventeenth century the town underwent its greatest architectural development. In 1650, there were forty-seven guilds here

250. Gothic-Renaissance town hall, Bardejov

251. Bastion of the medieval fortifications of the town of Bardejov

and from 1667 there was a university — the Protestant college, with faculties of theology and law. Its Renaissance building is among the finest examples of architecture in the town. Prešov was the centre of the rising of the estates led by Thököly, and after its suppression, an Imperial court martial headed by General Caraffa had twenty-four citizens of Prešov and about 300 others cruelly tortured and executed. This tragic event is recalled by a bas-relief on the wall of the college and also by Caraffa's fifteenth-century jail which was known as the "Prešov Slaughter-house". Despite these bitter experiences the town again played a part in the struggle against the Habsburgs in 1704 under Ferencz Rákóczy II. His family were the owners of a richly decorated two-storey palace which now houses the Museum of the Slovak Soviet Republic. After a period of decline, the town underwent considerable economic development towards the end of the eighteenth century. It became the headquarters of the Šariš district and since the middle of the last century an industrial centre, too. During the revolutionary events in Slovakia after the First World War, Prešov played an important part when a socialist state — the Slovak Soviet Republic — was proclaimed there on 16 June 1919. Although this attempt failed, it left deep imprints on the minds and hearts of the masses of the people and was an encouragement to them in times of persecution. Among the remarkable features of the town's historic urban reservation are the Gothic parish church of St. Nicholas which dates from the middle of the fourteenth century, the sixteenth-century town hall, rebuilt in Baroque style, the Rococo-Neo-Classical administrative centre built in 1790 and the Jonáš Záborský

Theatre with its Neo-Classical façade. The town is the centre of the cultural and economic life in the northern part of East Slovakia and it is the heart of the Ukrainian national minority in Czechoslovakia.

On the way to Sabinov, a medieval trade centre with many interesting historic buildings and fortifications, we pass through the former royal town of Veľký Šariš which at one time became subject to Šariš Castle. All that remains to remind us of the town's former glory are the ruins of Rákóczy's Castle, where, in 1701, the Imperial forces captured Ferencz Rákóczy.

Bardejov, further to the north, is reached across the ridge of the Čerchov Hills. This historic urban reservation with its well-preserved fortifications, numerous bastions and Gothic as well as Renaissance burghers' houses, can also boast of a Gothic-Renaissance town hall from the years 1505 to 1509 with two gables and well-preserved Renaissance plaster work. The Church of St. Giles, built in Gothic style, dates from the thirteenth to the fifteenth century, and has rich furnishings with valuable paintings and sculptures on the altars. The Gothic monastery and Franciscan Church also date from the fifteenth century. Bardejov spa whose healing springs were already known in 1247, has been enhanced by the building of an open-air museum of East Slovak folk architecture. Many interesting buildings from the whole region have been transferred here. Remarkable, too, are the ruins of the frontier castle of Zborov overlooking the trade route into Poland. An alley of a hundred lime trees

252. Slovak open-air museum at Bardejov Spa

used to lead to the Renaissance chateau in the village beneath the castle. This was a favourite spot of Ferencz Rákóczy II who used to write his letters here, datelining them "Datum Zboroviae sub centum tiliis". Only part of this memorable alley survived the First World War. Nor was the region spared during the Second World War, which left a toll of many villages laid waste and countless graves. The great memorial to nine thousand Soviet dead at Svidník cemetery is a reminder for all time of the heroism of those who fought to destroy fascism.

Travelling through a romantic region dotted with wooden Orthodox churches, including the cupola church at Korejovce with its magnificent iconostasis dating from the second half of the eighteenth century, we come to Vyšný Komárnik. From the villages of Ladomirová and Nižný Komárnik, beneath the Dukla Pass there stretches the scene of the Carpathian Dukla military campaign in which three thousand Czechoslovak and Soviet soldiers laid down their lives in the common struggle during the Second World War. The heavy tanks and artillery placed in fighting positions, including a great deal of destroyed enemy equipment have a deep effect on all who come here to pay homage to the courageous liberators of the first stretches of Czechoslovakia. The central memorial at the Dukla Pass with its mausoleum and the figure of a Slovak mother offering flowers to a Soviet soldier eloquently express the gratitude of the Czech and Slovak people for the opportunity to develop the progressive legacy of the nations' past.

254. Part of the iconostasis in the Church of Our Lady at Korejovce

◀ *253. Wooden Orthodox Church of Our Lady at Korejovce*

255. *Morské Oko (Eye of the Sea) — natural lake in the Vihorlat Mountains*

NOTES TO THE ILLUSTRATIONS

where the original rotunda of St. Wenceslas once stood, the foundations of which were uncovered by archaeologists beneath the floor of St. Wenceslas's Chapel. The lower part of the walls of this place of worship are encrusted with jaspers and amethysts. The cycle of murals dating from the 1370's depicts the Passion of Christ. The murals over the cornice are the work of an early 16th-century Czech artist known as the Master of Litoměřice. In the foreground is a scene depicting the arrival of Prince Wenceslas at the Imperial Assembly in Regensburg.

18. The interior of the Vladislav Hall in the Royal Palace of Prague Castle. The Vladislav Hall was built at the turn of the 15th and 16th centuries by the court architect Benedict Ried (d.1534) for Vladislav Jagiello. It is 62 metres long and 16 metres wide and was roofed with a unique net vault with dynamic curving ribs. In some of the individual details of this part of Prague Castle Renaissance elements can be picked out. The hall was originally used for great celebrations and tournaments.

19. One of the curiosities of Prague is the Golden Lane in the precincts of Prague Castle — an odd grouping of tiny houses built over the years against the castle's northern fortification wall. In the reign of Rudolph II members of the castle guard and goldsmiths used to live here.

20. View of the Golden Lane with its mixture of Renaissance and Baroque houses, linked on the left by the covered gallery of the castle's peripheral fortification wall. In the background can be seen the Renaissance Queen Anne's Summer Palace known as the Belvedere.

21. The Renaissance Queen Anne's Summer Palace, the Belvedere, opens by means of an arcaded loggia into the royal garden. The palace was built by Ferdinand I and constructed according to a design by Paolo della Stella (d.1552). From Stella's workshop also came the Renaissance stone reliefs decorating the walls of the summer palace. The first floor with its keel-shaped roof was the work of Boniface Wohlmut from 1557—1565. The Belvedere was restored between 1953 and 1955. In front of it is the bronze "Singing Fountain" by Francesco Terzio, cast in 1564 by Tomáš Jaroš of Brno.

22. This diamond-studded monstrance is a unique example of the work of Baroque jewellers. It is part of the valuable collection of liturgical furnishings in the treasury of Prague's Loreto.

23. The front of the Loreto Church at Hradčany occupies the eastern side of Loreto Square, one of the most enchanting spots in Prague. The complex of the Loreto monastery came into being in the course of the seventeenth and the first half of the eighteenth century. Its façade was built from 1720 to 1722 by Kilián Ignác Dientzenhofer (1689—1751), the most outstanding architect of Prague Baroque. The Loreto is famous not only for its treasury, but also for its chimes.

24. Master of the Třeboň Altarpiece: "The Resurrection of Christ". Altarpiece. Canvas on fir panel, about 1380. National Gallery, Prague.

25. Master of the Lamentation of Žebrák: "The Lamentation of Christ of Žebrák". Relief carved in lime wood, about 1510. National Gallery, Prague.

26. On the terraces beneath Prague Castle there are many picturesque gardens. Among the most charming are the Kolovrat Garden and the Ledeburg Garden with its *salla terrena*, built by G. Santini in 1712—1713.

27. From the heights above the left bank of the River Vltava there is an enchanting view of the Old Town situated on the right bank. Among the houses rise the towers of many churches, the most striking of which is the Gothic Týn Church. The Vltava is spanned by many bridges. In the foreground is the Mánes Bridge and behind it the Gothic Charles Bridge dating from the second half of the fourteenth century.

28. Charles Bridge in Prague, linking the Old Town with the Lesser Town, was built on the orders of Emperor Charles IV under the direction of Peter Parler. It replaced the Romanesque Judith Bridge destroyed by floods in 1342. The bridge is adorned by thirty statues or groups of statuary, mostly dating from the seventeenth and the first half of the eighteenth century, creating a kind of gallery of Czech Baroque sculpture. Among the most striking works of eighteenth-century Czech sculpture is the statue of St. Lutgard (right), an early work of Matthias Bernard Braun dating from 1710.

29. Passing over Charles Bridge and through the gateway of the Old Town Bridge Tower, one comes to the Square of the Knights Hospitallers on the right bank of the River Vltava. The great bridge tower was built by Peter Parler's lodge at the end of the fourteenth and the beginning of the fifteenth century. The tower is richly decorated with sculpture which was partially damaged when the Swedes attacked the Old Town in 1648. In memory of the attack which was repulsed a plaque was placed in the wall by the Prague burghers between 1650 and 1654. To the left of the tower, the Old Town bridgehead is closed on one side by the Monastery of the Knights Hospitallers and the Church of St. Francis, the oldest building in Prague topped with a cupola. It was built between 1679—1689 according to the plans of G. B. Mathey.

30. The Old-New Synagogue in the Old Town of Prague is an early-Gothic double-naved building dating from the end of the third quarter of the thirteenth century. It is one of the very few buildings that remain to recall what was once the Jewish Town. In the background is the Rococo building which used to be the Jewish Town Hall and dates from the second half of the eighteenth century.

31. The Old Jewish Cemetery in Prague originated in the fifteenth century. It was gradually extended. Today this comparatively small area contains more than twenty thousand tombstones. They range

from simple tablets to great stone tombs of important personalities of Prague's Jewish community from the fifteenth to the eighteenth century.

32. The dominant feature of Prague's Old Town Square is the complex of the Old Town Hall and the Church of Our Lady Before Týn. In the left foreground can be seen a detail of the ancient astronomical clock originally constructed at the beginning of the fifteenth century and frequently rebuilt and restored afterwards. The calendar plaque with its circular pictures representing the months of the year is the work of the painter Josef Mánes from 1865. In the background is the twin-towered front of the Týn Church built on the site of an older church by Peter Parler and his lodge in the second half of the fourteenth century and completed during the fifteenth century.

33. Statues of antique gods and goddesses decorating the garden stairway of the early Baroque villa at Troja, Prague. The statuary from 1685 to 1703 is the work of Johann Georg and Paul Heermann.

34. The Emmaus Church of Our Lady and the Slav Patron-saints from the second half of the fourteenth century. The architecture of the spire-like construction is the work of the contemporary architect, F. M. Černý, carried out from 1964 to 1967.

35. The new Czechoslovak Television Centre at Kavčí Hory, Prague, is an outstanding example of modern Czechoslovak architecture.

36. Prague and the River Vltava. To the left, above the Gothic Charles Bridge, can be seen Petřín Hill balanced on the other side by the complex of Prague Castle with the towers of St. Vitus's Cathedral and the twin towers of the Romanesque basilica of St. George. In the Lesser Town beneath the castle can be seen the great dome of St. Nicholas's Church, built by Kryštof and Kilián Ignác Dientzenhofer in the first half of the 18th century. The belfry is the work of Anselmo Lurago.

37. The Great and Little Blaník Hills which are closely linked with the history of the Czech nation and enveloped in legends rise up over fields, woods and meadows in the south-eastern part of Central Bohemia.

38. Křivoklát Castle, lying in the hilly country which was a favourite hunting ground of Czech rulers, was known as far back as the beginning of the twelfth century. During the reign of Wenceslas I (d.1253) and Přemysl Otakar II (1253—1278), the small wooden castle was rebuilt into a splendid early Gothic residence, later undergoing late Gothic restorations at the end of the fifteenth and the beginning of the sixteenth century.

39. Křivoklát — the castle chapel. This chapel is the result of late Gothic restoration work. It was roofed with net-vaulting and richly decorated with stonework of fantastic and naturalistic forms. The east end of the chapel contains a late Gothic winged altarpiece dating from after 1490. The architecture of the altarpiece culminates in the richly carved superstructure.

40. The Prague Gate at Rakovník — the work of master-builders Jan and Jakub Městecký — was part of the partially preserved medieval town fortifications. It was restored in 1903.

41. Krakovec Castle, south of Rakovník, was built in the 1380's. It is an outstanding work from the circle of the court lodge of King Wenceslas IV. John Huss stayed at Krakovec Castle before making his last journey to Constance.

42. The confluence of Bohemia's two greatest rivers, the Elbe and the Vltava, is a state nature reservation with many moisture-loving types of plants and marshy virgin forests.

43. Gothic stained glass window with the figure of The Man of Sorrows from Slivenec parish Church is a typical example of the so-called "Beautiful Style" from around the year 1400. Applied Arts Museum, Prague.

44. The deanery Church of St. Bartholomew at Kolín. The three early Gothic hall-type naves with two west towers were built in the second half of the thirteenth century. After a great fire in the middle of the fourteenth century, the original presbytery was replaced, under Peter Parler's direction, by a cathedral choir with a system of flying buttresses and a ring of chapels. The bell-tower dates from 1504.

45. The town of Nymburk was founded before the year 1276 by Přemysl Otakar II near a ford crossing the River Elbe. The greater part of the imposing ring of peripheral fortifications with brick walls, dating from the fourteenth century and strengthened with a number of prismatic towers, have been preserved to this day. The large parish church towering above the town's fortifications was built in red brick, which is typical for medieval architecture of this town, during the thirteenth and fourteenth centuries.

46. Kutná Hora miners receiving their mining charter from King Wenceslas II. Miniature from a copy of the Kutná Hora Mining Charter of 1525. State Library of Czechoslovakia, Prague.

47. The Gothic Church of St. Barbara at Kutná Hora is one of the main landmarks of this famous medieval mining town. This huge five-naved structure with its cathedral ambulatory was started in the fourteenth century. After a pause during the Hussite Wars, it was completed by Matthias Rejsek and Benedict Ried who, at the beginning of the sixteenth century, roofed the three hall-type naves with a dynamic net-vaulting. The space in front of the Cathedral is occupied by the large early Baroque building of the Jesuit College dating from the second half of the seventeenth century.

48. The Italian Court at Kutná Hora was founded by King Wenceslas II (d.1305). The tremendous wealth of the Kutná Hora silver mines was concentrated here. It was in workshops on the ground floor of the Italian Court that the famous Prague *groschen* were minted from Kutná Hora silver. The Italian Court was adapted by King Wenceslas IV (1378—1419). The chapel with its articulated bay

and the vaulted halls in the first floor date from the same period.

49. Konopiště Castle is situated to the south of Prague and was founded in the second half of the thirteenth century. The original early Gothic building was remarkable for its powerful towers which defended the entire area of the castle. It received its present form during restoration work carried out after 1887 at the expense of the new owner of the estate, the Archduke Francis Ferdinand d'Este, according to the plans of the architect J. Mocker. Access to the castle is provided by a Baroque gateway adorned with works of sculpture by Matthias Bernard Braun.

50. Konopiště — the great hall with frescoes by J. Lux on the ceiling. Restoration work carried out after 1887 gave Konopiště its present character of a splendid residence. The heir to the Austro-Hungarian throne, Francis Ferdinand d'Este, built up a great collection of paintings, works of sculpture, weapons, furniture and various examples of arts and crafts with which he filled the luxuriously furnished chambers of the castle.

51. A canyon carved by the Berounka River close to Srbsko in the Bohemian Karst with interesting warmth-loving steppeland and woodland flora.

52. The royal Castle of Karlštejn, built from 1348 to 1357 by King and Emperor Charles IV as a splendid residence and a treasury for the Imperial crown jewels.

53. Master Theodoric: "St. Jerome" — a Gothic panel painting decorating the Chapel of the Holy Rood at Karlštejn Castle. Beech wood. Before 1365.

54. The Chapel of the Holy Rood in the main tower of Karlštejn Castle, with its original decoration and a unique collection of 129 panel paintings by the court painter of Emperor Charles IV, Master Theodoric. The chapel was built as a treasury for the Imperial jewels and Charles's collection of holy relics.

55. The mill at Bláhova Lhota near Sedlčany — a timber-framed building dating from the beginning of the seventeenth century, with late Gothic portals brought from elsewhere, is a typical example of the folk architecture of the south of Central Bohemia.

56. The huge Baroque Chateau of Dobříš was built in 1745—1765 according to a design by the French architect Jules Robert de Cotte (1683—1767). Before the part of the chateau facing the gardens is a French terraced park. The fountain with statues representing gods of the water is the work of the Prague sculptor Ignác Platzer (1717—1787).

57. The vast artificial lake formed by Orlík dam on the middle reaches of the River Vltava, surrounded by beautiful scenery is a Mecca for tourists, especially in the summer months.

58. The royal Castle of Zvíkov was built on a headland over the confluence of the Rivers Vltava and Otava. Its setting on steep granite rocks made this castle an impregnable fortress accessible only from the south along a narrow isthmus between the two rivers. The extensive royal palace with its arcaded courtyard was built in the 50's and 60's of the thirteenth century, during the reign of King Přemysl Otakar II. The main defences of the castle, including a powerful keep with a wedge, date from the same period. The upper floor of the tower, in Renaissance style, is from the end of the sixteenth century. In the foreground can be seen the fourteenth-century outer gateway.

59. Žďákov Bridge — a modern steel construction with a single span 100 metres above the bottom of Orlík reservoir.

60. The town of Písek was founded before the year 1254, possibly towards the end of the reign of King Wenceslas I (d.1253). But the real builder of the town was Přemysl Otakar II (1253—1278). Most of the early Gothic buildings in Písek date from that time. In the foreground of the picture can be seen the stone bridge over the River Otava from the third quarter of the thirteenth century, the oldest bridge in the Czech Lands. Above the bridge is the former royal castle, built when the town was first established. The most striking feature of the town is the tall tower of the deanery church attached to the early Gothic building at the end of the fifteenth century. To the left are the two towers of the Baroque town hall, built in the 1750's.

61. The town of Tábor in South Bohemia became famous in the fifteenth century as the centre of the Hussite revolutionary movement. The western side of Tábor's main square is occupied by the late Gothic town hall, completed at the beginning of the sixteenth century. It received its present form when Neo-Gothic restoration work was carried out by the architect Niklas. The town hall now houses the Museum of the Hussite Revolutionary Movement.

62. Tábor — Bechyně Gate and the Kotnov castle tower which is the only witness to the town's most distant past. It was part of the castle of the Lords of Ústí, built here in the first quarter of the fourteenth century. The Bechyně Gate was built later when the Hussite town of Tábor was fortified in the fifteenth century to withstand the attacks of enemies of the Hussite movement.

63. Czechoslovakia's biggest fishpond — Rožmberk Pond in the Třeboň area, covering an area of 711 hectares, was constructed in 1584—1590 by the designer of the entire system of South Bohemian ponds, the Regent of the Rožmberk estates, Jakub Krčín of Jelčany. Its great dyke, lined with centuries-old lime trees, is two and a half kilometres long, ten metres high and up to fifty metres wide.

64. The South Bohemian town of Třeboň is famous for the beauty of its surroundings and its wealth of historic buildings among which are the town's late Gothic fortifications including well-preserved gunbastions and gates. They date from 1525—1527.

65. The original early Gothic Castle of Jindřichův Hradec, built in the thirteenth century, was reconstructed in the second half of the sixteenth century

into a comfortable Renaissance residence for the Lords of Hradec.

66. The diamond vaulting in the entrance hall of House No. 46 at Slavonice in the south-eastern part of South Bohemia is evidence of advanced late Gothic architecture of the first quarter of the sixteenth century. The little town of Slavonice, lying close to the Austrian frontier, is famous for its late Gothic and Renaissance burghers' houses.

67. Slavonice, a Gothic and Renaissance town on the old provincial frontier route. The houses on the square have richly decorated attics and gables, their façades are adorned with graffito work dating from the second half of the sixteenth century.

68. Zbudov Moor, typical South Bohemian moorland north of České Budějovice.

69. Hluboká Castle — originally an early Gothic royal castle from the thirteenth century — was rebuilt from 1841 to 1871 by the architects F. Beer and D. Deworetzský in English Tudor Gothic style. Its interior is filled with paintings, works of statuary and valuable furniture.

70. The reception hall of Hluboká Castle with its period furnishings, ebony furniture and a portrait of Princess Paulina Schwarzenberg.

71. Unknown master: "Virgin and Child". Panel painting from the Hospital Church of the Holy Trinity in České Budějovice, an outstanding example of Czech Gothic panel painting from the early fifteenth century. Mikoláš Aleš Gallery, Hluboká.

72. České Budějovice. Late Gothic armoury with a stepped gable and a shooting gallery, later used as a store-house for salt. In the neighbourhood is part of the Dominican monastery with the Church of the Presentation of Our Lady, founded in 1265 on orders from King Přemysl Otakar II.

73. The great even-sided square in České Budějovice, the metropolis of South Bohemia, is one of the biggest squares in Europe. It came into being at the same time as the town, in the year 1265. České Budějovice was always the main bastion of royal power in South Bohemia. The Baroque fountain with the figure of Samson taming a lion is the work of F. Baugut and J. Dietrich.

74. Český Krumlov, a historic town with a large castle, used to be the economic, administrative and cultural centre of the extensive feudal estates of the Rožmberks, a south Bohemian noble family. Countless historic buildings and unspoilt surroundings all go to create the unique atmosphere of this town.

75. The former Cistercian abbey of Zlatá Koruna (Golden Crown) founded by the Czech King Přemysl Otakar II in 1263. The vast complex of monastery buildings with the monumental Abbey Church was built in the second half of the thirteenth century and in the fourteenth century.

76. The monastery library at Vyšší Brod, founded in 1757. The frescoes on the ceiling dating from the beginning of the nineteenth century are the work of L. Vávra. The original cabinets contain valuable old manuscripts and printed books.

77. "Missale pro prelatis pontificantibus", the initial "I" with a fictitious portrait of a Benedictine Abbot kneeling before St. John the Evangelist. Below, on the shield, is the emblem of the donor, the head of a Moor with long ears. A miniature from around 1400. The manuscript, which belonged to Vyšší Brod Monastery, is now in the library of the National Museum, Prague.

78. The pilgrimage Church of Our Lady at Kájov, with two hall-type naves, dating from 1471—1485, is among the finest examples of South Bohemian late Gothic, typical of which is the use of two-naved halls.

79. Lipno reservoir on the upper reaches of the River Vltava. This great expanse of water amidst the mountains of the southern part of the Šumava range is the biggest lake in Czechoslovakia. Its beautiful surroundings attract countless tourists.

80. The vaulting of the nave and presbytery of the Church of St. Mary Magdalene at Chvalšiny is among the finest examples of South Bohemian late Gothic architecture.

81. Prachatice, a historic town on the Golden Route, was, until the seventeenth century, an important centre of the salt trade. Later stagnation of the town meant that individual houses and the town centre as a whole were not reconstructed and therefore they have kept their medieval and Renaissance appearance. The north-eastern part of the square contains the oldest stone houses dating from the fifteenth century. In the background is the late Gothic parish church of St. James.

82. A farmer's house at Volary, a typical mountain timber construction of the alpine type, its living quarters and farm buildings creating a single unit under one roof.

83. Boubín — a mountain in the Šumava range (1362 m) — above the valley of the Teplá (Warm) Vltava. On its south-western slopes is a mountainous virgin forest containing fir and pine trees, some of them as much as from 300 to 400 years old. State nature reservation.

84. Peat bog near Kvilda with its rare moorland flora.

85. The little mountain River Vydra is the principal source of the River Otava. Its rocky bed creates many rapids and cascades.

86. The Renaissance town hall at Kašperské Hory dating from 1597. At the end of the seventeenth century, it acquired three Baroque gables topped with little turrets. It is the most attractive building in this small town deep in the Šumava Mountains.

87. Ruins of the royal Castle of Kašperk in the midst of the wooded summits of the Ždánovské Hills. It was built for King and Emperor Charles IV from 1356 to 1361 by Vít Hedvábný. The powerful castle served to defend the nearby gold mines and the not far distant provincial frontier.

88. The village of Albrechtice near Sušice in the Šumava foothills with its small early Gothic church of Our Lady, built in the thirteenth century.

89. The square at Sušice, a town giving access to the

central part of the Šumava Mountains. The façade of the medieval deanery (left) ends in a high, late Renaissance attic; the Rozacín House (right) is decorated with graffiti dating from around the year 1600. In the background is the tower of the parish church, topped with an articulated Baroque dome.

90. Rábí, a fourteenth- and fifteenth-century Gothic castle with a cleverly planned system of fortifications, was built to protect an important trade route and the gold beds of the River Otava. Its silhouette dominates the surrounding landscape.

91. Panorama of the Šumava range as seen from the wooded summit of Mount Pancíř, not far from Železná Ruda.

92. Železná Ruda, a summer and winter sports resort in the western part of the Šumava range. The Church of Our Lady of Assistance, dating from 1727—1732, is a central structure with a twelve-sided ground-plan and an onion-shaped dome.

93. The royal town of Klatovy in the Šumava foothills was founded in the sixties of the thirteenth century on orders from King Přemysl Otakar II. The town is dominated by the Renaissance Black Tower (1547—1557) which is adjoined by the town hall. To the left are the towers of the Baroque Jesuit Church which is among Klatovy's finest historic buildings.

94. Domažlice, a town established near the provincial route and the toll houses by King Přemysl Otakar II around the year 1260. The elongated town square is lined with gabled Baroque houses and the high cylindrical tower of the deanery Church of the Birth of the Virgin Mary, built immediately after the foundation of the town.

95. Republic Square in Pilsen is the centre of the metropolis of the West Bohemian region, founded at the end of the thirteenth century. In the centre of the square stands the Gothic deanery church of St. Bartholomew, built in the fourteenth century. On the north side is the town hall dating from 1559, a fine example of Czech early Renaissance.

96. Kozel Castle near Šťáhlavy was built from 1784 to 1789 for Count Černín by the Prague master-builder, Wenceslas Haberditz. It is decorated in Louis Seize style. The author of the ornamental and figural paintings within the castle was the Prague artist A. Tuvora (1787—1788). The picture shows the main hall of the castle with its Rococo furniture and murals.

97. The late Neo-Classical Castle of Kynžvart near Marienbad, built between 1833 and 1839. An originally Baroque building, it was restored by the architect Petro Nobile as a summer residence for the Austrian State Chancellor, Metternich.

98. The West Bohemian town of Cheb is famous for its many fine examples of ancient architecture. Best known are the group of Gothic houses, dating from the end of the fourteenth century and known as the "Špalíček", with partially timbered walls and with façades subjected only to minor adaptations. The fountain with the statue of Roland dates from 1591.

99. This little Baroque cabinet, inlaid with a mosaic of wood from about the year 1650, is a typical example of the work of seventeenth-century cabinet-makers in Cheb. Applied Arts Museum, Prague.

100. Marienbad (Mariánské Lázně) in West Bohemia, has been famous as a watering-place since the beginning of the nineteenth century. The Neo-Classical Colonnade of the Ferdinand Spring was built in 1826—1827.

101. Soos Moor, a state nature reserve in the valley of Vonšovský Brook. An interesting phenomenon here are the "marshy volcanoes", mofettes, from which emanates carbon dioxide.

102. Loket-on-Ohře Castle in North-West Bohemia was built by Czech kings as early as the first half of the thirteenth century. The castle was reconstructed during the reign of Wenceslas IV (about the year 1390). Today it houses a museum of porcelain. The town beneath the castle is a historic urban reservation with a number of fine burghers' houses.

103. Porcelain vase from the late Rococo period, gilded and painted with a floral design. Stará Role, near Carlsbad (about 1850). From the collection of the Applied Arts Museum, Prague.

104. Carlsbad (Karlovy Vary), the world famous spa with rich thermal springs. The town was established in 1358 by King and Emperor Charles IV. The majority of the buildings in the town which form the typical Carlsbad panorama date from the end of the nineteenth and the beginning of the twentieth centuries. The twin-spired Baroque church (left) was built by Kilián Ignác Dientzenhofer between 1731 and 1737.

105. The Baroque Castle of Libochovice on the left bank of the River Ohře. This four-winged building enclosing a rectangular courtyard is the work of the architect A. Porta from 1682—1690. The decorative façade of the building faces an extensive park.

106. The Ohře valley close to Kadaň.

107. The deanery church of St. Nicholas at Louny with three hall-type naves and a net-vaulting is among the finest examples of Czech late Gothic. It was built in 1520—1538.

108. The Romanesque crypt of the Premonstratensian Abbey Church at Doksany dating from the period after the year 1200, is roofed with original cross-vaulting supported by single and double columns and pillars.

109. Mount Říp is linked with many legends about the beginnings of Czech history. On the summit of this basalt hill stands the Romanesque rotunda of St. George built in 1126 by Prince Soběslav to commemorate the victory of Czech troops at the Battle of Chlumec.

110. The Master of the Litoměřice Altarpiece: "Christ before Caiaphas". Detail of a wing of the wooden altarpiece, after 1500. Regional Gallery, Litoměřice.

111. Litoměřice with its picturesque setting on the right bank of the River Elbe is one of the oldest towns in Bohemia. The dominant feature of Litoměřice is the early Baroque episcopal Church of St. Stephen,

built between 1663 and 1670 by D. Orsi and G. Broggio.

112. Milešovka, the highest hill in the Central Bohemian Highlands (837 m), a wooded cone-shaped hill with a botanical reservation. The view from Milešovka is one of the loveliest in Central Europe.

113. The Holy Trinity column in the castle square at Teplice, dating from 1718. The dramatic liveliness of the whole composition, of the individual statues and details, shows that this is the work of the great Czech Baroque sculptor, M. B. Braun.

114. Pravčická Gate, a sandstone rock formation in what is known as the Czech-Saxon Switzerland, close to Hřensko. It is one of the most interesting natural formations in this area.

115. Early Gothic royal Castle of Bezděz dating from 1264—1279, and founded by Přemysl Otakar II, is situated on a high hill dominating the surrounding landscape. The palace and castle chapel are among the finest examples of Czech early Gothic.

116. Television centre and hotel on the summit of Mount Ještěd near Liberec. Designed by the architects K. Hubáček and Z. Patrmann. An example of modern Czechoslovak architecture, 1969.

117. Valley of the River Jizera near Spálov above Železný Brod with the typical scenery of the surroundings.

118. The orangery in the park of the romantic Chateau of Sychrov near Turnov. The structure was built in 1852 in Neo-Renaissance style by Josef Pruvot, architect to the noble family of Rohan. The chateau was also constructed in the nineteenth century, according to a design of the architect B. Grueber.

119. North Bohemian landscape near Česká Lípa.

120. The Lord's Rock in the eastern part of the Central Bohemian Highlands. The remnants of a basalt rock form a group of three-sided to sexagonal columns which were easily broken off during quarrying. State nature reserve.

121. The Gothic Castle of Frýdlant, built in the second half of the thirteenth century, underwent several stages of reconstruction which gave the castle complex its present appearance. It won fame as the titular seat of the Duchy of Frýdlant, belonging to the military leader during the Thirty Years' War, Albrecht of Wallenstein. The castle's halls contain a rare collection of paintings, arms and furniture.

122. Trosky, a picturesque ruined Gothic castle in the central part of the Czech Paradise. The castle was built in the second half of the fourteenth century.

123. Kost Castle, built from the fourteenth to the sixteenth century — a powerful Gothic-Renaissance fortress with residential quarters in the White Tower. In the Šelmberk Palace within the castle is a gallery of Czech late Gothic art.

124. Dlask farmstead, No. 12 at Dolánky near Turnov. A two-storey framed structure dating from 1716, it is a typical example of folk architecture in the Czech Paradise where wooden beams, lengthwise ground-plan, and side-balconies on the first floor facing on to the courtyard are common.

125. Prachovské Rocks create a strange town of sandstone rock formations with canyons and mazes, caves and needle-like projections, as well as enormous boulders. The entire area of Prachovské Rocks has been declared a state nature reserve.

126. The village of Ústí near Stará Paka with its framed cottages.

127. Kuks in East Bohemia is one of the most valuable historic reservations in the Czech Lands. It is famous for the collection of statues by Matthias Bernard Braun who also carved his "Allegory of Slyness" from a series of depictions of the vices outside the Kuks hospital. Sandstone. About 1719.

128. The Kuks Hospital with the Church of the Holy Trinity, built according to a design by G. B. Alliprandi in 1707—1716 for Count F. A. Sporck is among the finest and unique examples of Czech Baroque. The terraces in front of the hospital are adorned with the allegorical groups of statuary representing the vices, virtues and blessings, by the greatest of Czech Baroque sculptors, M. B. Braun.

129. Bethlehem Wood near Kuks is filled with outstanding works by the sculptor Matthias Bernard Braun and his workshop. "The Nativity". Relief carving of a biblical scene. Sandstone. 1726—1731.

130. Baroque goblet with a mythological scene representing the tritons is a typical example of Czech Baroque glass. The painting on glass with black fired colour is the work of Ignác Preissler. East Bohemia, about 1725. Applied Arts Museum, Prague.

131. The Krkonoše (Giant) Mountains, the highest range in the Czech Lands. View from Sněžka (Snow Peak) to Obří (Giant's) Chalet. The altitude of Sněžka — 1603 m — indicates that the Giant Mountains are of medium height. They are a centre for winter sports and for climbs and rambles all the year round. They are a protected mountain area.

132. Teplice Rocks near the upper reaches of the River Metuje. These strange formations are the result of the deep erosion of sandstone boulders. A state nature reserve.

133. Otto Gutfreund: "Granny" — sandstone memorial in Ratibořice Valley near Česká Skalice, the setting of the story *Granny* by the Czech authoress, Božena Němcová.

134. The square at Náchod with the deanery Church of St. Lawrence. The towers, known as Adam and Eve, have wooden upper floors. Above is the Renaissance-Baroque castle which contains a splendid collection of Brussels tapestries.

135. Renaissance houses in the square at Nové Město-on-Metuje which originated in the mid-sixteenth century. To the left is the tower of the Renaissance castle. The town was founded in the year 1501. After a fire in 1526 it was rebuilt as a single urban unit in the Renaissance style. For its purity of style

it is a splendid example of Central European architecture.

136. Wooden Church of St. John the Baptist at Slavoňov dating from 1553. The interior is adorned with rustic folk paintings. The prismatic bell-tower was built at the same time as the church.

137. Gothic brick Church of the Holy Spirit, dating from the fourteenth and fifteenth centuries at Hradec Králové. The long three naves are roofed with cross-ribbed vaulting supported by three pairs of pillars.

138. The square at Hradec Králové with the old town hall, sixteenth-century White Tower and the Church of the Holy Spirit.

139. The Gothic-Renaissance Castle of Kunětická Hora near Pardubice. The oldest part of the building was constructed after the year 1491 when the castle was bought by William of Pernštejn. Thus a large late Gothic fortress came into being, which dominated the surrounding landscape along the River Elbe from the high hill on which it was set. The halls of the castle are roofed with interesting diamond vaulting. The castle was restored according to the plans of the architect Dušan Jurkovič.

140. Kunvald, a village in the Orlické (Eagle) Mountains where, in 1457, the Czech Reformed Church of the Unity of Bohemian Brethren was established. Among its leading representatives in the seventeenth century was Jan Amos Komenský (Comenius).

141. The Renaissance town hall in the East Bohemian town of Chrudim, built in 1560. The plague column dedicated to the Transfiguration of Our Lord dates from 1719—1734.

142. The entrance to the Castle of Litomyšl, built between 1568 and 1573 by the Imperial architects, G. B. Avostalis de Sala and O. Avostalis for Vratislav of Pernstein. The castle has an arcaded courtyard and interesting graffito decorations. It was in the Baroque brewery, opposite the castle, that the great Czech composer, Bedřich Smetana, was born in 1824.

143. Brno, the historic capital city of Moravia with its Gothic, Renaissance and Baroque buildings. Dominating the town, an important industrial centre, are Špilberk Fortress and Petrov Hill where the Church of St. Peter and St. Paul stands.

144. The courtyard of the Moravian Museum in Brno, once the Dietrichstein Palace, and the Baroque fountain with the statue of Mercury by the sculptor Ignác Bendl (1693—1699). In the background is the Church of St. Peter and St. Paul, the oldest part of which was built at the beginning of the fourteenth century. It was restored in the nineteenth century.

145. Master of the Rajhrad Altarpiece: "Bearing of the Cross". Panel of the Rajhrad Altarpiece. Canvas on fir panel, tempera. Before 1420. Moravian Gallery, Brno. The Master of the Rajhrad Altarpiece was an outstanding Czech panel painter of the pre-Hussite period.

146. Golden pendant with an almandine and pearls. Culture of the Great Moravian Empire. A find from Mikulčice. Moravian Museum, Brno. The rich archaeological finds from South Moravia provide evidence of the high level of culture of the inhabitants of the Great Moravian Empire in the ninth and at the beginning of the tenth century.

147. Renaissance garden of Telč Castle which was founded in the second half of the sixteenth century. The garden is enclosed by the wings of the castle's arcades. The presbytery of the chapel also faces the garden. Telč Castle is one of the finest examples of Czech Renaissance art. From the sixties of the sixteenth century the Rožmberk master-builder, Balthazar Maio da Ronio, worked here.

148. Telč, a Gothic-Renaissance town in South Moravia, has an elongated town square lined with the façades of houses that have Renaissance attics, Baroque gables and medieval arcades. The historic urban reservation of the South Moravian town of Telč is a great attraction for art lovers because of the number of ancient buildings that have been preserved in such a compact arrangement.

149. The residential palace of Pernštejn Castle. The castle was founded in the second half of the thirteenth century as a feudal fortress perched high on a headland. It was rebuilt in late Gothic style at the end of the fifteenth and in the first half of the sixteenth century. Its fine architecture is enhanced by valuable paintings and works of sculpture.

150. The Cistercian abbey at Žďár-on-Sázava was founded in the mid-thirteenth century. After the year 1254, its early Gothic church was built. This was rebuilt in Baroque-Gothic by G. Santini in the first half of the eighteenth century.

151. The Moravian Karst. A system of underground and surface Karst formations with caves, the subterranean River Punkva and the Macocha Abyss, 138 metres deep.

152. The caves of the Moravian Karst have beautiful and interesting stalactite and stalagmite formations.

153. The modern altar in the Baroque Church of St. Peter and St. Paul at Jedovnice near Blansko is the work of the Prague painter M. Medek and the sculptor J. Koblasa from 1966.

154. The Church of the Birth of Our Lady at Křtiny originated in the years 1728—1750, according to a design by G. Santini. It is one of the finest examples of dynamic Baroque to be found in Moravia. Some of Moravia's outstanding eighteenth-century artists were responsible for its interior decoration.

155. The minaret in the castle park at Lednice, South Moravia. It was built in Moorish style for the Princes of Liechtenstein by J. Hardtmuth between 1797 and 1802, and is one of many buildings that adorn the vast park of Lednice Castle.

156. The wine cellars in the ancient Moravian-Slovakian wine-growing village of Petrov near Strážnice. The façades of the cellars are decorated with motifs from local folklore.

157. The River Dyje near Mušov. In the background

are the limestone Pavlovské Hills, part of the outer branch of the Carpathians.

158. Windmill at Kuželov in Moravian Slovakia dating from 1842. It is one of the most interesting examples of Moravian folk architecture.

159. Milotice near Kyjov. The original Renaissance castle was rebuilt in the course of the seventeenth and eighteenth centuries as an ostentatious Baroque noble residence for the Serényi family. J. Emanuel Fischer, son of the famous Johann Bernard Fischer of Erlach, probably had a hand in planning the restoration.

160. The Peace Mound near the village of Práce. Memorial to unknown soldiers who laid down their lives in the Battle of the Three Emperors at Slavkov (Austerlitz) in 1805. Built in 1911—1912 according to a design by the architect J. Fanta. The statuary was the work of the sculptor Č. Vosmík.

161. The Gothic Castle of Buchlov with remains of late Romanesque and early Gothic structures used to guard Moravia's frontier. This powerful Moravian medieval fortress was built before the middle of the thirteenth century. Later it underwent several phases of restoration.

162. The Vassals' Hall of the Archbishop's Palace at Kroměříž with frescoes by F. A. Maulbertsch, dating from 1759, which are among the finest examples of Central European Rococo. The stucco decoration of the walls which bears all the marks of Viennese Rococo of the time of Maria Theresa is of a later date.

163. The Baroque cemetery at Střílky (1730—1743). The unique layout is enhanced by statues of angels, symbols of faith, hope and charity, as well as allegorical depictions of the virtues and vices, and stone vases with reliefs. The sculptor is B. Fritsch.

164. Gottwaldov, a modern city with a vast footwear industry. It embodies a remarkable town-planning concept, combining the city with its green setting. The individual buildings and their surroundings are both functional and aesthetic, and residential districts blend harmoniously into the factory areas.

165. One of North Moravia's most striking towns is Olomouc which is the centre of the surrounding district. The centre of Olomouc itself is the square with its Gothic-Renaissance town hall and medieval astronomical clock dating from the end of the fifteenth century. The group of statuary representing the Holy Trinity, by V. Render from the years 1716—1754, is a fine example of Baroque art.

166. Master of the Torun Madonna: "Virgin and Child", known as the "Šternberk Madonna". Limestone. In the collection of the state Castle of Šternberk, Moravia. This statue is among the finest works of the so-called "Beautiful Style" from the turn of the fourteenth and fifteenth centuries.

167. The Gothic Castle of Bouzov, built around 1300. During the Thirty Years' War it was destroyed by Swedish troops. It was rebuilt between 1896 and 1912 in Neo-Gothic romantic style as an ostentatious residence of the Order of Teutonic Knights.

168. Renaissance chateau at Velké Losiny on the southern slopes of the Jeseníky Mountains. The original building was constructed from 1580 to 1589. It was enlarged at the end of the seventeenth century by the addition of three early Baroque wings, the buildings of which were used for economic purposes. The original style of the interior is unusually well preserved.

169. Velké Losiny. The courtyard of the chateau with its two-storey arcaded galleries bears a distinct resemblance to Italian Renaissance.

170. Červenohorské sedlo (Red Mountain Saddle) 1010 m — a centre for tourists and winter sports enthusiasts, the starting-point for trips along the main ridge of the Jeseníky.

171. Praděd (1492 m), the highest mountain of the Jeseníky range. It is a centre of a popular North Moravian recreational area.

172. The Castle of Hradec, near Opava, famous for the fact that Beethoven stayed there. The Neo-Gothic brick gateway dates from the end of the nineteenth century. Several earlier restorations of the castle, which is surrounded by an extensive English-style park, have left valuable architectural monuments of Gothic, Renaissance, Baroque and Neo-Classical styles.

173. The romantic valley of the River Moravice set in the framework of deciduous woods.

174. Ostrava, North Moravia's largest city, is the centre of hard coal mining and of the metallurgical industry.

175. The little wooden sixteenth-century Church of St. Catherine at Ostrava-Hrabová — one of the few historic buildings preserved in the Ostrava area.

176. Nový Jičín was founded on an ancient route linking Olomouc with Cracow. The north-eastern side of the square with the "Old Post Office" was built in 1563 in Tuscan Renaissance style. The two-storey loggia has archivolts faced with carved stone. In the background can be seen the Renaissance church tower dating from 1587—1618. The Mary column (right) dates from 1710.

177. Štramberk. A town known as the "Moravian Bethlehem" contains a number of timbered Walachian houses which give the whole town a most picturesque appearance. It is dominated by a tall cylindrical watch-tower, once part of the seignorial castle, built in the first half of the fourteenth century.

178. The western part of the Carpathians, the Moravian-Silesian Beskydy Mountains, with the Lysá Hora group (1324 m). The mountainous vegetation consists of extensive mixed woods and rare flora.

179. Rožnov-under-Radhošť. The Walachian Open-air Museum with its collection of typical folk architecture from the Beskydy ethnographical area.

Slovakia:

180. Slovak landscape with the peaks of the High Tatra mountains.

181. Bratislava lies in the western part of the Danubian lowlands. This strategically important site, guarding the left bank of the Danube, was already inhabited in the very distant past. The first to settle here were Celtic tribes and then the Romans. In the tenth and eleventh centuries this was one of the centres of the Great Moravian Empire. Today it is the capital city of the Slovak Socialist Republic. The historic core of this former free royal town contains many treasures of architecture. The city of Bratislava is dominated by its castle, once the seat of provincial rulers, beneath which rises St. Martin's Church. Here, the kings of Hungary were crowned until the middle of the nineteenth century.

182. First mention of Bratislava Castle dates from 907 A.D. But its site has a much older history. Archaeological research has recently brought to light traces of ninth-century Slav fortified settlement. In the course of the fifteenth century, a great Gothic castle was built on the site of earlier structures. Rebuilding continued in the sixteenth and seventeenth centuries. After the middle of the eighteenth century considerable reconstruction was carried out on the orders of the Empress Maria Theresa. Among the architects to have a hand in the work were J. N. Jadot, N. F. Pacassi, J. B. Martinelli and F. A. Hillebrandt. The castle was badly damaged by fire in 1811. Recently, a large-scale reconstruction of the castle and the whole area around it was carried out.

183. The ceiling of a chamber on the first floor of the east wing of the palace in Bratislava Castle, with lunette vaulting and rich stucco decorations. The ornamentation dates from the Renaissance reconstruction of the castle carried out by the Habsburg Emperor Ferdinand I from 1552 to 1562.

184. Ľudovít Fulla ∙ Mosaic, 1968. Bratislava Castle.

185. South entrance to Bratislava Castle. In front of it is the court of honour which received its present form in the 1760's during the restoration ordered by Maria Theresa. It is closed on either side by propylaea. To the right are the single-storey guardhouses.

186. The Primate's Palace is the most significant example of a palace building in Bratislava. From 1778 to 1781 it was built for the Archbishop of Esztergom, Bathyány, by his architect, Melchior Hefele. In 1805, the Peace of Bratislava between Austria and France was signed in this building. Nineteenth-century engraving.

187. The front of the Primate's Palace in Bratislava, with its central protruding wing completed by a tympanum, is articulated strictly in the spirit of French Neo-Classicism. The decorative vases and allegorical statues are the work of the sculptor E. K. Messerschmidt. The frescoes in the chapel are by F. A. Maulbertsch. In the reception rooms there is a fine collection of English tapestries illustrating the ancient Greek legend of Hero and Leander.

188. The Church of the Holy Trinity in Bratislava was built between 1717 and 1727. It is among the finest Baroque buildings in the city. The illusive painting in the cupola is the work of the Italian painter Galli Bibiena from 1736 to 1740.

189. The Michael Gate, Bratislava, is the best preserved part of the medieval system of fortifications dating from the fourteenth century. The octagonal superstructure of the tower is in Renaissance style and the Rococo onion-shaped roof dates from 1758.

190. The Square of April 4, Bratislava, with the town hall. An older building of the magistrate's office was rebuilt for this purpose in the first half of the fifteenth century. The oriel above the main portal leading on to the square dates from 1457. In 1581, the stonemason Bartholomew of Wolfsthal added a Renaissance arcaded corridor to the north wing of the town hall. The tower was restored in 1733. In the square there is a fountain with the statue of Roland, defender of the rights of cities. The statue is the work of O. Luttringer of Deutsch-Altenburg from 1752.

191. Sanctuary in the presbytery of the Gothic Church of St. Martin. This building with three hall-type naves dates from the fourteenth and fifteenth centuries. The interior has been given a Gothic appearance and Neo-Gothic furnishings.

192. Devín Castle near Bratislava at the confluence of the Rivers Danube and Morava. Earlier, on the same site there was a prehistoric fortified settlement, later on, a Roman military post and then one of the most important fortresses of the Great Moravian Empire. The powerful watch-tower on the summit of a rocky cliff dates from the thirteenth century.

193. West Slovak landscape on the slopes of the Small Carpathians, a range of mountains attracting ramblers and holiday-makers. The south-eastern slopes are covered with extensive vineyards constituting Czechoslovakia's most important wine-growing area.

194. Plavecký Castle on the north-western foothills of the Small Carpathians used to protect the open and exposed territory close to the frontier. First mention of this castle dates from 1296; it was probably built not long before this. In 1707 it was abandoned and has been in ruins since that time.

195. The University Church of St. John the Baptist at Trnava was built from 1629 to 1637 by the Italian architects R. and A. Spezza. The rich stucco decorations are the work of G. B. Rossi, G. Tornini and P. A. Conti. It is one of the finest early Baroque buildings in Slovakia.

196. The Small Carpathians — a range of mountains with deciduous and mixed woods lying north-east of Bratislava — form the southern tip of the Carpathian chain.

197. Smolenice, a romantic castle built on the ruins of a medieval fortress according to a design by the architect J. Hubert in the first half of the twentieth century. Now the centre of Slovak research workers.

198. Fortified parish Church of St. Ladislaus at Čachtice,

built from 1373 to 1390, restored in Baroque style in 1687 and 1759. The Gothic stone wall with its portal dating from 1496 protected the area around the church, chapel and cemetery.

199. Trenčín Castle on the left bank of the central reaches of the River Váh. This medieval castle originated on the site of an older fortified settlement. At the beginning of the fourteenth century it was the seat of the ruler of the surrounding region, Matúš Čák. The castle was inhabited until the end of the eighteenth century. Beneath the castle are the twin towers of the former Jesuit Church, built between 1653 and 1657 and rebuilt after a fire between 1709 and 1713. On a rock beneath Trenčín Castle is an inscription from the year 179 A.D. commemorating the victory of the Romans over barbarian tribes.

200. The actual core of the Trenčín Castle with its early Gothic prismatic tower and the palace of Barbara of Cilli, wife of the Emperor Sigismund, dating from around 1430.

201. Radvaň-on-Danube. The Castle of Virt, originally a Baroque curia from around 1720, rebuilt at the beginning of the nineteenth century as a Neo-Classical noble residence. At the present time it serves as an attractive restaurant and wine cellar.

202. The Danube lowlands on the southern fringe of the Ipeľská Plateau. Sandy beach near Kováčová.

203. The Danubian port of Komárno and its Renaissance-Baroque fortress on the site of an old royal castle. This was an important defence post from the times of Turkish invasions and the Napoleonic Wars, as well as during the struggle of the Hungarian people for freedom in 1848 and 1849. The photograph shows the inner part of the town and the Baroque parish Church of St. Andrew, built between 1748 and 1756 and restored between 1850 and 1860, following a fire.

204. Two-tier Rococo iconostasis in the Orthodox Church at Komárno. The individual icons are set in richly decorated rocaille frames. The archivolt of the tympanum of the Czar's door is filled with a painting representing the enthroned Pantocrator. Around 1770.

205. Nitra. General panorama of the town and castle. In the background is Mount Zobor. In the early Middle Ages the town was the centre of the Principality of Nitra and the seat of rulers of the Great Moravian Empire.

206. Nitra College of Agriculture, built from 1961 to 1968 according to a design of the architects V. Dědeček and R. Miňovský.

207. Nitra Castle originated in the eleventh century on the site of an old Slavonic fortified settlement. Following many changes and adaptations, part of the Gothic fortifications, the Baroque defence system, the Cathedral, the Bishop's Palace and various other buildings have been preserved. The photograph shows the Vasil Tower dating from the first third of the fifteenth century.

208. Topoľčianky. The church, originally Gothic, built in the fifteenth and sixteenth centuries, was rebuilt in Renaissance and Baroque styles. From 1825 to 1839, the south entry wing was built by the architect J. Hild. The buildings of the castle are surrounded by an English-style park with statuary by the sculptor A. Strobl.

209. The arboretum at Mlyňany. A unique park with thousands of different shrubs, trees and plants from all parts of the world which have been successfully acclimatized. The Botanical Gardens of the Slovak Academy of Sciences.

210. "The Man of Sorrows". A folk sculpture from the second third of the nineteenth century. Stone. Horné Obdokovce, near Topoľčany.

211. Strečno. Ruined Gothic castle from the beginning of the fourteenth century perched on a steep rock over the River Váh. Tradition has it that Matúš Čák of Trenčín was its founder. The castle was enlarged in the fifteenth and sixteenth centuries. During the Second World War French guerilla fighters took part here in the Slovak National Uprising.

212. Vrátná Valley, with its limestone rock formations in the Small Fatra Mountains is a popular holiday area.

213. Rajecké Teplice. A modern spa in the valley of the River Rajčanka with thermal springs and a swimming pool filled with thermal water.

214—215. Vrátná Valley and the mountain village of Štefanová. In nearby Terchová the Slovak hero, Juraj Jánošík, was born in 1688. He led a band of outlaws who, at the beginning of the eighteenth century, fought against feudal oppression in the area around the upper reaches of the River Váh.

216. Jánošík's band of outlaws. Folk painting on glass from the end of the eighteenth or the beginning of the nineteenth century. Slovak National Museum, Martin.

217. Orava Castle. The oldest early Gothic part of the castle dates from the second half of the thirteenth century. The castle complex was considerably extended during the late Gothic and Renaissance periods. It was an important strategic fortress on the Slovak-Polish border.

218. Orava Dam on the upper reaches of the River Orava is one of the largest artificial lakes in the whole of Czechoslovakia, covering an area of thirty-five square kilometres.

219. The little River Turiec in the valley near Sklené between Žiar and the Kremnica Hills.

220. The valley of the Smrečianka, a wild mountain stream which rises on the slopes of the Ostrý Roháč mountain range. In the Middle Ages iron ore was mined here.

221. Čičmany, a Central Slovak village in the Strážovské Hills, is famous for its folk architecture. In the village several types of timbered cottages, with shingle roofs and ornamental painting on the façades, have been preserved.

222. The square of the medieval mining town of Kremnica. An interesting feature of the town's historic

core is the two-naved castle church of St. Catherine with its double Gothic fortifications. In the famous mint silver *groschen* and gold Kremnica ducats were struck. The Holy Trinity plague column is the work of D. Stanetti from the years 1765—1772.

223. Bojnice. The original castle on a raised terrace over the River Nitra was founded in the thirteenth century. The present appearance of the castle resulted from adaptations carried out from 1899 to 1910, according to the designs of the Hungarian architect J. Hubert. The collections contained in Bojnice Castle are also famous.

224. The ancient mining town of Banská Štiavnica dating from the first half of the thirteenth century. The historic urban reservation consists of many valuable buildings representing different architectural styles. Above the town is the Maidens' Castle, a watchtower with four cylindrical bastions placed at the four corners of the building from the years 1564 to 1571.

225. The Gothic castle of Zvolen in Central Slovakia, built around the year 1370 by King Louis the Great of Hungary in the style of Italian city castles. Important Renaissance adaptations gave the castle an advanced system of Quattrocento fortifications. In the middle of the fifteenth century, Jan Jiskra of Brandýs, the leader of the remaining Hussite forces, made his home here.

226. Museum and memorial to the Slovak National Uprising in Banská Bystrica. The whole project was completed in 1969. The architect responsible was D. Kuzma.

227. Banská Bystrica, the town which during the Second World War became famous as the centre of the Slovak National Uprising, is one of the oldest towns in Slovakia. The photograph shows part of the square with the Gothic-Renaissance Thurzo House.

228. The Low Tatras — a mountain range running between the upper reaches of the rivers Váh and Hron — form the most extensive mountain range in Slovakia with splendid Karst formations. The continuous belt of forests that covers these mountains and the varied flora and fauna give a unique character to the area's natural beauties.

229. The ancient mining community of Vyšná Boca. Characteristic of the local folk architecture are the timbered cottages on stone foundations with hipped and gambrel roofs and small cone-shaped projections. The village is a good starting point for hikers and winter sports enthusiasts.

230. Vrbické Lake in the upper part of the Demänovská Valley provides evidence of the one-time glaciers in the Ďumbier group — the highest mountains in the Low Tatras (2045 m). Around the lake are icy moraines and erratic boulders.

231. The ridges of the High Tatras. The highest mountains in Czechoslovakia with many lakes, waterfalls, deep valleys and snow fields, form a protected national park. On the southern slopes of the High Tatras there are many fine holiday and health resorts.

232. Štrbské Pleso. Health and holiday resort in the western part of the High Tatras with a great modern winter sports area; it is situated beside a lake of the same name at an altitude of 1351 m. A dominant feature is the hotel Kriváň (in Art Nouveau style) built in 1905—1906.

233. Javorina Hunting Lodge beneath Ľadový Štít (Ice Peak) on the Czechoslovak-Polish frontier. A complex of timbered buildings from the end of the Silesian-Polish style of folk architecture.

234. The limestone and dolomite peaks of the Belanské Tatry link up with the High Tatras in a north-easterly direction along the state frontier. A typical feature here are the Karst formations.

235. The Renaissance Chateau of Betlanovce, built between 1564 and 1568. One of the first unfortified chateaux to be built in Slovakia, it has preserved its original ground-plan of the interior with a large entrance hall. The smooth façades with a wooden balcony are topped with the original attics with arched gables.

236. The town bell-tower at Spišská Sobota, built in 1598 by the Kežmarok master-builder U. Materer. The Renaissance appearance was later changed to Baroque.

237. The Carthusian Červený Kláštor (Red Monastery) on the River Dunajec. It was established in 1319 and when the Hussites attacked Spiš in the fifteenth century it was destroyed. The Carthusian monks then restored the monastery and the Church of St. Anthony in late Gothic style. The whole complex of buildings changed hands several times and it underwent its last major repairs after the Second World War. The monastery is today a museum and a first class hotel.

238. The Dunajec Valley with the Three Crowns group of mountains. On both sides of the river stretches the Pieniny National Park with limestone rocks and rare plants. Close to Červený Kláštor is the place where rafts are docked on which one can float down the Dunajec through the romantic passes of the Pieniny.

239. The town of Levoča in North-Eastern Slovakia was the centre of the Spiš region. The Gothic-Renaissance town hall standing in the middle of the large square underwent several phases of restoration in the Baroque period and in the nineteenth and twentieth centuries. What was once the town hall now houses the Spiš Museum. The prismatic bell-tower dates from 1656—1661 and though it is a separate building it is linked with the town hall by a passageway.

240. The high altar of St. James the Greater in Levoča parish church is an outstanding example of late Gothic Slovak woodcarving. It was created by Master Pavol of Levoča between 1507 and 1518. In the centre is the winged altarpiece with three larger-than-life statues of Our Lady, St. James the Greater and St. John the Evangelist. Beneath them, on the predella, is a carved scene representing the Last Supper. The altar, which is 18 metres 62 centi-

metres high, is one of the biggest Gothic altars in Europe.

241. Levoča, the left folding wing of the altar of St. James the Greater in the parish church. A detail from the relief depicting the "Beheading of St. James". Lime wood, polychromy.

242. St. George, icon from the wooden church at Nová Sedlica, early eighteenth century. Now housed in the Slovak National Gallery, Bratislava. The icon in its original Baroque frame is one of a large group of panel paintings which decorate churches in the eastern part of the Slovak Republic.

243. Spišská Kapitula. Formerly a fortified ecclesiastical community, the core of which consists of the three-naved Romanesque basilica of St. Martin dating from 1245—1273. Next to the Church of St. Martin stands the late Gothic chapel of the Zápolya family (right) which dates from 1488—1493. The fortifications were built at the end of the sixteenth and in the second half of the seventeenth century.

244. The huge ruins of Spiš Castle, the fortress which once was the seat of the Spiš district administration, dominate the extensive region beneath it. The oldest preserved parts of the upper castle — the palace, the cylindrical tower and the fortifications are still in Romanesque style and date from before the middle of the thirteenth century. The castle was gradually extended and fortified until it became the biggest and most extensive fortress in Slovakia. It had five courtyards, several dozen rooms and several lines of ramparts. After a great fire in 1780, the castle was abandoned.

245. The Gothic castle of Krásna Hôrka in the Rožňava basin. It was founded some time after 1318 and was restored several times in Renaissance and Baroque styles. Collections in the interior include ancient weapons, the original castle kitchen, paintings, porcelain and furniture.

246. The Protestant section of the cemetery at Hrhov in the midst of the Slovak Karst. The simple wooden tombs are interesting examples of folk craftsmanship.

247. Košice, St. Elizabeth's Cathedral. The building was started at the beginning of the fourteenth century and completed around the year 1508. The three hall-type naves are roofed with late Gothic vaulting. The interior furnishings of the Cathedral are of great value and include several splendid late Gothic altars. Outstanding is the high altar of St. Elizabeth

of Hungary, dating from the last quarter of the fifteenth century. The statuary on this altar is probably the work of the monk Erhardt of Ulm. Košice Cathedral is among the finest examples of Slovak Gothic architecture.

248. The south front of St. Elizabeth's Cathedral bears traces of the puristic changes made in the period of the extensive restoration carried out from 1877 to 1896 under the direction of Professor F. Schmidt.

249. Prešov. A Gothic town built on a crossroads of medieval trade routes has undergone many complicated architectural developments. The most remarkable of its ancient public buildings is the Rákóczy House with its rich Renaissance attics and ornamental graffito work. Today it houses the Municipal Museum and its rich collections.

250. The square of the East Slovak town of Bardejov, with its Gothic-Renaissance town hall built at the beginning of the sixteenth century by the master-builders Alexander and Alexi. Renaissance restoration work was carried out in 1641. Today the building serves as the Museum of the Šariš District.

251. Northern semi-circular bastion, part of the medieval fortifications of the town of Bardejov, was repaired during restoration work on historic buildings from 1949 to 1960. On the right, the town Church of St. Giles, built in the year 1415. The vaulting of the presbytery was reconstructed in 1464 by Master Štefan of Košice who raised the height of the central nave and re-vaulted it. The interior of the church contains a number of original late Gothic altars.

252. Bardejov spa — a summer holiday resort and spa in the vicinity of the town of Bardejov. The first Slovak open-air museum which has been established here contains examples of folk architecture of the East Carpathian type.

253. The Orthodox Church of Our Lady at Korejovce is a typical example of the wooden ecclesiastical architecture of East Slovakia. This timbered building dates from 1761. The interior is divided into an entrance porch under the tower, a square nave and a presbytery. The shingle roofs are of cupola-shape. Next to the church stands the wooden bell-tower.

254. The Church of Our Lady at Korejovce. Part of the iconostasis with an eighteenth-century picture of the Madonna which is a typical example of East Slovak icon painting of this period.

255. Morské Oko (Eye of the Sea) — a natural lake high up in the densely wooded Vihorlat Mountains.

INDEX OF PLACES

INDEX OF PERSONS